THREE MO

THREE MORE PLAYS

BY

SEAN O'CASEY

THE SILVER TASSIE
PURPLE DUST
RED ROSES FOR ME

With an introduction by
J. C. Trewin

MACMILLAN

ST MARTIN'S PRESS

SBN 333 08946 4

First Edition of *The Silver Tassie* 1928
First Edition of *Purple Dust* 1940
First Edition of *Red Roses For Me* 1942
First Edition of *Three More Plays* 1965
Reprinted 1969, 1971, 1973

Published by
MACMILLAN LONDON LTD
London and Basingstoke
Associated companies in New York
Dublin Melbourne Johannesburg and Madras

Printed in Great Britain by
RICHARD CLAY (THE CHAUCER PRESS) LTD
Bungay, Suffolk

CONTENTS

INTRODUCTION

THROUGHOUT his long life as a dramatist Sean O'Casey has watched the world from the bridge of vision. It is a phrase he uses in the first act of *Red Roses For Me* where Ayamonn says: 'Tomorrow night, in the old place, near the bridge, the bridge of vision where we first saw Aengus and his coloured birds of passion . . .'. At the beginning of the third act we find a weary group on a Liffey bridge: slum folk, listless unemployed, women selling their violets or their cakes and apples (from 'a drab-coloured basket in which the cakes and apples are spending an idle and uneasy time'). Suddenly, as the scene moves on, men and women renew their youth and vigour in a few transfiguring moments. The Liffey is on fire; the Dublin world is now gold and silver and burnished bronze. Roof, column, steeple, are aureoled. The transformed Finnoola cries: 'She's glowin' like a song sung be Osheen himself, with the golden melody of his own harp helpin'.' Presently the fantasy develops into O'Casey's stage direction:

Finnoola has been swaying her body to the rhythm of the song, and now, just as the last part is ending, she swings out on to the centre of the bridge in a dance. The tune, played on a flute by someone, somewhere, is that of a Gavotte, or an air of some dignified and joyous dance, and, for a while, it is played in fairly slow time. After some time it gets quicker, and Ayamonn dances out to meet her. They dance opposite each other, the people around clapping their hands to the tap of the dancers' feet. The two move around in this spontaneous dance, she in a golden pool of light, he in a violet-coloured shadow, now and again changing their movements so that she is in the violet-coloured shadow, and he in the golden pool.

Red Roses For Me was published in 1942. Its third act derives from the experience that Johnny Casside, who is Sean O'Casey, had as a youth on a late spring evening at the turn of the century when he came down with his empty handcart to the Liffey quays and saw Dublin glorified in the sunset. More than four decades later, O'Casey established the recollection in a chapter of *Pictures in the Hallway*, the second volume of his autobiography: the chapter is called, unexpectedly, 'All Heaven and Harmsworth Too'. Basically it is the same experience (though here the music is that of a hurdy-gurdy playing a dance tune in a violet shadow), and there is much of the same pageantry of phrase, a vision, exalted and ecstatic, of 'Dublin in the grip of God.'

Sean O'Casey has always known this transforming ecstasy, something the Elizabethans would have recognised upon Bankside. Dramatists then walked the stage in kingly-flashing coats. A relatively minor craftsman, Thomas Dekker, in his play of *Old Fortunatus*, could throw off the glittering speech that ends with 'the ball of gold that set all Troy on fire'. The same instinct had caused Marlowe's Dido to say:

> I would have given Achates store of gold,
> And Ilioneus gum and Libyan spice;
> The common soldiers rich embroidered coats,
> And silver whistles to control the winds...

Elizabethans and Jacobeans prized this sensuous relish in a play. They seldom wrote in a desperately gnomic patter, and they would distribute their largesse generously. Thus Shakespeare allows Euphronius, Antony's schoolmaster — a personage of fifteen lines or so who does no more than bear a message — to say to Octavius Caesar:

I was of late as petty to his ends
As is the morn-dew on the myrtle leaf
To his grand sea.

O'Casey, an Elizabethan out of time, has been just as prodigal with his bounty. Thus it is a Second Workman that says in *Purple Dust*:

It sthretches out to the sight of a big dim ship with a followin' fleet in the great dim distance, with a stern-fac'd man in the blue-gold coat of the French Armee, standin' alone on th' bridge of the big dim ship, his eyes fixed fast on the shore that was fallin' undher the high-headed, rough-tumblin' waves o' the sea!

The more we read him and listen to him — listening is important, for O'Casey is a dramatist of the theatre — the more we are held by the splendour of the word: he has never left his bridge of vision. Naturally he has been labelled. The late Hilton Brown said, in another context, that we are 'a great people for labels, and we furnish them with well-nigh imperishable gum.' One of these, plastered on O'Casey long ago, proclaimed that he had written nothing but *Juno and the Paycock* and *The Plough and the Stars*. It still endures. A decade ago a writer with the best intentions recalled *The Silver Tassie*, after twenty-three years, as 'all about Irish gunmen and the Black-and-Tans. The memory it leaves is of grim, lean men wearing mackintoshes and carrying revolvers in their trousers pockets'. The writer could hardly have been remembering the *Tassie*, but he knew the O'Casey label and he gummed it on.

Though *Juno* and *The Plough and the Stars* are, of course, major works — often and uncertainly called realistic[1] — we have to

---

[1] 'The beauty, fire, and poetry of drama have perished in the storm of fake realism.' — O'Casey in *The Flying Wasp* (Macmillan, 1937).

remember that O'Casey has been a dramatist for forty years and that he has written a score of plays, long and short. All this time his speech at its most impassioned could have joined the torch-flare from the prow of the Bankside stage. We can mark it in the present volume: plays published in 1928 (*The Silver Tassie*), in 1940 (*Purple Dust*; written in 1937–38), and in 1942 (*Red Roses For Me*). In two of these, besides the dazzle of heightened speech, we get the sharp Elizabethan juxtaposition of tragedy and comedy: consider the last act of the *Tassie* in the dance-hall. And in the stage direction quoted earlier from *Red Roses For Me* — any chapter on O'Casey must become a mosaic — we observe the phrase, 'The tune, played on a flute by someone, some-where . . .'. What is that but Glendower's promise in *Henry IV, Part I*:

> And those musicians that shall play to you
> Hang in the air a thousand leagues from hence,
> And straight they shall be here. . .

or maybe, in another line (from *The Tempest*), 'This is the tune of our catch, play'd by the picture of nobody'?

Of these three — the 'tragi-comedy,' 'the wayward comedy,' and the 'play in four acts' — the first, *The Silver Tassie*, O'Casey's earliest break from accepted form, has been the most controversial, and the last, *Red Roses For Me*, the most generally applauded: it brought the dramatist back to the London stage after a long gap. *Purple Dust* still needs an entirely satisfying British production. Even so, I have known certain scenes (as in the Mermaid revival of 1962) to rise grandly from a text that, like all the later plays, is a steady challenge to the theatre of the imagination.

We need not return now to the Yeats–O'Casey dispute that kept *The Silver Tassie* from performance at the Abbey Theatre in 1928. At this distance, though Yeats's attitude remains inexplicable,[1] it is better to recall the dramatist's chivalry in the *Rose and Crown* chapter, 'Black Oxen Passing By,' which ends with the words, 'His greatness is such, thought Sean, that the Ireland which tormented him will be forced to remember him for ever.'

The Silver Tassie is a play in which O'Casey knew precisely what he wanted to do, and how to do it: to show the horror of war and its aftermath. He worked not in the common mode of the theatre but in a medium that seemed to wed flame and ice. Harley Granville-Barker, in his Romanes Lecture, *On Poetry in Drama* (1937) described the 'remarkable second act' in which O'Casey employed 'symbolism of scene and character, choric rhythms of speech and movement, the insistence of rhyme, the dignity of ritual, every transcendental means available in his endeavour to give us, seated in our comfortable little theatre, some sense of the chaos of war.'

I came up from the West in December 1929 to catch the *Tassie* on the last night of its London run. There had been no snug lying in the Abbey; but that most courageous of managers, Charles B. Cochran, had presented the play at the Apollo in Shaftesbury Avenue with a gallantry that O'Casey would appreciate. During the afternoon I had met a glib little piece, tuned to ephemeral fashion, that would run unchecked for a long time. Not a word of it lingers. *The Tassie* — though it had survived at the Apollo for only a few weeks — was an experience that would always prickle in the mind. If none would have said that the young Charles Laughton was precisely cast for a lusty Dublin footballer who returns from the war, paralysed from the

---

[1] A. V. Cookman, writing in *The Times* for O'Casey's eightieth birthday, said of *The Silver Tassie*: 'It was ... an experiment of absorbing interest, and that Yeats should have rejected such an experiment for the Abbey, with consequences hardly less sad for the theatre than for the author, still teases the mind.'

waist downwards, he acted with his nerves; after thirty-five years I can see that tortured eye and hear that husky voice. Barry Fitzgerald and Sidney Morgan brought full relish to the double turn of Sylvester and Simon; but more than anything I can re-create the second act in the war zone. There, before the 'jagged and lacerated ruin of what was once a monastery' (the set, governed by a great howitzer, was Augustus John's), were the intoning Croucher, the chanted choruses, the wild humours, the terrors, the repetitions, the litany to the gun ('Dreams in bronze and dreams in stone have gone to make thee delicate and strong to kill'), and the minute of calm when a soldier chants of 'a greenfinch resting in a drowsy, brambled lane of Cumberland.' The act — as Raymond Massey's production proved[1] — is meant to be heard and seen. Visually as well as verbally, it is the work of a magnificent dramatist. Nothing had brought war more fiercely to the English stage since the soldier Williams had spoken in *Henry V* by the camp-fire in the daybreak of Agincourt: '. . . When all those legs, and arms, and heads, chopp'd off in the battle, shall join together at the latter day, and cry all "We died at such a place"; some swearing, some crying for a surgeon; some upon their wives left poor behind them; some upon the debts they owe; some upon their children rawly left.' Robert Speaight (and the dramatist would return to this years later in *Rose and Crown*) wrote of the *Tassie*: 'O'Casey has seen into the heart of the horror of war, and wrenched out its dreadful secret: that the co-heirs with Christ destroy one another in the sight of the Son of Man.'

Purple Dust, the 'wayward comedy' written about a decade

---

[1] Bernard Shaw wrote to Cochran (November 1929): 'If someone would build you a huge Woolworth theatre (all seats sixpence) to start with O'Casey and O'Neill, and no plays by men who had ever seen a five pound note before they were thirty or been inside a school after they were thirteen, you would be buried in Westminster Abbey.'

later but not published until 1940 or performed in England (at Liverpool) until 1945, delighted New York playgoers more than it has yet pleased the English: they seem here to have mislaid their sense of humour. The fantasy is set in the remote Irish village of Clune na Geera where Stoke and Poges, a pair of English plutocrats, seek the simple country life — endeavouring to exist, with attendant harpies and a superb covey of Irish workmen, in the shell of a Tudor mansion that has been crumbling to purple dust and murmuring ashes. Its fall is not far off ('Wait until God sends the heavy rain, and the floods come!'). At the last a Figure who 'seems to look like the turbulent waters of the rising river' brings his warning:

The river has broken her banks and is rising high; high enough to come tumbling in on top of you. Cattle, sheep, and swine are moaning in the whirling flood. Trees of an ancient heritage, that looked down on all below them, are torn from the power of the place they were born in, and are tossing about in the foaming energy of the waters. Those who have lifted their eyes unto the hills are firm of foot, for in the hills is safety; but a trembling perch in the highest place on the highest house shall be the portion of those who dwell in the valleys below!

In a last stage direction 'the green waters tumble into the room through the entrance from the hall.'

O'Casey means the river of Time. He was writing at an hour of stern change, of the flaking away of the Empire and the wearing to dust of old and cherished tradition ('dusty bygones' as Ayamonn says in *Red Roses For Me*). Even if it is entirely possible to appreciate the play without realising this, for anyone who seeks to read between the lines here is the dramatist's own word:[1] 'There are those who clutch at things that are departing, and try to hold them back. So do Stoke and Poges, digging up old bones, and trying to glue them together again. They try to shelter

[1] *Under a Colored Cap* (Macmillan, 1963).

from the winds of change but Time wears away the roof, and Time's river eventually sweeps the purple dust away.'

If the fantasy has not yet had its full due, it is because no English stage production — and I have met some good tries — has achieved both the eloquence and the comic inspiration: I wish I had seen Miles Malleson and the late Walter Hudd, as Stoke and Poges, developing in a full performance the ingenuities so happy at rehearsal. Further, it is hard to fix an audience at an hour when — transiently at least — many playgoers care little for the texture and lustre and rhythm of language, the sway and lift of a sentence, a dramatist's 'gold embroidery out o' dancing words'. While it is a joy to watch Stoke and Poges in farcical agony, it ought to enchant us to hear the language with which they are dazzled. Thus the First Workman will say:

> This is a wondherful house, so it is. It's an honour to be workin' in it. After hundhreds o' years standin' in frost, rain, and snow, frontin' th' winds o' the world, it's a marvel it isn't flat on its face, furnishin' only an odd shelther for a sthray fox; but here it stands, an' we all waitin' for a windy winther ud stagger it an' send it tottherin' down.

And the Second Workman is always likely to put down his brick-filled barrow with the words:

> That was in the days of Finn Mac Coole, before his hair was scarred with a hint o' grey; the mighty Finn, I'm sayin', who stood as still as a stone in th' heart of a hill to hear the cry of a curlew over th' cliffs o' Erris, the song of the blackbird, the cry o' the hounds hotfoot afther a boundin' deer, the steady wail o' the waves tumblin' in on a lonely shore; the mighty Finn who'd surrendher an emperor's pomp for a place with the bards, and the gold o' the King o' Greece for a night asleep be the sthream of Assaroe!

When I heard a few scenes in rehearsal at a church hall in Kingsway (that afternoon the author was there himself) the dull little room glittered as if it were spread with cloth of gold. *Purple Dust* (I remember such actors at various times as Maurice Jones and Cyril Luckham, Ronald Fraser and Peter Bowles) can also be extremely and diversely comic.

Our third play, in order of writing, is the highly personal *Red Roses For Me*. Once more O'Casey uses Dublin — as another age would use Venice or Athens or Amalfi — as a hearth for the glowing imagination: 'A gold-speckled candle, white as snow, was Dublin once; yellowish now, leanin' sideways, an' gutherin' down to a last shaky glimmer in the wind of life.' If we have read the autobiographies, and especially *Pictures in the Hallway*, we know the background of Ayamonn — who is much like the young O'Casey — and of his mother. We understand why Ayamonn, at the very beginning of the first act, is wearing Richard of Gloucester's cloak and declaiming from *Henry VI, Part III* — an unexpected choice — 'What, will th' aspiring blood of Lancaster sink to the ground?' In life 'Johnny Casside' would have been Henry VI, but no matter. The chapter of *Pictures in the Hallway* is entitled 'Shakespeare Taps at the Window'; and if the Royal Shakespeare Company had wanted an epigraph for its production of *The Wars of the Roses*, it could have done no better than this:

Battles, castles, and marching armies; kings, queens, knights, and esquires in robes today and in armour tomorrow, shouting their soldiers on to the attack, or saying a last lone word before poor life gave out; of mighty men of valour joining this king and reneging that one; of a king gaining a crown and of a king losing it; of kings and knights rushing on their foes and of kings and captains flying frantic from them...

There are no castles or kings or knights in *Red Roses For Me*;[1] but there is certainly a battle. Ayamonn, doomed Dublin

' The song of 'Red Roses For Me' is quoted in the thirteenth chapter of *Pictures in the Hallway*, 'Touched by the Theatre'.

idealist, a Protestant in love with a Catholic, sees the shape of a
new world in the shilling-a-week for which the railwaymen are
striking. As with the other plays in this volume we may think
first of *Red Roses* for one scene in particular. In the *Tassie* it is
the second act; in *Purple Dust* it is the ultimate symbolism; in
Red Roses it is the third act on the bridge of vision ('Sons an'
daughters of princes are we all, an' one with the race of Milesius'). I wrote after the Embassy Theatre production of 1946:
'Our stage demands irradiating speech. Excitement on the first
night of *Red Roses For Me* was answer enough to those plain,
blunt spadesmen of the theatre who are also blind and deaf.'

   Behind all is O'Casey's great heart and compassionate mind.
And over all is the knowledge that Shakespeare and the Elizabethans have been tapping at the window-pane, that Sean
O'Casey has stood with them upon the bridge of vision. Ayamonn says of Shakespeare: 'He's part of the kingdom of heaven
in the nature of everyman.' Elsewhere is the simple phrase,
'No one knows what a word may bring forth.' Let us say now
that, of the dramatists of our time, Sean O'Casey has known most
certainly what the word can do.

   1964   J. C. TREWIN

THE SILVER TASSIE

A Tragi-Comedy in Four Acts

STAGE VERSION

TO

EILEEN

WITH THE YELLOW DAFFODILS

IN THE GREEN VASE

NOTES

THE Croucher's make-up should come as close as possible to a death's head, a skull; and his hands should show like those of a skeleton's. He should sit somewhere *above* the group of Soldiers; preferably to one side, on the left, from view-point of audience, so as to overlook the Soldiers. He should look languid, as if very tired of life.

The group of Soldiers — Act Two — should enter in a close mass, as if each was keeping the other from falling, utterly weary and tired out. They should appear as if they were almost locked together.

The Soldiers' last response to the Staff-Wallah's declaration, namely, 'To the Guns!' should have in these three words the last high notes of 'The Last Post'.

The song sung at the end of the play should be given to the best two (or one) singers in the cast. If, on the other hand, there be no passable singer among the players, the song should be omitted.

Perhaps a more suitable Spiritual than 'Sweet Chariot' would be chosen for Harry to sing. For instance, 'Keep Inchin' Along', or 'Keep Me from Sinkin' Down'.

The Chants in the play are simple Plain Song. The first chant is given in full as an example of the way in which they are sung. In the others, the dots . . . indicate that the note preceding them should be sustained till the music indicates a change. There are three parts in each chant: the Intonation; the Meditation; and the Ending. After a little practice, they will be found to be easy to sing. The Soldiers having the better voices should be selected to intone the chants, irrespective of the numbers allotted to them as characters in the book of the play.

CHARACTERS IN THE PLAY

(As they appear)

Sylvester Heegan
Mrs. Heegan, *his wife*
Simon Norton
Susie Monican
Mrs. Foran
Teddy Foran, *her husband*
Harry Heegan, D.C.M., *Heegan's son*
Jessie Taite
Barney Bagnal
The Croucher
1st Soldier
2nd Soldier
3rd Soldier
4th Soldier
The Corporal
The Visitor
The Staff-Wallah
1st Stretcher-Bearer
2nd Stretcher-Bearer
1st Casualty
2nd Casualty
Surgeon Forby Maxwell
The Sister of the Ward

Act I.—Room in Heegans' home.
Act II.—Somewhere in France (*later on*).
Act III.—Ward in a Hospital (*a little later on*).
Act IV.—Room in Premises of Avondale Football Club
(*later on still*).

ACT I

The eating, sitting, and part sleeping room of the Heegan family. A large window at back looks on to a quay, from which can be seen the centre mast of a steamer, at the top of which gleams a white light. Another window at right looks down on a side street. Under the window at back, plumb in the centre, is a stand, the legs gilded silver and the top gilded gold; on the stand is a purple velvet shield on which are pinned a number of silver medals surrounding a few gold ones. On each side of the shield is a small vase holding a bunch of artificial flowers. The shield is draped with red and yellow ribbons. To the left of the stand is a bed covered with a bedspread of black striped with vivid green. To the right of the stand is a dresser and chest of drawers combined. The fireplace is to the left. Beside the fireplace is a door leading to a bedroom, another door which gives access to the rest of the house and the street, on the right. At the corner left is a red coloured stand resembling an easel, having on it a silver-gilt framed picture photograph of Harry Heegan in football dress, crimson jersey with yellow collar and cuffs and a broad yellow belt, black stockings, and yellow football boots. A table on which are a half-pint bottle of whisky, a large parcel of bread and meat sandwiches, and some copies of English illustrated magazines.

Sylvester Heegan and Simon Norton are sitting by the fire. Sylvester Heegan is a stockily built man of sixty-five; he has been a docker all his life since first the muscles of his arms could safely grip a truck, and even at sixty-five the steel in them is only beginning to stiffen.

Simon Norton is a tall man, originally a docker too, but by a little additional steadiness, a minor effort towards self-education, a natural, but very slight superior nimbleness of mind, has risen in the Company's estimation and has been given the position of checker, a job entailing as many hours of work as a docker, almost as much danger, twice as much responsibility, and a corresponding reduction in his earning powers. He is not so warmly, but a little more circumspectly dressed than Sylvester, and in his manner of conduct and speech there is a hesitant suggestion of greater refinement than in those of Sylvester, and a still more vague indication that he is aware of it. This timid semi-conscious sense of superiority, which Simon sometimes forgets, is shown frequently by a complacent stroking of a dark beard which years are beginning to humiliate. The night is cold, and Simon and Sylvester occasionally stretch longingly towards the fire. They are fully dressed and each has his topcoat and hat beside him, as if ready to go out at a moment's notice. Susie Monican is standing at the table polishing a Lee-Enfield rifle with a chamois cloth; the butt of the rifle is resting on the table. She is a girl of twenty-two, well-shaped limbs, challenging breasts, all of which are defiantly hidden by a rather long dark blue skirt and bodice buttoning up to the throat, relieved by a crimson scarf around her neck, knotted in front and falling down her bosom like a man's tie. She is undeniably pretty, but her charms are almost completely hidden by her sombre, ill-fitting dress, and the rigid manner in which she has made her hair up declares her unflinching and uncompromising modesty. Just now she is standing motionless, listening intently, looking towards the door on right.

Mrs. Heegan is standing at the window at right, listening too, one hand pulling back the curtain, but her attention, taken from the window, is attracted to the door. She is older than Sylvester, stiffened with age and rheumatism; the end of her life is unknowingly lumbering towards a rest: the impetus necessity has given to continual toil and striving is beginning to slow down, and everything she has to do is done with a quiet mechanical persistence. Her inner ear cannot hear even a faint echo of a younger day. Neither Sylvester nor Simon has noticed the attentive attitude of Mrs. Heegan or Susie, for Sylvester, with one arm outstretched crooked at the elbow, is talking with subdued intensity to Simon.

Sylvester. I seen him do it, mind you. I seen him do it.

Simon. I quite believe you, Sylvester.

Sylvester. Break a chain across his bisseps! [*With pantomime action*] Fixes it over his arm . . . bends it up . . . a little strain . . . snaps in two . . . right across his bisseps!

Susie. Shush you, there!

[*Mrs. Heegan goes out with troubled steps by door. The rest remain still for a few moments.*

Sylvester. A false alarm.

Simon. No cause for undue anxiety; there's plenty of time yet.

Susie [*chanting as she resumes the polishing of rifle*]:

Man walketh in a vain shadow, and disquieteth himself in vain:
He heapeth up riches, and cannot tell who shall gather them.

[*She sends the chant in the direction of Sylvester and Simon, Susie coming close to the two men and sticking an angry face in between them.*

Susie. When the two of yous stand quiverin' together on the dhread day of the Last Judgement, how will the two of yous feel if yous have nothin' to say but 'he broke a chain across his bisseps'? Then the two of you'll know that the wicked go down into hell, an' all the people who forget God!

[*She listens a moment, and leaving down the rifle, goes out by door left.*

Sylvester. It's persecutin', that tambourine theology of Susie's. I always get a curious, sickenin' feelin', Simon, when I hear the Name of the Supreme Bein' tossed into the quietness of a sensible conversation.

Simon. The day he won the Cross Country Championship of County Dublin, Syl, was a day to be chronicled.

Sylvester. In a minor way, yes, Simon. But the day that caps the chronicle was the one when he punched the fear of God into the heart of Police Constable 63 C under the stars of a frosty night on the way home from Terenure.

Simon. Without any exaggeration, without any exaggeration, mind you, Sylvester, that could be called a memorable experience.

Sylvester. I can see him yet [*he gets up, slides from side to side, dodging and parrying imaginary blows*] glidin' round the dazzled Bobby, cross-ey'd tryin' to watch him.

Simon [*tapping his pipe resolutely on the hob*]. Unperturbed, mind you, all the time.

Sylvester. An' the hedges by the road-side standin' stiff in the silent cold of the air, the frost beads on the branches glistenin' like toss'd-down diamonds from the breasts of the stars, the quietness of the night stimulated to a fuller stillness by the mockin' breathin' of Harry, an' the heavy, ragin' pantin' of the Bobby, an' the quickenin' beats of our own hearts afraid, of hopin' too little or hopin' too much.

[*During the last speech by Sylvester, Susie has come in with a bayonet, and has commenced to polish it.*

Susie. We don't go down on our knees often enough; that's why we're not able to stand up to the Evil One: we don't go down on our knees enough. . . . I can hear some persons fallin' with a splash of sparks into the lake of everlastin' fire. . . . An account of every idle word shall be given at the last day.

[*She goes out again with rifle.*

Susie [*bending towards Simon and Sylvester as she goes*]. God is listenin' to yous; God is listenin' to yous!

Sylvester. Dtch, dtch, dtch. People ought to be forcibly restrained

from constantly cannonadin' you with the name of the
Deity.

Simon. Dubiety never brush'd a thought into my mind, Syl,
while I was waitin' for the moment when Harry would stretch
the Bobby hors dee combaa on the ground.

Sylvester [*resuming his pantomime actions*]. There he was staggerin',
beatin' out blindly, every spark of energy panted out of him,
while Harry feinted, dodg'd, side-stepp'd, then suddenly sail'd
in an' put him asleep with . . .

Simon. A right-handed hook to the jaw! ⎫
Sylvester. A left-handed hook to the jaw! ⎭ [*together*].

Sylvester [*after a pause*]. A left-handed hook to the jaw, Simon.

Simon. No, no, Syl, a right-handed hook to the jaw.

[*Mrs. Foran runs quickly in by the door with a frying-pan in her
hand, on which is a steak. She comes to the fire, pushing, so as
to disturb the two men. She is one of the many gay, careworn
women of the working-class.*

Mrs. Foran [*rapidly*]. A pot of clothes is boilin' on the fire above,
an' I knew yous wouldn't mind me slappin' a bit of a steak on
here for a second to show him, when he comes in before he
goes away, that we're mindful of his needs, an' I'm hopeful of
a dream tonight that the sea's between us, not lookin' very
haggard in the mornin' to find the dream a true one. [*With
satisfied anticipation*]

For I'll be single again, yes, I'll be single again;
An' I eats what I likes, . . . an' I drinks what I likes,
An' I likes what I likes, when I'm ——

[*Stopping suddenly*] What's the silence for?

Sylvester [*slowly and decidedly*]. I was at the fight, Simon, an' I
seen him givin' a left-handed hook to the jaw.

Mrs. Foran. What fight?

Simon [*slowly and decidedly*]. I was there too, an' I saw him down
   the Bobby with a right-handed hook to the jaw.

Mrs. Foran. What Bobby?   [*A pause.*

Sylvester. It was a close up, an' I don't know who'd know better
   if it wasn't the boy's own father.

   Mrs. Foran. What boy . . . what father?

Sylvester. Oh, shut up, woman, an' don't be smotherin' us with
   a shower of questions.

Susie [*who has entered on the last speech, and has started to polish a
   soldier's steel helmet*]. Oh, the miserableness of them that don't
   know the things that belong unto their peace. They try one
   thing after another, they try everything, but they never think
   of trying God. [*Coming nearer to them.*] Oh, the happiness of
   knowing that God's hand has pick'd you out for heaven. [*To
   Mrs. Foran*] What's the honey-pot kiss of a lover to the kiss
   of righteousness and peace?

                  [*Mrs. Foran, embarrassed, goes over to window.*

Susie [*turning to Simon*]. Simon, will you not close the dandy
   door of the public-house and let the angels open the pearly
   gates of heaven for you?

Sylvester. We feel very comfortable where we are, Susie.

Susie. Don't mock, Sylvester, don't mock. You'd run before a
   great wind, tremble in an earthquake, and flee from a fire; so
   don't treat lightly the still, small voice calling you to repen-
   tance and faith.

Sylvester [*with appeal and irritation*]. Oh, do give over worryin' a
   man, Susie.

Susie. God shows His love by worrying, and worrying, and
   worrying the sinner. The day will come when you will call
   on the mountains to cover you, and then you'll weep and
   gnash your teeth that you did not hearken to Susie's warning.
   [*Putting her hands appealingly on his shoulders*] Sylvester, if you

pray long enough, and hard enough, and deep enough, you'll get the power to fight and conquer Beelzebub.

Mrs. Foran. I'll be in a doxological mood tonight, not because the kingdom of heaven'll be near me, but because my husband'll be far away, and tomorrow [singing]:

> I'll be single again, yes, single again;
> An' I goes where I like, an' I does what I likes,
> An' I likes what I likes now I'm single again!

Simon. Go on getting Harry's things ready, Susie, and defer the dosing of your friends with canticles till the time is ripe with rest for them to listen quietly.

[*Simon and Sylvester are very self-conscious during Susie's talk to them. Simon empties his pipe by tapping the head on the hob of the grate. He then blows through it. As he is blowing through it, Sylvester is emptying his by tapping it on the hob; as he is blowing it Simon taps his again; as Simon taps Sylvester taps with him, and then they look into the heads of the pipes and blow together.*]

Susie. It must be mercy or it must be judgement: if not mercy today it may be judgement tomorrow. He is never tired of waiting and waiting and waiting; and watching and watching and watching; and knocking and knocking and knocking for the sinner — you, Sylvester, and you, Simon — to turn from his wickedness and live. Oh, if the two of you only knew what it was to live! Not to live leg-staggering an' belly-creeping among the pain-spotted and sin-splashed desires of the flesh; but to live, oh, to live swift-flying from a holy peace to a holy strength, and from holy strength to a holy joy, like the flashing flights of a swallow in the deep beauty of a summer sky.

[*Simon and Sylvester shift about, self-conscious and uneasy.*
Susie [*placing her hand first on Simon's shoulder and then on Sylvester's*]. The two of you God's elegant swallows; a saved pair;

a loving pair strong-wing'd, freed from the gin of the snarer,
tip of wing to tip of wing, flying fast or darting swift together
to the kingdom of heaven.

Simon [*expressing a protecting thought to Sylvester*]. One of the two
of us should go out and hunt back the old woman from the
perishing cold of watching for the return of Harry.

Sylvester. She'll be as cold as a naked corpse, an' unstinted
watchin' won't bring Harry back a minute sooner. I'll go an'
drive her back. [*He rises to go*] I'll be back in a minute, Susie.

Simon [*hurriedly*]. Don't bother, Syl, I'll go; she won't be farther
than the corner of the street; you go on toasting yourself where
you are. [*He rises*] I'll be back in a minute, Susie.

Mrs. Foran [*running to the door*]. Rest easy the two of you, an' I'll
go, so as to give Susie full time to take the sin out of your
bones an' put you both in first-class form for the kingdom of
heaven.   [*She goes out.*

Susie. Sinners that jeer often add to the glory of God: going out,
she gives you, Sylvester, and you, Simon, another few moments, precious moments — oh, how precious, for once gone,
they are gone for ever — to listen to the warning from heaven.

Simon [*suddenly*].Whisht, here's somebody coming, I think?

Sylvester. I'll back this is Harry comin' at last.

                          [*A pause as the three listen.*

Sylvester. No, it's nobody.

Simon. Whoever it was 's gone by.

Susie. Oh, Syl, oh, Simon, don't try to veil the face of God with
an evasion. You can't, you can't cod God. This may be your
last chance before the pains of hell encompass the two of you.
Hope is passing by; salvation is passing by, and glory arm-in-
arm with her. In the quietness left to you go down on your
knees and pray that they come into your hearts and abide with
you for ever. . . . [*With fervour, placing her left hand on Simon's*

shoulder and her right hand on Sylvester's, and shaking them] Get down on your knees, get down on your knees, get down on your knees and pray for conviction of sin, lest your portion in David become as the portion of the Canaanites, the Amorites, the Perizzites, and the Jebusites!

Sylvester. Eh, eh, Susie; cautious now — you seem to be for-gettin' yourself.

Simon. Desist, Susie, desist. Violence won't gather people to God. It only ingenders hostility to what you're trying to do.

Sylvester. You can't batter religion into a man like that.

Simon. Religion is love, but that sort of thing is simply a nulli-fication of religion.

Susie. Bitterness and wrath in exhortation is the only hope of rousing the pair of yous into a sense of coming and everlasting penalties.

Sylvester. Well, give it a miss, give it a miss to me now. Don't try to claw me into the kingdom of heaven. An' you only succeed in distempering piety when you try to mangle it into a man's emotions.

Simon. Heaven is all the better, Susie, for being a long way off.

Sylvester. If I want to pray I do it voluntarily, but I'm not going to be goaded an' goaded into it.

Susie. I go away in a few days to help to nurse the wounded, an' God's merciful warnings may depart along with me, then sin'll usher the two of you into Gehenna for all eternity. Oh, if the two of you could only grasp the meaning of the word eternity! [*Bending down and looking up into their faces*] Time that had no beginning and never can have an end — an' there you'll be — two cockatrices creeping together, a desolation, an astonish-ment, a curse and a hissing from everlasting to everlasting.

[*She goes into room.*

Sylvester. Cheerful, what! Cockatrices — be-God, that's a good one, Simon!

Simon. Always a trying thing to have to listen to one that's trying to push the kingdom of God into a reservation of a few yards.

Sylvester. A cockatrice! Now where did she manage to pick up that term of approbation, I wonder?

Simon. From the Bible. An animal somewhere mentioned in the Bible, I think, that a serpent hatched out of a cock's egg.

Sylvester. A cock's egg! It couldn't have been the egg of an ordinary cock. Not the male of what we call a hen?

Simon. I think so.

Sylvester. Well, be-God, that's a good one! You know Susie'll have to be told to disintensify her soul-huntin', for religion even isn't an excuse for saying that a man'll become a cocatrice.

Simon. In a church, somehow or other, it seems natural enough, and even in the street it's all right, for one thing is as good as another in the wide-open ear of the air, but in the delicate quietness of your own home it, it ——

Sylvester. Jars on you!

Simon. Exactly!

Sylvester. If she'd only confine her glory-to-God business to the festivals, Christmas, now, or even Easter, Simon, it would be recommendable; for a few days before Christmas, like the quiet raisin' of a curtain, an' a few days after, like the gentle lowerin' of one, there's nothing more . . . more ——

Simon. Appropriate. . . .

Sylvester. Exhilaratin' than the singin' of the Adestay Fidellis.

Simon. She's damned pretty, an' if she dressed herself justly, she'd lift some man's heart up, an' toss down many another. It's a mystery now, what affliction causes the disablement, for most women of that kind are plain, an' when a woman's born plain she's born good. I wonder what caused the peculiar bend in Susie's nature? Narrow your imagination to the limit and you couldn't call it an avocation.

Sylvester [*giving the head of his pipe a sharp, quick blow on the palm of his hand to clear it*]. Adoration.

Simon. What?

Sylvester. Adoration, Simon, accordin' to the flesh. . . . She fancied Harry and Harry fancied Jessie, so she hides her rage an' loss in the love of a scorchin' Gospel.

Simon. Strange, strange.

Sylvester. Oh, very curious, Simon.

Simon, It's a problem, I suppose.

Sylvester. An inconsolable problem, Simon.

[*Mrs. Foran enters by door, helping in Mrs. Heegan, who is pale and shivering with cold.*

Mrs. Heegan [*shivering and shuddering*]. U-u-uh, I feel the stream of blood that's still trickling through me old veins icifyin' fast; u-uh.

Mrs. Foran. Madwoman, dear, to be waitin' out there on the quay an' a wind risin' as cold as a stepmother's breath, piercin' through your old bones, mockin' any effort a body would make to keep warm, an' [*suddenly rushing over to the fireplace in an agony of dismay, scattering Simon and Sylvester, and whipping the frying-pan off the fire*] — The steak, the steak; I forgot the blasted steak an' onions fryin' on the fire! God Almighty, there's not as much as a bead of juice left in either of them. The scent of the burnin' would penetrate to the street, an' not one of you'd stir a hand to lift them out of danger. Oh, look at the condition they're in. Even the gospel-gunner couldn't do a little targert practice by helpin' the necessity of a neighbour. [*As she goes out*] I can hear the love for your neighbours almost fizzlin' in your hearts.

Mrs. Heegan [*pushing in to the fire, to Simon and Sylvester*]. Push
to the right and push to the left till I get to the fosterin' fire.
Time eatin' his heart out, an' no sign of him yet. The two of
them, the two of my legs is numb . . . an' the wind's risin'
that'll make the sea heave an' sink under the boat tonight,
under shaded lights an' the submarines about. [*Susie comes in,
goes over to window, and looks out.*] Hours ago the football match
must have been over, an' no word of him yet, an' all drinkin'
if they won, an' all drinkin' if they lost; with Jessie hitchin'
on him, an' no one thinkin' of me an' the maintenance
money.

Sylvester. He'll come back in time; he'll have to come back; he
must come back.

Simon. He got the goals, Mrs. Heegan, that won the last two
finals, and it's only fair he'd want to win this, which'll mean
that the Cup won before two —

Sylvester [*butting in*]. Times hand runnin'.

Simon. Two times consecutively before, makin' the Cup the
property of the Club.

Sylvester. Exactly!

Mrs. Heegan. The chill's residin' in my bones, an' feelin's left
me just the strength to shiver. He's overstayed his leave a lot,
an' if he misses now the tide that's waitin', he skulks behind
desertion from the colours.

Susie. On Active Service that means death at dawn.

Mrs. Heegan. An' my governmental money grant would stop at
once.

Susie. That would gratify Miss Jessie Taite, because you put her
weddin' off with Harry till after the duration of the war, an'
cut her out of the allowance.

Sylvester [*with a sickened look at Simon*]. Dtch, dtch, dtch, the way
the women nag the worst things out of happenings! [*To the*

women] My God Almighty, he'll be back in time an' fill yous all with disappointment.

Mrs. Heegan. She's coinin' money workin' at munitions, an' doesn't need to eye the little that we get from Harry; for one evening hurryin' with him to the pictures she left her bag behind, an' goin' through it what would you think I found?

Susie. A saucy book, now, or a naughty picture?

Mrs. Heegan. Lion and Unicorn standin' on their Jew ay mon draw. With all the rings an' dates, an' rules an' regulations.

Simon. What was it, Mrs. Heegan?

Mrs. Heegan. Spaced an' lined; signed an' signatured; nestlin' in a blue envelope to keep it warm.

Sylvester [*testily*]. Oh, sing it out, woman, an' don't be takin' the value out of what you're goin' to tell us.

Mrs. Heegan. A Post Office Savings Bank Book.

Sylvester. Oh, hairy enough, eh?

Simon. How much, Mrs. Heegan?

Mrs. Heegan. Pounds an' shillings with the pence missin'; backed by secrecy, an' security guaranteed by Act of Parliament.

Sylvester [*impatiently*]. Dtch, dtch. Yes, yes, woman, but how much was it?

Mrs. Heegan. Two hundred an' nineteen pounds, sixteen shillings, an' no pence.

Sylvester. Be-God, a nice little nest-egg, right enough!

Susie. I hope in my heart that she came by it honestly, and that she remembers that it's as true now as when it was first spoken that it's harder for a camel to go through the eye of a needle than for a rich person to enter the kingdom of heaven.

Simon. And she hidin' it all under a veil of silence, where there wasn't the slightest fear of any of us bein' jealous of her.

[*A tumult is heard on the floor over their heads, followed by a crash of breaking delf. They are startled, and listen attentively.*

Mrs. Heegan [*breaking the silence*]. Oh, there he's at it again. An'
she sayin' that he was a pattern husband since he came home
on leave, merry-making with her an' singin' dolorously the
first thing every mornin'. I was thinkin' there'd be a rough
house sometime over her lookin' so well after his long absence . . . you'd imagine now, the trenches would have given
him some idea of the sacredness of life!

[*Another crash of breaking delfware.*

Mrs. Heegan. An' the last week of his leave she was too fond of
breakin' into song in front of him.

Sylvester. Well, she's gettin' it now for goin' round heavin' her
happiness in the poor man's face.

[*A crash, followed by screams from Mrs. Foran.*

Susie. I hope he won't be running down here as he often does.

Simon [*a little agitated*]. I couldn't stay here an' listen to that;
I'll go up and stop him: he might be killing the poor woman.

Mrs. Heegan. Don't do anything of the kind, Simon; he might
down you with a hatchet or something.

Simon. Phuh, I'll keep him off with the left and hook him with
the right. [*Putting on his hat and coat as he goes to the door.*] Looking prim and careless'll astonish him. Monstrous to stay here,
while he may be killing the woman.

Mrs. Heegan [*to Simon as he goes out*]. For God's sake mind yourself, Simon.

Sylvester [*standing beside closed door on right with his ear close to one
of the panels, listening intently*]. Simon's a tidy little man with
his fists, an' would make Teddy Foran feel giddy if he got
home with his left hook. [*Crash.*] I wonder is that Simon
knockin' down Foran, or Foran knockin' down Simon?

Mrs. Heegan. If he came down an' we had the light low, an' kept
quiet, he might think we were all out.

Sylvester. Shush. I can hear nothin' now. Simon must have awed

him. Quiet little man, but when Simon gets goin'. Shush? No,
nothin' . . . Something unusual has happened O, oh, be-God!
[*The door against which Sylvester is leaning bursts suddenly in.
Sylvester is flung headlong to the floor, and Mrs. Foran, her hair
falling wildly over her shoulders, a cut over her eye, frantic with
fear, rushes in and scrambles in a frenzy of haste under the bed.
Mrs. Heegan, quickened by fear, runs like a good one, followed by
Susie, into the room, the door of which they bang after them.
Sylvester hurriedly fights his way under the bed with Mrs. Foran.*
Mrs. Foran [*speaking excitedly and jerkily as she climbs under the bed*].
Flung his dinner into the fire — and started to smash the little
things in the room. Tryin' to save the dresser, I got a box in
the eye. I locked the door on him as I rushed out, an' before I
was half-way down, he had one of the panels flyin' out with —
a hatchet!
Sylvester [*under the bed — out of breath*]. Whythehell didn'tyou
sing out beforeyousent thedoor flyin' inontop o' me!
Mrs. Foran. How could I an' I flyin' before danger to me — life?
Sylvester. Yes, an'you'got meinto a nice extremity now!
Mrs. Foran. An' I yelled to Simon Norton when he had me —
down, but the boyo only ran the faster out of the — house!
Sylvester. Oh, an' the regal-like way he went out to fight! Oh,
I'm findin' out that everyone who wears a cocked hat isn't a
Napoleon!
[*Teddy Foran, Mrs. Foran's husband, enters by door, with a large,
fancy, vividly yellow-coloured bowl, ornamented with crimson
roses, in one hand and a hatchet in the other. He is big and power-
ful, rough and hardy. A man who would be dominant in a public-
house, and whose opinions would be listened to with great respect.
He is dressed in the khaki uniform of a soldier home on leave.*
Teddy. Under the bed, eh? Right place for a guilty conscience. I
should have thrown you out of the window with the dinner

you put before me. Out with you from under there, an' come
up with your husband.

Susie [*opening suddenly door right, putting in her head, pulling it back
and shutting door again*]. God is looking at you, God is looking
at you!

Mrs. Foran. I'll not budge an inch from where I am.

Teddy [*looking under the bed and seeing Sylvester*]. What are you
doin' there encouragin' her against her husband?

Sylvester. You've no right to be rippin' open the poor woman's
life of peace with violence.

Teddy [*with indignation*]. She's my wife, isn't she?

Mrs. Foran. Nice thing if I lose the sight of my eye with the cut
you gave me!

Teddy. She's my wife, isn't she? An' you've no legal right to be
harbourin' her here, keepin' her from her household duties.
Stunned I was when I seen her lookin' so well after me long
absence. Blowin' her sighin' in me face all day, an' she sufferin'
the tortures of hell for fear I'd miss the boat!

Sylvester. Go on up to your own home; you've no right to be
violatin' this place.

Teddy. You'd like to make her your cheery amee, would you?
It's nappo, there, nappo, you little pip-squeak. I seen you an'
her goin' down the street arm-in-arm.

Sylvester. Did you expect to see me goin' down the street leg-
in-leg with her?

Teddy. Thinkin' of her Ring-papers instead of her husband. [*To
Mrs. Foran*] I'll teach you to be rippling with joy an' your husband goin' away! [*He shows the bowl.*] Your weddin' bowl,
look at it; pretty, isn't it? Take your last eyeful of it now, for
it' goin' west quick!

Susie [*popping her head in again*]. God is watching you, God is
watching you!

Mrs. Foran [*appealingly*]. Teddy, Teddy, don't smash the poor weddin' bowl.

Teddy [*smashing the bowl with a blow of the hatchet*]. It would be a pity, wouldn't it? Damn it, an' damn you. I'm off now to smash anything I missed, so that you'll have a gay time fittin' up the little home again by the time your loving husband comes back. You can come an' have a look, an' bring your mon amee if you like.

[*He goes out, and there is a pause as Mrs. Foran and Sylvester peep anxiously towards the door.*

Sylvester. Cautious, now cautious; he might be lurking outside that door there, ready to spring on you the minute you show'd your nose!

Mrs. Foran. Me lovely little weddin' bowl, me lovely little weddin' bowl!

[*Teddy is heard breaking things in the room above.*

Sylvester [*creeping out from under the bed*]. Oh, he is gone up. He was a little cow'd, I think, when he saw me.

Mrs. Foran. Me little weddin' bowl, wrapp'd in tissue paper, an' only taken out for a few hours every Christmas — me poor little weddin' bowl.

Susie [*popping her head in*]. God is watching — oh, he's gone!

Sylvester [*jubilant*]. Vanished! He was a little cow'd, I think, when he saw me.

[*Mrs. Heegan and Susie come into the room.*

Mrs. Foran. He's makin' a hash of every little thing we have in the house, Mrs. Heegan.

Mrs. Heegan. Go inside to the room, Mrs. Foran, an' if he comes down again, we'll say you ran out to the street.

Mrs. Foran [*going into room*]. My poor little weddin' bowl that I might have had for generations!

Susie [*who has been looking out of the window, excitedly*]. They're comin', they're comin': a crowd with a concertina; some of them carrying Harry on their shoulders, an' others are carrying that Jessie Taite too, holding a silver cup in her hands. Oh, look at the shameful way she's showing her legs to all who like to have a look at them!

Mrs. Heegan. Never mind Jessie's legs — what we have to do is to hurry him out in time to catch the boat.

[*The sound of a concertina playing in the street outside has been heard, and the noise of a marching crowd. The crowd stop at the house. Shouts are heard —* 'Up the Avondales!'; 'Up Harry Heegan and the Avondales!' *Then steps are heard coming up the stairs, and first Simon Norton enters, holding the door ceremoniously wide open to allow Harry to enter, with his arm around Jessie, who is carrying a silver cup joyously, rather than reverentially, elevated, as a priest would elevate a chalice. Harry is wearing khaki trousers, a military cap stained with trench mud, a vivid orange-coloured jersey with black collar and cuffs. He is twenty-three years of age, tall, with the sinewy muscles of a manual worker made flexible by athletic sport. He is a typical young worker, enthusiastic, very often boisterous, sensible by instinct rather than by reason. He has gone to the trenches as unthinkingly as he would go to the polling booth. He isn't naturally stupid; it is the stupidity of persons in high places that has stupefied him. He has given all to his masters, strong heart, sound lungs, healthy stomach, lusty limbs, and the little mind that education has permitted to develop sufficiently to make all the rest a little more useful. He is excited now with the sweet and innocent insanity of a fine achievement, and the rapid lowering of a few drinks.*

[*Jessie is twenty-two or so, responsive to all the animal impulses of life. Ever dancing around, in and between the world, the flesh, and the devil. She would be happy climbing with a boy among the heather on Howth Hill, and could play ball with young men on*

the swards of the Phoenix Park. She gives her favour to the promi-
nent and popular. Harry is her favourite: his strength and speed
have won the Final for his club, he wears the ribbon of the D.C.M.
It is a time of spiritual and animal exaltation for her.

[*Barney Bagnal, a soldier mate of Harry's, stands a little shyly near*
the door, with a pleasant, good-humoured grin on his rather broad
face. He is the same age as Harry, just as strong, but not so quick,
less finely formed, and not so sensitive; able to take most things
quietly, but savage and wild when he becomes enraged. He is fully
dressed, with topcoat buttoned on him, and he carries Harry's on
his arm.

Harry [*joyously and excited*]. Won, won, won, be-God; by the
odd goal in five. Lift it up, lift it up, Jessie, sign of youth, sign
of strength, sign of victory!

Mrs. Heegan [*to Sylvester*]. I knew, now, Harry would come back
in time to catch the boat.

Harry [*to Jessie*]. Leave it here, leave it down here, Jessie, under
the picture, the picture of the boy that won the final.

Mrs. Heegan. A parcel of sandwiches, a bottle of whisky, an'
some magazines to take away with you an' Barney, Harry.

Harry. Napoo sandwiches, an' napoo magazines: look at the cup,
eh? The cup that Harry won, won by the odd goal in five!
[*To Barney*] The song that the little Jock used to sing, Barney,
what was it? The little Jock we left shrivellin' on the wire after
the last push.

Barney. 'Will ye no come back again?'

Harry. No, no, the one we all used to sing with him. 'The Silver
Tassie'. [*Pointing to cup*] There it is, the Silver Tassie, won by
the odd goal in five, kicked by Harry Heegan.

Mrs. Heegan. Watch your time, Harry, watch your time.

Jessie. He's watching it, he's watching it — for God's sake don't
get fussy, Mrs. Heegan.

Harry. They couldn't take their beatin' like men. . . . Play the game, play the game, why the hell couldn't they play the game? [*To Barney*] See the President of the Club, Dr. Forby Maxwell, shaking hands with me, when he was giving me the cup, 'Well done, Heegan!' The way they yell'd and jump'd when they put in the equalizing goal in the first half!

Barney. Ay, a fluke, that's what it was; a lowsey fluke.

Mrs. Heegan [*holding Harry's coat up for him to put it on*]. Here, your coat, Harry, slip it on while you're talkin'.

Harry [*putting it on*]. All right, keep smiling, don't fuss. [*To the rest*] Grousing the whole time they were chasing the ball; an' when they lost it, 'Referee, referee, offside, referee . . . foul there; ey, open your eyes, referee!'

Jessie. And we scream'd and shouted them down with 'Play the game, Primrose Rovers, play the game!'

Barney. You ran them off their feet till they nearly stood still.

Mrs. Foran [*has been peeping twice in timidly from the room and now comes in to the rest*]. Somebody run up an' bring Teddy down for fear he'd be left behind.

Sylvester [*to Harry*]. Your haversack an' trench tools, Harry; haversack first, isn't it?

Harry [*fixing his haversack*]. Haversack, haversack, don't rush me. [*To the rest*] But when I got the ball, Barney, once I got the ball, the rain began to fall on the others. An' the last goal, the goal that put us one ahead, the winning goal, that was a-a-eh-a stunner!

Barney. A beauty, me boy, a hot beauty.

Harry. Slipping by the back rushing at me like a mad bull, steadying a moment for a drive, seeing in a flash the goalie's hands sent with a shock to his chest by the force of the shot, his half-stunned motion to clear, a charge, and then carrying him, the ball and all with a rush into the centre of the net!

Barney [*enthusiastically*]. Be-God, I did get a thrill when I seen you puttin' him sittin' on his arse in the middle of the net!

Mrs. Foran [*from the door*]. One of yous do go up an' see if Teddy's ready to go.

Mrs. Heegan [*to Harry*]. Your father'll carry your kit-bag, an' Jessie'll carry your rifle as far as the boat.

Harry [*irritably*]. Oh, damn it, woman, give your wailin' over for a minute!

Mrs. Heegan. You've got only a few bare minutes to spare, Harry.

Harry. We'll make the most of them, then. [*To Barney*] Out with one of them wine-virgins we got in 'The Mill in the Field', Barney, and we'll rape her in a last hot moment before we set out to kiss the guns!

[*Simon has gone into room and returned with a gun and a kit-bag. He crosses to where Barney is standing.*

Barney [*taking a bottle of wine from his pocket*]. Empty her of her virtues, eh?

Harry. Spill it out, Barney, spill it out. . . . [*Seizing Silver Cup, and holding it towards Barney*] Here, into the cup, be-God. A drink out of the cup, out of the Silver Tassie!

Barney [*who has removed the cap and taken out the cork*]. Here she is now. . . . Ready for anything, stripp'd to the skin!

Jessie. No double-meaning talk, Barney.

Susie [*haughtily, to Jessie*]. The men that are defending us have leave to bow themselves down in the House of Rimmon, for the men that go with the guns are going with God.

[*Barney pours wine into the cup for Harry and into a glass for himself.*

Harry [*to Jessie*]. Jessie, a sup for you. [*She drinks from the cup.*] An' a drink for me. [*He drinks.*] Now a kiss while our lips are wet. [*He kisses her.*] Christ, Barney, how would you like to be re-treating from the fairest face and [*lifting Jessie's skirt a little*] — and the trimmest, slimmest little leg in the parish? Napoo' Barney, to everyone but me!

Mrs. Foran. One of you go up, an' try to get my Teddy down.

Barney [*lifting Susie's skirt a little*]. Napoo, Harry, to everyone but ——

Susie [*angrily, pushing Barney away from her*]. You khaki-cover'd ape, you, what are you trying to do? Manhandle the lassies of France, if you like, but put on your gloves when you touch a woman that seeketh not the things of the flesh.

Harry [*putting an arm round Susie to mollify her*]. Now, Susie, Susie, lengthen your temper for a passing moment, so that we may bring away with us the breath of a kiss to the shell-bullied air of the trenches. . . . Besides, there's nothing to be ashamed of — it's not a bad little leggie at all.

Susie [*slipping her arm round Harry's neck, and looking defiantly at Barney*]. I don't mind what Harry does; I know he means no harm, not like other people. Harry's different.

Jessie. You'll not forget to send me the German helmet home from France, Harry?

Susie [*trying to rest her head on Harry's breast*]. I know Harry, he's different. It's his way. I wouldn't let anyone else touch me, but in some way or another I can tell Harry's different.

Jessie [*putting her arm round Harry under Susie's in an effort to dislodge it*]. Susie, Harry wants to be free to keep his arm round me during his last few moments here, so don't be pulling him about!

Susie [*shrinking back a little*]. I was only saying that Harry was different.

Mrs. Foran. For God's sake, will someone go up for Teddy, or he won't go back at all!

Teddy [*appearing at door*]. Damn anxious for Teddy to go back! Well, Teddy's goin' back, an' he's left everything tidy upstairs so that you'll not have much trouble sortin' things out. [*To Harry*] The Club an' a crowd's waitin' outside to bring us to the boat before they go to the spread in honour of the final. [*Bitterly*] A party for them while we muck off to the trenches!

Harry [*after a slight pause, to Barney*]. Are you game, Barney?

Barney. What for?

Harry. To go to the spread and hang the latch for another night?

Barney [*taking his rifle from Simon and slinging it over his shoulder*]. No, no, nappo desertin' on Active Service. Deprivation of pay an' the rest of your time in the front trenches. No, no. We must go back.

Mrs. Heegan. No, no, Harry. You must go back.

Simon,
Sylvester, } [*together*]. You must go back.
and Susie

Voices of crowd outside. They must go back!

[*The ship's siren is heard blowing.*

Simon. The warning signal.

Sylvester. By the time they get there, they'll be unslinging the gangways!

Susie [*handing Harry his steel helmet*]. Here's your helmet, Harry.

[*He puts it on.*

Mrs. Heegan. You'll all nearly have to run for it now!

Sylvester. I've got your kit-bag, Harry.

Susie. I've got your rifle.

Simon. I'll march in front with the cup, after Conroy with the concertina.

Teddy. Come on: ong avong to the trenches!

Harry [*recklessly*]. Jesus, a last drink, then! [*He raises the Silver Cup, singing*]:

> Gae bring to me a pint of wine,
> And fill it in a silver tassie;

Barney [*joining in vigorously*]:
> . . . . a silver tassie.

Harry:

> That I may drink before I go,
> A service to my bonnie lassie.

Barney:

> . . . . bonnie lassie.

Harry:

> The boat rocks at the pier o' Leith,
> Full loud the wind blows from the ferry;
> The ship rides at the Berwick Law,
> An' I must leave my bonnie Mary!

Barney:

> . . . . . . leave my bonnie Mary!

Harry:

> The trumpets sound, the banners fly,
> The glittering spears are ranked ready;

Barney:

> . . . glittering spears are ranked ready;

Harry:

> The shouts of war are heard afar,
> The battle closes thick and bloody.

Barney:

> ...... closes thick and bloody.

Harry:

> It's not the roar of sea or shore,
> That makes me longer wish to tarry,
> Nor shouts of war that's heard afar —
> It's leaving thee, my bonnie lassie!

Barney:

> ... leaving thee, my bonnie lassie!

Teddy. Come on, come on.

> [*Simon, Sylvester, and Susie go out.*

Voices outside:

> Come on from your home to the boat;
> Carry on from the boat to the camp.

[*Teddy and Barney go out. Harry and Jessie follow; as Harry reaches the door, he takes his arm from round Jessie and comes back to Mrs. Heegan.*

Voices outside. From the camp up the line to the trenches.

Harry [*shyly and hurriedly kissing Mrs. Heegan*]. Well, goodbye, old woman.

Mrs. Heegan. Goodbye, my son.

[*Harry goes out. The chorus of 'The Silver Tassie', accompanied by a concertina, can be heard growing fainter till it ceases. Mrs. Foran goes out timidly. Mrs. Heegan pokes the fire, arranges the things in the room, and then goes to the window and looks out. After a pause, the loud and long blast of the ship's siren is heard. The light on the masthead, seen through the window, moves slowly away, and Mrs. Heegan with a sigh, 'Ah dear', goes over*

*to the fire and sits down. A slight pause, then Mrs. Foran returns
to the room.*

Mrs. Foran. Every little bit of china I had in the house is lyin'
above in a mad an' muddled heap like the flotsum an' jetsum
of the seashore!

Mrs. Heegan [*with a deep sigh of satisfaction*]. Thanks be to Christ
that we're after managin' to get the three of them away safely.

ACT II

In the war zone: a scene of jagged and lacerated ruin of what was once a monastery. At back a lost wall and window are indicated by an arched piece of broken coping pointing from the left to the right, and a similar piece of masonry pointing from the right to the left. Between these two lacerated fingers of stone can be seen the country stretching to the horizon where the front trenches are. Here and there heaps of rubbish mark where houses once stood. From some of these, lean, dead hands are protruding. Further on, spiky stumps of trees which were once a small wood. The ground is dotted with rayed and shattered shell-holes. Across the horizon in the red glare can be seen the criss-cross pattern of the barbed wire bordering the trenches. In the sky sometimes a green star, sometimes a white star, burns. Within the broken archway to the left is an arched entrance to another part of the monastery, used now as a Red Cross Station. In the wall, right, near the front is a stained-glass window, background green, figure of the Virgin, white-faced, wearing a black robe, lights inside making the figure vividly apparent. Farther up from this window is a life-size crucifix. A shell has released an arm from the cross, which has caused the upper part of the figure to lean forward with the released arm outstretched towards the figure of the Virgin. Underneath the crucifix on a pedestal, in red letters, are the words: PRINCEPS PACIS. *Almost opposite the crucifix is a gunwheel to which Barney is tied. At the back, in the centre, where the span of the arch should be, is the shape of a big howitzer gun, squat, heavy underpart, with a long, sinister barrel now pointing towards the front at an angle of forty-five degrees. At the base of the gun a piece of wood is placed on which is chalked,* HYDE PARK CORNER. *On another piece of wood*

47

near the entrance of the Red Cross Station is chalked, NO HAWKERS OR STREET CRIES PERMITTED HERE. *In the near centre is a brazier in which a fire is burning. Crouching above, on a ramp, is a soldier whose clothes are covered with mud and splashed with blood. Every feature of the scene seems a little distorted from its original appearance. Rain is falling steadily; its fall worried now and again by fitful gusts of a cold wind. A small organ is heard playing slow and stately notes as the curtain rises.*

After a pause, the Croucher, without moving, intones dreamily:

Croucher. And the hand of the Lord was upon me, and carried me out in the spirit of the Lord, and set me down in the midst of a valley.

And I looked and saw a great multitude that stood upon their feet, an exceeding great army.

And he said unto me, Son of man, can this exceeding great army become a valley of dry bones?

[*The music ceases, and a voice, in the part of the monastery left standing, intones:* Kyr . . . ie . . . e . . . eleison. Kyr . . . ie . . . e . . . eleison, *followed by the answer:* Christe . . . eleison.

Croucher [*resuming*]. And I answered, O Lord God, thou knowest. And he said, prophesy, and say unto the wind, come from the four winds a breath and breathe upon these living that they may die.

[*As he pauses the voice in the monastery is heard again:* Gloria in excelsis Deo et in terra pax hominibus bonae voluntatis.

Croucher [*resuming*]. And I prophesied, and the breath came out of them, and the sinews came away from them, and behold a shaking, and their bones fell asunder, bone from his bone, and they died, and the exceeding great army became a valley of dry bones.

[*The voice from the monastery is heard, clearly for the first half of the*

sentence, then dying away towards the end: Accendat in nobis
Dominus ignem sui amoris, et flammam aeternae caritatis.

[*A group of soldiers come in from fatigue, bunched together as if for
comfort and warmth. They are wet and cold, and they are sullen-
faced. They form a circle around the brazier and stretch their hands
towards the blaze.*

1st Soldier. Cold and wet and tir'd.

2nd Soldier. Wet and tir'd and cold.

3rd Soldier. Tir'd and cold and wet.

4th Soldier [*very like Teddy*]. Twelve blasted hours of ammunition
transport fatigue!

1st Soldier. Twelve weary hours.

2nd Soldier. And wasting hours.

3rd Soldier. And hot and heavy hours.

1st Soldier. Toiling and thinking to build the wall of force that
blocks the way from here to home.

2nd Soldier. Lifting shells.

3rd Soldier. Carrying shells.

4th Soldier. Piling shells.

1st Soldier. In the falling, pissing rine and whistling wind.

2nd Soldier. The whistling wind and falling, drenching rain.

3rd Soldier. The God-dam rain and blasted whistling wind.

1st Soldier. And the shirkers sife at home coil'd up at ease.

2nd Soldier. Shells for us and pianos for them.

3rd Soldier. Fur coats for them and winding-sheets for us.

4th Soldier Warm.

2nd Soldier. And dry.

1st Soldier. An' 'appy.   [*A slight pause.*

Barney. An' they call it re-cu-per-at-ing!

1st Soldier [*reclining near the fire*]. Gawd, I'm sleepy.

2nd Soldier [*reclining*]. Tir'd and lousy.

3rd Soldier [*reclining*]. Damp and shaking.

4th Soldier [*murmuringly, the rest joining him*]. Tir'd and lousy, an'
   wet an' sleepy, but mother call me early in the morning.
1st Soldier [*dreamily*]. Wen I thinks of 'ome, I thinks of a field of
   dysies.
The Rest [*dreamily*]. Wen 'e thinks of 'ome, 'e thinks of a field
   of dysies.
1st Soldier [*chanting dreamily*]:

> I sees the missus paryding along Walham Green,
> Through the jewels an' silks on the costers' carts,
> Emmie a-pulling her skirt an' muttering,
> 'A balloon, a balloon, I wants a balloon',
> The missus a-tugging 'er on, an' sying,
> 'A balloon, for shime, an' your father fighting:
> You'll wait till 'e's 'ome, an' the bands a-plying!'

[*He pauses.*

   [*Suddenly*] But wy'r we 'ere, wy'r we 're — that's wot we
   wants to know!
2nd Soldier. God only knows — or else, perhaps, a red-cap.
1st Soldier [*chanting*]:

> Tabs'll murmur, 'em an' 'aw, an' sy: 'You're 'ere
>   because you're
> Point nine double o, the sixth platoon an' forty-eight
>   battalion,
> The Yellow Plumes that pull'd a bow at Crecy,
> And gave to fame a leg up on the path to glory;
> Now with the howitzers of the Twenty-first Division,
> Tiking life easy with the Army of the Marne,
> An' all the time the battered Conchie squeals,
> "It's one or two men looking after business." '

3rd Soldier. An' saves his blasted skin!

1st Soldier [*chanting*]. The padre gives a fag an' softly whispers:

> 'Your king, your country an' your muvver 'as you 'ere.'
> An' last time 'ome on leave, I awsks the missus:
> 'The good God up in heaven, Bill, 'e knows,
> An' I gets the seperytion moneys reg'lar.'

> [*He sits up suddenly.*

> But wy're we 'ere, wy'r we 'ere, – that's wot I wants
> to know!

The Rest [*chanting sleepily*]. Why 's 'e 'ere, why 's 'e 'ere — that's
wot 'e wants to know!

Barney [*singing to the air of second bar in chorus of 'Auld Lang Syne'*].
We're here because we're here, because we're here, because
we're here!

[*Each slides into an attitude of sleep — even Barney's head droops a
little. The Corporal, followed by the Visitor, appears at back. The
Visitor is a portly man with a rubicund face; he is smiling to
demonstrate his ease of mind, but the lines are a little distorted with
an ever-present sense of anxiety. He is dressed in a semi-civilian,
semi-military manner — dark worsted suit, shrapnel helmet, a
haversack slung round his shoulder, a brown belt round his middle,
black top boots and spurs, and he carries a cane. His head is bent
between his shoulders, and his shoulders are crouched a little.*

Visitor. Yes, tomorrow, I go a little farther. Penetrate a little
deeper into danger. Foolish, yes, but then it's an experience;
by God, it's an experience. The military authorities are damned
strict — won't let a . . . man . . . plunge!

Corporal. In a manner of speakin', sir, only let you see the arses
of the guns.

Visitor [*not liking the remark*]. Yes, no; no, oh yes. Damned strict, won't let a . . . man . . . plunge! [*Suddenly, with alarm*] What's that, what was that?

Corporal. Wha' was what?

Visitor. A buzz, I thought I heard a buzz.

Corporal. A buzz?

Visitor. Of an aeroplane.

Corporal. Didn't hear. Might have been a bee.

Visitor. No, no; don't think it was a bee. [*Arranging helmet with his hands*] Damn shrapnel helmet; skin tight; like a vice; hurts the head. Rather be without it; but, regulations, you know. Military authorities damn particular — won't let a . . . man . . . plunge!

Visitor [*seeing Barney*]. Aha, what have we got here, what have we got here?

Corporal [*to Barney*]. 'Tshun! [*To the Visitor*] Regimental misdemeanour, sir.

Visitor [*to Barney*]. Nothing much, boy, nothing much?

Barney [*chanting softly*]:

> A Brass-hat pullin' the bedroom curtains
> Between himself, the world an' the Estaminay's
>   daughter,
> In a pyjama'd hurry ran down an' phon'd
> A Tommy was chokin' an Estaminay cock,
> An' I was pinch'd as I was puttin' the bird
> Into a pot with a pint of peas.

Corporal [*chanting hoarsely*]:

> And the hens all droop, for the loss has made
> The place a place of desolation!

Visitor [*reprovingly, to the Corporal*]. Seriously, Corporal, seriously please. Sacred, sacred: property of the citizen of a friendly

State, sacred. On Active Service, serious to steal a fowl, a cock. [*To Barney*] The uniform, the cause, boy, the corps. Infra dignitatem, boy, infra dignitatem.

Barney. Wee, wee.

Visitor [*pointing to reclining soldiers*]. Taking it easy, eh?

Corporal. Done in; transport fatigue, twelve hours.

Visitor. Um, not too much rest, corporal. Dangerous. Keep 'em moving much as possible. Too much rest — bad. Sap, sap, sap.

Corporal [*pointing to the left*]. Bit of monastery left intact. Hold services there; troops off to front line. Little organ plays.

Visitor. Splendid. Bucks 'em up. Gives 'em peace.

[*A Staff Officer enters suddenly, passing by the Visitor with a spring-ing hop, so that he stands in the centre with the Visitor on his right and the Corporal on his left. He is prim, pert, and polished, superfine khaki uniform, gold braid, crimson tabs, and gleaming top-boots. He speaks his sentences with a gasping importance.*

Corporal [*stiffening*]. 'Shun! Staff!

Soldiers [*springing to their feet — the Croucher remains as he is, with a sleepy alertness*]. Staff! 'Shun!

Corporal [*bellowing at the Croucher*]. Eh, you there: 'shun! Staff !

Croucher [*calmly*]. Not able. Sick, Privilege. Excused duty.

Staff-Wallah [*reading document*]:

Battery Brigade Orders, F.A., 31 D 2.

Units presently recuperating, parade eight o'clock P.M.

Attend Lecture organised by Society for amusement and mental development, soldiers at front.

Subject: Habits of those living between Frigid Zone and Arctic Circle.

Lecturer: Mr. Melville Sprucer.

Supplementary Order: Units to wear gas-masks.

As you were.

[*The Staff-Wallah departs as he came with a springing hop. The Visitor and the Corporal relax, and stroll down towards the R.C. Station. The soldiers relax too, seeking various positions of ease around the fire.*

Visitor [*indicating R.C. Station*]. Ah, in here. We'll just pop in here for a minute. And then pop out again.

[*He and the Corporal go into the R.C. Station. A pause.*

1st Soldier [*chanting and indicating that he means the Visitor by looking in the direction of the R.C. Station*]:

> The perky bastard's cautious nibbling
> In a safe, safe shelter at danger queers me.
> Furiously feeling he's up to the neck in
> The whirl and the sweep of the front-line fighting.

2nd Soldier [*chanting*]:

> In his full-blown, chin-strapp'd, shrapnel helmet,
> He'll pat a mug on the back and murmur,
> 'Here's a stand-fast Tauntonshire before me',
> And the mug, on his feet, 'll whisper 'yessir'.

3rd Soldier [*chanting*]:

> Like a bride, full-flush'd, 'e'll sit down and listen
> To every word of the goddam sermon,
> From the cushy-soul'd, word-spreading, yellow-
>   streaked dud.

Barney [*chanting*]. Who wouldn't make a patch on a Tommy's backside.   [*A pause.*

1st Soldier. 'Ow long have we been resting 'ere?

2nd Soldier. A month.

3rd Soldier. Twenty-nine days, twenty-three hours, and [*looking at watch*] twenty-three minutes.

4th Soldier. Thirty-seven minutes more'll make it thirty days.
Croucher:

> Thirty days hath September, April, June, and Novem-
>   ber —
> November — that's the month when I was born —
>   November.
> Not the beginning, not the end, but the middle of
>   November.
> Near the valley of the Thames, in the middle of
>   November.
> Shall I die at the start, near the end, in the middle of
>   November?

1st Soldier [*nodding towards the Croucher*]. One more scrap, an'
    'e'll be Ay one in the kingdom of the bawmy.
2nd Soldier. Perhaps they have forgotten.
3rd Soldier. Forgotten.
4th Soldier. Forgotten us.
1st Soldier. If the blighters at the front would tame their grousing.
The Rest. Tame their grousing.
2nd Soldier. And the wounded cease to stare their silent scorning.
The Rest. Passing by us, carried cushy on the stretchers.
3rd Soldier. We have beaten out the time upon the duckboard.
4th Soldier. Stiff standing watch'd the sunrise from the firestep.
2nd Soldier. Stiff standing from the firestep watch'd the sunset.
3rd Soldier. Have bless'd the dark wiring of the top with curses.
2nd Soldier. And never a ray of leave.
3rd Soldier. To have a quiet drunk.
1st Soldier. Or a mad mowment to rustle a judy.

> [*3rd Soldier takes out a package of cigarettes; taking one himself he
>   hands the package round. Each takes one, and the man nearest to
>   Barney, kneeling up, puts one in his mouth and lights it for him.*

They all smoke silently for a few moments, sitting up round the fire.

2nd Soldier [*chanting very earnestly and quietly*]:

> Would God I smok'd an' walk'd an' watch'd th'
> Dance of a golden Brimstone butterfly,
> To the saucy pipe of a greenfinch resting
> In a drowsy, brambled lane in Cumberland.

1st Soldier:

> Would God I smok'd and lifted cargoes
> From the laden shoulders of London's river-way;
> Then holiday'd, roaring out courage and movement
> To the muscled machines of Tottenham Hotspur.

3rd Soldier:

> To hang here even a little longer,
> Lounging through fear-swell'd, anxious moments;
> The hinderparts of the god of battles
> Shading our war-tir'd eyes from his flaming face.

Barney:

> If you creep to rest in a clos'd-up coffin,
> A tail of comrades seeing you safe home;
> Or be a kernel lost in a shell exploding —
> It's all, sure, only in a lifetime.

All Together:

> Each sparrow, hopping, irresponsible,
> Is indentur'd in God's mighty memory;
> And we, more than they all, shall not be lost
> In the forgetfulness of the Lord of Hosts.

[*The Visitor and the Corporal come from the Red Cross Station.*

Visitor [*taking out a cigarette-case*]. Nurses too gloomy. Surgeons too serious. Doesn't do.

Corporal. All lying-down cases, sir. Pretty bad.

Visitor [*who is now standing near the crucifix*]. All the more reason make things merry and bright. Lift them out of themselves. [*To the soldiers*] See you all tomorrow at lecture?

1st Soldier [*rising and standing a little sheepishly before the Visitor*]. Yessir, yessir.

The Rest. Yessir, yessir.

The Visitor. Good. Make it interesting. [*Searching in pocket*] Damn it, have I none? Ah, saved.

[*He takes a match from his pocket and is about to strike it carelessly on the arm of the crucifix, when the 1st Soldier, with a rapid frightened movement, knocks it out of his hand.*

1st Soldier [*roughly*]. Blarst you, man, keep your peace-white paws from that!

2nd Soldier. The image of the Son of God.

3rd Soldier. Jesus of Nazareth, the King of the Jews.

1st Soldier [*reclining by the fire again*]. There's a Gawd knocking abaht somewhere.

4th Soldier. Wants Him to be sending us over a chit in the shape of a bursting shell.

The Visitor. Sorry put it across you. [*To Corporal*] Too much time to think. Nervy. Time to brood, brood; bad. Sap. Sap. Sap. [*Walking towards where he came in*] Must return quarters; rough and ready. Must stick it. There's a war on. Cheerio. Straight down road instead of round hill: shorter?

Corporal. Less than half as long.

The Visitor. Safe?

Corporal. Yes. Only drop shells off and on, cross-roads. Ration party wip'd out week ago.

The Visitor. Go round hill. No hurry. General Officer's orders,
  no unnecessary risks. Must obey. Military Authorities damned
  particular — won't let a . . . man . . . plunge!

[*He and the Corporal go off. The soldiers in various attitudes are
  asleep around the fire. After a few moments' pause, two Stretcher-
  Bearers come in slowly from left, carrying a casualty. They pass
  through the sleeping soldiers, going towards the Red Cross Station.
  As they go they chant a verse, and as the verse is ending, they are
  followed by another pair carrying a second casualty.*

1st Bearers [*chanting*]:

> Oh, bear it gently, carry it soft —
> A bullet or a shell said stop, stop, stop.
> It's had its day, and it's left the play,
> Since it gamboll'd over the top, top, top.
> It's had its day, and it's left the play,
> Since it gamboll'd over the top.

2nd Bearers [*chanting*]:

> Oh, carry it softly, bear it gently —
> The beggar has seen it through, through, through.
> If it 'adn't been 'im, if it 'adn't been 'im,
> It might 'ave been me or you, you, you.
> If it 'adn't been 'im, if it 'adn't been 'im,
> It might 'ave been me or you.

Voice [*inside R.C. Station*]. Easy, easy there; don't crowd.
1st Stretcher-Bearer [*to man behind*]. Woa, woa there, Bill, 'ouse
  full.
Stretcher-Bearer [*behind, to those following*]. Woa, woa; traffic
  blocked.

                              [*They leave the stretchers on the ground.*
The Wounded on the Stretchers [*chanting*]:

Carry on, carry on to the place of pain,
Where the surgeon spreads his aid, aid, aid.
And we show man's wonderful work, well done,
To the image God hath made, made, made,
And we show man's wonderful work, well done,
To the image God hath made!

When the future hours have all been spent,
And the hand of death is near, near, near,
Then a few, few moments and we shall find
There'll be nothing left to fear, fear, fear,
Then a few, few moments and we shall find
There'll be nothing left to fear.

The power, the joy, the pull of life,
The laugh, the blow, and the dear kiss,
The pride and hope, the gain and loss,
Have been temper'd down to this, this, this,
The pride and hope, the gain and loss,
Have been temper'd down to this.

1st Stretcher-Bearer [*to Barney*]. Oh, Barney, have they liced you
  up because you've kiss'd the Colonel's judy?
Barney. They lit on me stealin' Estaminay poulthry.
1st Stretcher-Bearer. A hen?
2nd Stretcher-Bearer. A duck, again, Barney?
3rd Stretcher-Bearer. A swan this time.
Barney [*chanting softly*]:

A Brass-hat pullin' the bedroom curtains
Between himself, the world an' the Estaminay's daughter,
In a pyjama'd hurry ran down and phon'd
A Tommy was chokin' an Estaminay cock;

An' I was pinch'd as I was puttin' the bird
Into a pot with a pint of peas.

1st Stretcher-Bearer. The red-tabb'd squit!

2nd Stretcher-Bearer. The lousy map-scanner!

3rd Stretcher-Bearer. We must keep up, we must keep up the
morale of the awmy.

2nd Stretcher-Bearer [*loudly*]. Does e' eat well?

The Rest [*in chorus*]. Yes, 'e eats well!

2nd Stretcher-Bearer. Does 'e sleep well?

The Rest [*in chorus*]. Yes, 'e sleeps well!

2nd Stretcher-Bearer. Does 'e whore well?

The Rest [*in chorus*]. Yes, 'e whores well!

2nd Stretcher-Bearer. Does 'e fight well?

The Rest [*in chorus*]. Napoo; 'e 'as to do the thinking for the
Tommies!

Voice [*from the R.C. Station*]. Stretcher Party — carry on!

[*The Bearers stoop with precision, attach their supports to the
stretchers, lift them up and march slowly into the R.C. Station,
chanting.*

Stretcher-Bearers [*chanting*]:

Carry on — we've one bugled reason why —
We've 'eard and answer'd the call, call, call.
There's no more to be said, for when we are dead,
We may understand it all, all, all.
There's no more to be said, for when we are dead,
We may understand it all.

[*They go out, leaving the scene occupied by the Croucher and the
soldiers sleeping around the fire. The Corporal re-enters. He is
carrying two parcels. He pauses, looking at the sleeping soldiers
for a few moments, then shouts.*

Corporal [*shouting*]. Hallo, there, you sleepy blighters! Number 2!
a parcel; and for you, Number 3. Get a move on — parcels,

[*The Soldiers wake up and spring to their feet.*

Corporal. For you, Number 2. [*He throws a parcel to 2nd Soldier.*]
Number 3.

[*He throws the other parcel to 3rd Soldier.*

3rd Soldier [*taking paper from around his parcel*]. Looks like a bundle
of cigarettes.

1st Soldier. Or a pack of cawds.

4th Soldier. Or a prayer-book.

3rd Soldier [*astounded*]. Holy Christ, it is!

The Rest. What?

3rd Soldier. A prayer-book!

4th Soldier. In a green plush cover with a golden cross.

Croucher. Open it at the Psalms and sing that we may be saved
from the life and death of the beasts that perish.

Barney. Per omnia saecula saeculorum.

2nd Soldier [*who has opened his parcel*]. A ball, be God!

4th Soldier. A red and yellow coloured rubber ball.

1st Soldier. And a note.

2nd Soldier [*reading*]. To play your way to the enemies' trenches
when you all go over the top. Mollie.

1st Soldier. See if it 'ops.

[*The 2nd Soldier hops the ball, and then kicks it from him. The
Corporal intercepts it, and begins to dribble it across the stage.
The 3rd Soldier tries to take it from him. The Corporal shouts
'Offside, there!' They play for a few minutes with the ball,
when suddenly the Staff-Wallah springs in and stands rigidly
in centre.*

Corporal [*stiff to attention as he sees the Staff-Wallah*]. 'Shun. Staff!

[*All the soldiers stiffen. The Croucher remains motionless.*

Corporal [*shouting to the Croucher*]. You: 'shun. Staff!

Croucher. Not able. Sick. Excused duty.
Staff-Wallah [*reading document*]:

> Brigade Orders, C/X 143. B/Y 341. Regarding gas-masks.
> Gas-masks to be worn round neck so as to lie in front $2\frac{1}{2}$
> degrees from socket of left shoulder-blade, and $2\frac{3}{4}$ degrees
> from socket of right shoulder-blade, leaving bottom margin
> to reach $\frac{1}{4}$ of an inch from second button of lower end of
> tunic. Order to take effect from 6 A.M. following morning
> of date received. Dismiss!

> > [*He hops out again, followed by Corporal.*
1st Soldier [*derisively*]. Comprenneemoy.
3rd Soldier. Tray bong.
2nd Soldier [*who is standing in archway, back, looking scornfully
after the Staff-Wallah, chanting*]:

> Jazzing back to his hotel he now goes gaily,
> Shelter'd and safe where the clock ticks tamely.
> His backside warming a cushion, down-fill'd,
> Green clad, well splash'd with gold birds red-beak'd.

1st Soldier:

> His last dim view of the front-line sinking
> Into the white-flesh'd breasts of a judy;
> Cuddling with proud, bright, amorous glances
> The thing salved safe from the mud of the trenches.

2nd Soldier:

> His tunic reared in the lap of comfort
> Peeps at the blood-stain'd jackets passing,
> Through colour-gay bars of ribbon jaunty,
> Fresh from a posh shop snug in Bond Street.

Croucher:

Shame and scorn play with and beat them,
Till we anchor in their company;
Then the decorations of security
Become the symbols of self-sacrifice.

[*A pause.*

2nd Soldier:

A warning this that we'll soon be exiles
From the freedom chance of life can give,
To the front where you wait to be hurried breathless,
Murmuring how, how do you do, to God.

3rd Soldier:

Where hot with the sweat of mad endeavour,
Crouching to scrape a toy-deep shelter,
Quick-tim'd by hell's fast, frenzied drumfire
Exploding in flaming death around us.

2nd Soldier:

God, unchanging, heart-sicken'd, shuddering,
Gathereth the darkness of the night sky
To mask His paling countenance from
The blood dance of His self-slaying children.

3rd Soldier:

Stumbling, swiftly cursing, plodding,
Lumbering, loitering, stumbling, grousing,
Through mud and rain, and filth and danger,
Flesh and blood seek slow the front line.

2nd Soldier:

> Squeals of hidden laughter run through
> The screaming medley of the wounded
> Christ, who bore the cross, still weary,
> Now trails a rope tied to a field gun.

[*As the last notes of the chanting are heard the Corporal comes rapidly in; he is excited but steady; pale-faced and grim.*

Corporal. They attack. Along a wide front the enemy attacks. If they break through it may reach us even here.

Soldiers [*in chorus as they all put on gas-masks*]. They attack. The enemy attacks.

Corporal. Let us honour that in which we do put our trust.

Soldiers [*in chorus*]:

> That it may not fail us in our time of need.

[*The Corporal goes over to the gun and faces towards it, standing on the bottom step. The soldiers group around, each falling upon one knee, their forms crouched in a huddled act of obeisance. They are all facing the gun with their backs to the audience. The Croucher rises and joins them.*

Corporal [*singing*]:

> Hail, cool-hardened tower of steel emboss'd
> With the fever'd, figment thoughts of man;
> Guardian of our love and hate and fear,
> Speak for us to the inner ear of God!

Soldiers:

> We believe in God and we believe in thee.

Corporal:

> Dreams of line, of colour, and of form;
> Dreams of music dead for ever now;

Dreams in bronze and dreams in stone have gone
To make thee delicate and strong to kill.

Soldiers:

We believe in God and we believe in thee.

Corporal:

Jail'd in thy steel are hours of merriment
Cadg'd from the pageant-dream of children's play;
Too soon of the motley stripp'd that they may sweat
With them that toil for the glory of thy kingdom.

Soldiers:

We believe in God and we believe in thee.

Corporal:

Remember our women, sad-hearted, proud-fac'd.
Who've given the substance of their womb for shadows;
Their shrivel'd, empty breasts war tinselléd
For patient gifts of graves to thee.

Soldiers:

We believe in God and we believe in thee.

Corporal:

Dapple those who are shelter'd with disease,
And women labouring with child,
And children that play about the streets,
With blood of youth expiring in its prime.

Soldiers:

We believe in God and we believe in thee.

Corporal:

> Tear a gap through the soul of our mass'd enemies;
> Grant them all the peace of death;
> Blow them swiftly into Abram's bosom,
> And mingle them with the joys of paradise!

Soldiers:

> For we believe in God and we believe in thee.
> [*The sky has become vexed with a crimson glare, mixed with yellow
> streaks, and striped with pillars of rising brown and black smoke.
> The Staff-Wallah rushes in, turbulent and wild, with his uniform
> disordered.*

Staff-Wallah:

> The enemy has broken through, broken through, broken
>   through!
> Every man born of woman to the guns, to the guns.

Soldiers:

> To the guns, to the guns, to the guns!

Staff-Wallah:

> Those at prayer, all in bed, and the swillers drinking
>   deeply in the pubs.

Soldiers:

> To the guns, to the guns.

Staff-Wallah:

> All the batmen, every cook, every bitch's son that hides
> A whiff of courage in his veins,
> Shelter'd vigour in his body,
> That can run, or can walk, even crawl —
> Dig him out, dig him out, shove him on —

Soldiers:

 To the guns!

[*The Soldiers hurry to their places led by the Staff-Wallah to the gun. The gun swings around and points to the horizon; a shell is swung into the breech and a flash indicates the firing of the gun, searchlights move over the red glare of the sky; the scene darkens, stabbed with distant flashes and by the more vivid flash of the gun which the Soldiers load and fire with rhythmical movements while the scene is closing. Only flashes are seen; no noise is heard.*

ACT III

The upper end of an hospital ward. At right angles from back wall are two beds, one covered with a red quilt and the other with a white one. From the centre of the head of each bed is an upright having at the top a piece like a swan's neck, curving out over the bed, from which hangs a chain with a wooden cross-piece to enable weak patients to pull themselves into a sitting posture. To the left of these beds is a large glass double-door which opens on to the ground: one of the doors is open and a lovely September sun, which is setting, gives a glow to the garden.

Through the door two poplar trees can be seen silhouetted against the sky. To the right of this door is another bed covered with a black quilt. Little white discs are fixed to the head of each bed: on the first is the number 26, on the second 27, and on the third 28. Medical charts hang over each on the wall. To the right is the fireplace, facing down the ward. Farther on, to the right of the fire, is a door of a bathroom. In the corner, between the glass door and the fire, is a pedestal on which stands a statue of the Blessed Virgin; under the statue is written, 'Mater Misericordiae, ora pro nobis'. An easy-chair, on which are rugs, is near the fire. In the centre is a white, glass-topped table on which are medicines, drugs, and surgical instruments. On one corner is a vase of flowers. A locker is beside the head, and a small chair by the foot of each bed. Two electric lights, green-shaded, hang from the ceiling, and a bracket light with a red shade projects from the wall over the fireplace. It is dusk, and the two lights suspended from the ceiling are lighted. The walls are a brilliant white.

Sylvester is in the bed numbered '26'; he is leaning upon his elbow looking towards the glass door.

Simon, sitting down on the chair beside bed numbered '27', is looking into the grounds.

Sylvester [*after a pause*]. Be God, isn't it a good one!

Simon. Almost, almost, mind you, Sylvester, incomprehensible.

Sylvester. To come here and find Susie Monican fashion'd like a Queen of Sheba. God moves in a mysterious way, Simon.

Simon. There's Surgeon Maxwell prancing after her now.

Sylvester [*stretching to see*]. Heads together, eh? Be God, he's kissing her behind the trees! Oh, Susannah, Susannah, how are the mighty fallen, and the weapons of war perished!

[*Harry Heegan enters crouched in a self-propelled invalid chair; he wheels himself up to the fire. Sylvester slides down into the bed, and Simon becomes interested in a book that he takes off the top of his locker. Harry remains for a few moments beside the fire, and then wheels himself round and goes out as he came in; Sylvester raises himself in the bed, and Simon leaves down the book to watch Harry.*

Sylvester. Down and up, up and down.

Simon. Up and down, down and up.

Sylvester. Never quiet for a minute.

Simon. Never able to hang on to an easy second.

Sylvester. Trying to hold on to the little finger of life.

Simon. Half-way up to heaven.

Sylvester. And him always thinking of Jessie.

Simon. And Jessie never thinking of him.

[*Susie Monican, in the uniform of a V.A.D. nurse, enters the ward by the glass door. She is changed, for it is clear that she has made every detail of the costume as attractive as possible. She has the same assertive manner, but dignity and a sense of importance have* been added. *Her legs, encased in silk stockings, are seen (and shown) to advantage by her short and smartly cut skirt. Altogether she is now a very handsome woman. Coming in she glances at the bed numbered 28, then pauses beside Sylvester and Simon.*

Susie. How is Twenty-eight?

Simon and Sylvester [*together*]. Travelling again.

Susie. Did he speak at all to you?

Sylvester. Dumb, Susie, dumb.

Simon. Brooding, Susie; brooding, brooding.

Sylvester. Cogitatin', Susie; cogitatin', cogitatin'.

Susie [*sharply, to Sylvester*]. It's rediculous, Twenty-six, for you to be in bed. The Sister's altogether too indulgent to you. Why didn't you pair of lazy devils entice him down to sit and cogitate under the warm wing of the sun in the garden?

Sylvester. Considerin' the low state of his general health.

Simon. Aided by a touch of frost in the air.

Sylvester. Thinkin' it over we thought it might lead ——

Simon. To him getting an attack of double pneumonia.

Sylvester and Simon [*together*]. An' then he'd go off like — [*they blow through their lips*] poof — the snuff of a candle!

Susie. For the future, during the period you are patients here, I am to be addressed as 'Nurse Monican', and not as 'Susie'. Remember that, the pair of you, please

[*Harry wheels himself in again. crossing by her, and, going over to the fire, looks out into grounds.*

Susie [*irritatedly, to Sylvester*]. Number Twenty-six, look at the state of your quilt. You must make an effort to keep it tidy. Dtch, dtch, dtch, what would the Matron say if she saw it!

Simon [*with a nervous giggle*]. He's an uneasy divil, Nurse Monican.

Susie [*hotly, to Simon*]. Yours is as bad as his, Twenty-seven. You mustn't lounge on your bed; it must be kept perfectly tidy [*she smoothes the quilts*]. Please don't make it necessary to mention this again. [*To Harry*] Would you like to go down for a little while into the garden, Twenty-eight?

> [*Harry crouches silent and moody.*

Susie [*continuing*]. After the sober rain of yesterday it is good to feel the new grace of the yellowing trees, and to get the fresh smell of the grass.

> [*Harry wheels himself round and goes out by the left.*

Susie [*to Sylvester as she goes out*]. Remember, Twenty-six, if you're going to remain in a comatose condition, you'll have to keep your bed presentable.   [*A pause.*

Sylvester [*mimicking Susie*]. Twenty-six, if you're going to remeen in a comatowse condition, you'll have to keep your bed in a tidy an' awdahly mannah.

Simon. Dtch, dtch, dtch, Twenty-seven, it's disgriceful. And as long as you're heah, in the capacity of a patient, please remember I'm not be be addressed as 'Susie', but as 'Nurse Monican'.

Sylvester. Twenty-seven, did you tike the pills the doctah awdahed?

Voice of Susie, left. Twenty-six!

Sylvester. Yes, Nurse?

Voice of Susie. Sister says you're to have a bawth at once; and you, Twenty-seven, see about getting it ready for him.

> [*A fairly long pause.*

Sylvester [*angrily*]. A bawth: well, be God, that's a good one! I'm not in a fit condition for a bath!   [*Another pause.*

Sylvester [*earnestly, to Simon*]. You haven't had a dip now for nearly a week, while I had one only the day before yesterday in the late evening: it must have been you she meant, Simon.

Simon. Oh, there was no dubiety about her bellowing out Twenty-six, Syl.

Sylvester [*excitedly*]. How the hell d'ye know, man, she didn't mix the numbers up?

Simon. Mix the numbers up! How could the woman mix the numbers up?

Sylvester. How could the woman mix the numbers up! What could be easier than to say Twenty-six instead of Twenty-seven? How could the woman mix the numbers up! Of course the woman could mix the numbers up!

Simon. What d'ye expect me to do — hurl myself into a bath that was meant for you?

Sylvester. I don't want you to hurl yourself into anything; but you don't expect me to plunge into a bath that maybe wasn't meant for me?

Simon. Nurse Monican said Twenty-six, and when you can alter that, ring me up and let me know.

[*A pause; then Simon gets up and goes toward bathroom door.*

Sylvester [*snappily*]. Where are you leppin' to now?

Simon. I want to get the bath ready.

Sylvester. You want to get the bawth ready! Turn the hot cock on, and turn the cold cock on for Number Twenty-six, mixin' them the way a chemist would mix his medicines — sit still, man, till we hear the final verdict.

[*Simon sits down again. Susie comes in left, and, passing to the door leading to grounds, pauses beside Simon and Sylvester.*

Susie [*sharply*]. What are the two of you doing? Didn't I tell you, Twenty-six, that you were to take a bawth; and you, Twenty-seven, that you were to get it ready for him?

Sylvester [*sitting brightly up in bed*]. Oh, just goin' to spring up, Nurse Monican, when you popped in.

Susie. Well, up with you, then, and take it. [*To Simon*] You go and get it ready for him.   [*Simon goes into the bathroom.*

Sylvester [*venturing a last hope as Susie goes towards the entrance to grounds*]. I had a dip, Nurse, only the day before yesterday in the late evening.

Susie [*as she goes out*]. Have another one now, please.

[*The water can be heard flowing in the bathroom, and a light cloud
     of steam comes out by the door which Simon has left open.*

Sylvester [*mimicking Susie*]. Have another one, now, please! One
    to be taken before and after meals. The delicate audacity of the
    lip of that one since she draped her shoulders with a crimson
    cape!

[*Simon appears and stands leaning against the side of the bathroom
     door.*

Simon [*gloating*]. She's steaming away now, Sylvester, full cock.

Sylvester [*scornfully, to Simon*]. Music to you, the gurgling of the
    thing, music to you. Gaugin' the temperature for me. Dtch,
    dtch, dtch [*sitting up*], an hospital's the last place that God made.
    Be damn it, I wouldn't let a stuffed bird stay in one!

Simon. Come on, man, before the hot strength bubbles out of it.

Sylvester [*getting out of bed*]. Have you the towels hot an' everything
    ready for me to spring into?

Simon [*with a bow*]. Everything's ready for your enjoyment, Sir.

Sylvester [*as he goes towards the bathroom*]. Can't they be content
    with an honest to God cleanliness, an' not be tryin' to gild a
    man with soap and water.

Simon [*with a grin, as Sylvester passes*]. Can I do anything more for
    you, Sir?

Sylvester [*almost inarticulate with indignation, as he goes in*]. Now
    I'm tellin' you, Simon Norton, our cordiality's gettin' a little
    strained!

[*Harry wheels himself in, goes again to the fireplace, and looks into
     grounds. Simon watches him for a moment, takes a package of
     cigarettes from his pocket and lights one.*

Simon [*awkwardly, to Harry*]. Have a fag, Harry, oul' son?

Harry. Don't want one; tons of my own in the locker.

Simon. Like me to get you one?

Harry. I can get them myself if I want one. D'ye think my arms are lifeless as well as my legs?

Simon. Far from that. Everybody's remarking what a great improvement has taken place in you during the last few days.

Harry. Everybody but myself.

Simon. What with the rubbing every morning and the rubbing every night, and now the operation tomorrow as a grand finally, you'll maybe be in the centre of the football field before many months are out.

Harry [*irritably*]. Oh, shut up, man! It's a miracle I want — not an operation. The last operation was to give life to my limbs, but no life came, and again I felt the horrible sickness of life only from the waist up. [*Raising his voice*] Don't stand there gaping at me, man. Did you never before clap your eyes on a body dead from the belly down? Blast you, man, why don't you shout at me, 'While there's life there's hope'!

[*Simon edges away to his corner. Susie comes in by the glass door and goes over to the table.*

Harry [*to Susie*]. A package of fags. Out of the locker. Will you, Susie?

[*Susie goes to Harry's locker, gets the cigarettes and gives them to him. As he lights the cigarette, his right arm gives a sudden jerk.*

Susie. Steady. What's this?

Harry [*with a nervous laugh*]. Barred from my legs it's flowing back into my arms. I can feel it slyly creeping into my fingers.

Voice of Patient, out left [*plaintively*]. Nurse!

Susie [*turning her head in direction of the voice*]. Shush, you Twenty-three; go asleep, go asleep.

Harry. A soft, velvety sense of distance between my fingers and the things I touch.

Susie. Stop thinking of it. Brooding checks the chance of your recovery. A good deal may be imagination.

Harry [*peevishly*]. Oh, I know the different touches of iron [*he touches the bed-rail*]; of wood [*he touches the chair*]; of flesh [*he touches his cheek*]; and to my fingers they're giving the same answers — a feeling of numb distance between me and the touches of them all.

Voice of Patient, out left. Nurse!

Susie. Dtch, dtch. Go asleep, Twenty-three.

Voice, out left. The stab in the head is worse than ever, Nurse.

Susie. You've got your dose of morphia, and you'll get no more. You'll just have to stick it.

[*Resident Surgeon Forby Maxwell enters from the grounds. He is about thirty years of age, and good-looking. His white overalls are unbuttoned, showing war ribbons on his waistcoat, flanked by the ribbon of the D.S.O. He has a careless, jaunty air, and evidently takes a decided interest in Susie. He comes in singing softly.*

Surgeon Maxwell:

> Stretched on the couch, Jessie fondled her dress,
> That hid all her beauties just over the knee;
> And I wondered and said, as I sigh'd, 'What a shame,
> That there's no room at all on the couch there for me.'

Susie [*to Surgeon Maxwell*]. Twenty-three's at it again.

Surgeon Maxwell. Uh, hopeless case. Half his head in Flanders. May go on like that for another month.

Susie. He keeps the patients awake at night.

Simon. With his 'God have mercys on me', running after every third or fourth tick of the clock.

Harry. 'Tisn't fair to me, 'tisn't fair to me; I must get my bellyful of sleep if I'm ever going to get well.

Surgeon Maxwell. Oh, the poor devil won't trouble any of you much longer. [*Singing*]:

Said Jess, with a light in the side of her eyes,
'A shrewd, mathematical fellow like you,
With an effort of thought should be able to make
The couch wide enough for the measure of two.'

Susie. Dtch, dtch, Surgeon Maxwell.
Surgeon Maxwell [*singing*]:

I fixed on a plan, and I carried it through,
And the eyes of Jess gleam'd as she whisper'd to me:
'The couch, made for one, that was made to hold two,
Has, maybe, been made big enough to hold three!'

[*Surgeon Maxwell catches Susie's hand in his. Sylvester bursts in
from the bathroom, and rushes to his bed, colliding with the
Surgeon as he passes him.*

Surgeon Maxwell. Hallo, hallo there, what's this?
Sylvester [*flinging himself into bed, covering himself rapidly with the
clothes, blowing himself warm*]. Pooh, pooh, I feel as if I was sittin'
on the doorstep of pneumonia! Pooh, Oh!
Surgeon Maxwell [*to Sylvester*]. We'll have a look at you in a
moment, Twenty-six, and see what's wrong with you.

[*Sylvester subsides down into the bed, and Simon edges towards the
entrance to grounds, and stands looking into the grounds, or
watching Surgeon Maxwell examining Sylvester.*

Surgeon Maxwell [*to Harry, who is looking intently out into the
grounds*]. Well, how are we today, Heegan?
Harry. I imagine I don't feel quite so dead in myself as I've felt
these last few days back.
Surgeon Maxwell. Oh, well, that's something.
Harry. Sometimes I think I feel a faint, fluttering kind of a buzz
in the tops of my thighs.
Surgeon Maxwell [*touching Harry's thigh*]. Where, here?

Harry. No; higher up, doctor; just where the line is that leaves the one part living and the other part dead.

Surgeon Maxwell. A buzz?

Harry. A timid, faint, fluttering kind of a buzz.

Surgeon Maxwell. That's good. There might be a lot in that faint, fluttering kind of a buzz.

Harry [*after a pause*]. I'm looking forward to the operation tomorrow.

Surgeon Maxwell. That's the way to take it. While there's life there's hope [*with a grin and a wink at Susie*]. And now we'll have a look at Twenty-six.

   [*Harry, when he hears 'while there's life there's hope', wheels himself madly out left; half-way out he turns his head and stretches to look out into the grounds, then he goes on.*

Susie. Will the operation tomorrow be successful?

Surgeon Maxwell. Oh, of course; very successful.

Susie. Do him any good, d'ye think?

Surgeon Maxwell. Oh, blast the good it'll do him.

                           [*Susie goes over to Sylvester in the bed.*

Susie [*to Sylvester*]. Sit up. Twenty-six, Surgeon Maxwell wants to examine you.

Sylvester [*sitting up with a brave effort but a woeful smile*]. Righto. In the pink!

   [*Surgeon Maxwell comes over, twirling his stethoscope. Simon peeps round the corner of the glass door.*

Susie [*to Surgeon Maxwell*]. What was the cause of the row between the Matron and Nurse Jennings? [*To Sylvester*] Open your shirt, Twenty-six.

Surgeon Maxwell [*who has fixed the stethoscope in his ears, removing it to speak to Susie*]. Caught doing the tango in the Resident's arms in the Resident's room. Naughty girl, naughty girl.
[*To Sylvester*] Say 'ninety-nine'.

Sylvester. Ninety-nine.

Susie. Oh, I knew something like that would happen. Daughter of a Dean, too.

Surgeon Maxwell [*to Sylvester*]. Say 'ninety-nine'.

Sylvester. Ninety-nine. U-u-uh, it's gettin' very cold here, sitting up!

Surgeon Maxwell [*to Sylvester*]. Again. Don't be frightened; breathe quietly.

Sylvester. Ninety-nine. Cool as a cucumber, Doctor. Ninety-nine.

Surgeon Maxwell [*to Susie*]. Damn pretty little piece. Not so pretty as you, though.

Sylvester [*to Surgeon Maxwell*]. Yesterday Doctor Joyce, givin' me a run over, said to a couple of medical men that were with him lookin' for tips, that the thing was apparently yieldin' to treatment, and that an operation wouldn't be necessary.

Surgeon Maxwell. Go on; ninety-nine, ninety-nine.

Sylvester. Ninety-nine, ninety-nine.

Surgeon Maxwell [*to Susie*]. Kicks higher than her head, and you should see her doing the splits.

Sylvester [*to Surgeon Maxwell*]. Any way of gettin' rid of it'll do for me, for I'm not one of them that'll spend a night before an operation in a crowd of prayers.

Susie. Not very useful things to be doing and poor patients awaiting attention.

Surgeon Maxwell [*putting stethoscope into pocket*]. He'll do all right; quite fit. Great old skin. [*To Sylvester*] You can cover yourself up, now. [*To Susie*] And don't tell me, Nurse Susie, that you've never felt a thrill or left a bedside for a kiss in a corner. [*He tickles her under the arm.*] Kiss in a corner, Nurse!

Susie [*pleased, but coy*]. Please don't, Doctor Maxwell, please.

Surgeon Maxwell [*tickling her again as they go out*]. Kiss in a corner; ta-ra-ra-ra, kiss in a corner!   [*A pause.*

Sylvester [*to Simon*]. Simon, were you listenin' to that conversation?

Simon. Indeed I was.

Sylvester. We have our hands full, Simon, to keep alive. Think of sinkin' your body to the level of a hand that, ta-ra-ra-ra, would plunge a knife into your middle, haphazard, hurryin' up to run away after a thrill from a kiss in a corner. Did you see me dizzied an' wastin' me time pumpin' ninety-nines out of me, unrecognized, quiverin' with cold an' equivocation!

Simon. Everybody says he's a very clever fellow with the knife.

Sylvester. He'd gouge out your eye, saw off your arm, lift a load of vitals out of your middle, rub his hands, keep down a terrible desire to cheer lookin' at the ruin, an' say, 'Twenty-six, when you're a little better, you'll feel a new man!'

[*Mrs. Heegan, Mrs. Foran, and Teddy enter from the grounds. Mrs. Foran is leading Teddy, who has a heavy bandage over his eyes, and is dressed in the blue clothes of military hospitals.*

Mrs. Foran [*to Teddy*]. Just a little step here, Ted; upsh! That's it; now we're on the earth again, beside Simon and Sylvester. You'd better sit here.

[*She puts him sitting on a chair.*

Sylvester [*to Mrs. Heegan, as she kisses him*]. Well, how's the old woman, eh?

Mrs. Heegan. A little anxious about poor Harry.

Simon. He'll be all right. Tomorrow'll tell a tale.

Susie [*coming in, annoyed*]. Who let you up here at this hour? Twenty-eight's to have an operation tomorrow, and shouldn't be disturbed.

Mrs. Heegan. Sister Peter Alcantara said we might come up, Nurse.

Mrs. Foran [*loftily*]. Sister Peter Alcantara's authority ought to be good enough, I think.

Mrs. Heegan. Sister Peter Alcantara said a visit might buck him up a bit.

Mrs. Foran. Sister Peter Alcantara knows the responsibility she'd incur by keeping a wife from her husband and a mother from her son.

Susie. Sister Peter Alcantara hasn't got to nurse him. And remember, nothing is to be said that would make his habit of introspection worse than it is.

Mrs. Foran [*with dignity*]. Thanks for the warnin', Nurse, but them kind of mistakes is unusual with us.

[*Susie goes out left, as Harry wheels himself rapidly in. Seeing the group, he stops suddenly, and a look of disappointment comes on to his face.*]

Mrs. Heegan [*kissing Harry*]. How are you, son?

Mrs. Foran. I brought Teddy, your brother in arms, up to see you, Harry.

Harry [*impatiently*]. Where's Jessie? I thought you were to bring her with you?

Mrs. Heegan. She's comin' after us in a moment.

Harry. Why isn't she here now?

Mrs. Foran. She stopped to have a word in the grounds with someone she knew.

Harry. It was Barney Bagnal, was it? Was it Barney Bagnal?

Teddy. Maybe she wanted to talk to him about gettin' the V.C.

Harry. What V.C.? Who's gettin' the V.C.?

Teddy. Barney. Did he not tell you? [*Mrs. Foran prods his knee.*] What's up?

Harry [*intensely, to Teddy*]. What's he gettin' it for? What's he gettin' the V.C. for?

Teddy. For carryin' you wounded out of the line of fire. [*Mrs. Foran prods his knee.*] What's up?

Harry [*in anguish*]. Christ Almighty, for carryin' me wounded out of the line of fire!

Mrs. Heegan [*rapidly*]. Harry, I wouldn't be thinkin' of anything till we see what the operation'll do tomorrow.

Simon [*rapidly*]. God, if it gave him back the use even of one of his legs.

Mrs. Foran [*rapidly*]. Look at all the places he could toddle to, an' all the things he could do then with the prop of a crutch.

Mrs. Heegan. Even at the worst, he'll never be dependin' on any-one, for he's bound to get the maximum allowance.

Simon. Two quid a week, isn't it?

Sylvester. Yes, a hundred per cent total incapacitation.

Harry. She won't come up if one of you don't go down and bring her up.

Mrs. Heegan. She's bound to come up, for she's got your ukulele.

Harry. Call her up, Simon, call her up — I must see Jessie.

[*Simon goes over to the door leading to the grounds, and looks out.*

Mrs. Foran [*bending over till her face is close to Harry's*]. The drawn look on his face isn't half as bad as when I seen him last.

Mrs. Heegan [*bending and looking into Harry's face*]. Look, the hollows under his eyes is fillin' up, too.

Teddy. I'm afraid he'll have to put Jessie out of his head, for when a man's hit in the spine . . . [*Mrs. Foran prods his knee.*] What's up, woman?

Harry [*impatiently, to Simon*]. Is she coming? Can you see her anywhere?

Simon. I see someone like her in the distance, under the trees.

Harry. Call her; can't you give her a shout, man?

Simon [*calling*]. Jessie. Is that you, Jessie? Jessie-e!

Mrs. Heegan [*to Harry*]. What time are you goin' under the operation?

Harry [*to Simon*]. Call her again, call her again, can't you!

Simon [*calling*]. Jessie, Jessie-e!

Teddy. Not much of a chance for an injury to the spine, for . . .

Mrs. Foran [*putting her face close to Teddy's*]. Oh, shut up, you!

Harry. Why did you leave her in the grounds? Why didn't you wait till she came up with you?

Mrs. Foran [*going over to Simon and calling*]. Jessie, Jessie-e!

Jessie's Voice, in distance. Yehess!

Mrs. Foran [*calling*]. Come up here at once; we're all waitin' for you!

Jessie's Voice. I'm not going up!

Mrs. Foran [*calling*]. Bring up that ukulele here at once, miss!

Jessie's Voice. Barney'll bring it up!

[*Harry, who has been listening intently, wheels himself rapidly to where Simon and Mrs. Foran are, pushing through them hurriedly.*

Harry [*calling loudly*]. Jessie! Jessie! Jessie-e!

Mrs. Foran. Look at that, now; she's runnin' away, the young rip!

Harry [*appealingly*]. Jessie, Jessie-e!

[*Susie enters quickly from left. She goes over to Harry and pulls him back from the door.*

Susie [*indignantly*]. Disgraceful! Rousing the whole ward with this commotion! Dear, dear, dear, look at the state of Twenty-eight. Come along, come along, please; you must all go at once.

Harry. Jessie's coming up for a minute, Nurse.

Susie. No more to come up. We've had enough for one night, and you for a serious operation tomorrow. Come on, all out, please.

[*Susie conducts Mrs. Heegan, Mrs. Foran, and Teddy out left.*

Mrs. Foran [*going out*]. We're goin', we're goin', thank you. A nice way to treat the flotsum and jetsum of the battlefields!

Susie [*to Harry*]. To bed now, Twenty-eight, please. [*To Simon*] Help me get him to bed, Twenty-seven.

[*Susie pushes Harry to his bed, right; Simon brings portion of a bed-screen which he places around Harry, hiding him from view.*

Susie [*turning to speak to Sylvester, who is sitting up in bed, as she arranges screen*]. You're going to have your little operation in the morning, so you'd better go to sleep too.

[*Sylvester goes pale and a look of dismay and fear crawls over his face.*

Susie. Don't funk it now. They're not going to turn you inside out. It'll be over in ten minutes.

Sylvester [*with a groan*]. When they once get you down your only hope is in the infinite mercy of God!

Simon. If I was you, Sylvester, I wouldn't take this operation too seriously. You know th' oul' song — Let Me like a Soldier Fall! If I was you, I'd put it completely out of me mind.

Sylvester [*subsiding on to the pillow — with an agonised look on his face*]. Let me like a soldier fall! Did anyone ever hear th' equal o' that! Put it out of me mind completely! [*He sits up, and glares at Simon*]. Eh, you, look! If you can't think sensibly, then thry to think without talkin'! [*He sinks back on the pillow again.*] Let me like a soldier fall. Oh, it's not a fair trial for a sensible man to be stuck down in a world like this!

[*Sylvester slides down till he lies prone and motionless on the bed. Harry is in bed now. Simon removes the screen, and Susie arranges Harry's quilt for the night.*

Susie [*to Simon*]. Now run and help get the things together for supper. [*Simon goes out left.*] [*Encouragingly to Harry*] After the operation, a stay in the air of the Convalescent may work wonders.

Harry. If I could mingle my breath with the breeze that blows from every sea, and over every land, they wouldn't widen me into anything more than the shrivell'd thing I am.

Susie [*switching off the two hanging lights, so that the red light over the fireplace alone remains*]. Don't be foolish, Twenty-eight. Wheeling yourself about among the beeches and the pines, when the daffodils are hanging out their blossoms, you'll deepen your chance in the courage and renewal of the country.

[*The bell of a Convent in grounds begins to ring for Compline.*

Harry [*with intense bitterness*]. I'll say to the pine, 'Give me the grace and beauty of the beech'; I'll say to the beech, 'Give me the strength and stature of the pine'. In a net I'll catch butterflies in bunches; twist and mangle them between my fingers and fix them wriggling on to mercy's banner. I'll make my chair a Juggernaut, and wheel it over the neck and spine of every daffodil that looks at me, and strew them dead to manifest the mercy of God and the justice of man!

Susie [*shocked*]. Shush, Harry, Harry!

Harry. To hell with you, your country, trees, and things, you jibbering jay!

Susie [*as she is going out*]. Twenty-eight!

Harry [*vehemently*]. To hell with you, your country, trees, and things, you jibbering jay!

[*Susie looks at him, pauses for a few moments, as if to speak, and then goes out.*

[*A pause; then Barney comes in by door from grounds. An overcoat covers his military hospital uniform of blue. His left arm is in a sling. Under his right arm he carries a ukulele, and in his hand he has a bunch of flowers. Embarrassed, he goes slowly to Harry's bed, drops the flowers at the foot, then he drops the ukulele there.*

Barney [*awkwardly*]. Your ukulele. An' a bunch of flowers from Jessie.　　　　　　　　　　[*Harry remains motionless on the bed.*

Barney. A bunch of flowers from Jessie, and . . . your . . . ukulele.

[*The Sister of the Ward enters, left, going to the chapel for Compline. She wears a cream habit with a white coif; a large set of Rosary beads hangs from her girdle. She pauses on her way, and a brass Crucifix flashes on her bosom.*

Sister [*to Harry*]. Keeping brave and hopeful, Twenty-eight?

Harry [*softly*]. Yes, Sister.

Sister. Splendid. And we've got a ukulele too. Can you play it, my child?

Harry. Yes, Sister.

Sister. Splendid. You must play me something when you're well over the operation. [*To Barney*] Standing guard over your comrade, Twenty-two, eh?

Barney [*softly and shyly*]. Yes, Sister.

Sister. Grand. Forasmuch as ye do it unto the least of these my brethren, ye do it unto me. Well, God be with you both, my children. [*To Harry*] And Twenty-eight, pray to God for wonderful He is in His doing toward the children of men.

[*Calm and dignified she goes out into the grounds.*

Barney [*pausing as he goes out left*]. They're on the bed; the ukulele, and the bunch of flowers from . . . Jessie.

[*The Sisters are heard singing in the Convent the hymn of Salve Regina.*

Sisters:

Salve Regina, mater misericordiae;
Vitae dulcedo et spes nostra, salve!
Ad te clamamus, exules filii Hevae;
Ad te suspiramus, gementes et flentes in hac lacrymarum valle.
Eia ergo Advocata nostra,
Illos tuos misericordes oculos ad nos converte,
Et Jesum, benedictum fructum ventris tui —

Harry. God of the miracles, give a poor devil a chance, give a
  poor devil a chance!

Sisters:

> Nobis post hoc exsilium ostende,
> O clemens, o pia, o dulcis Virgo Maria!

ACT IV

A room of the dance hall of the Avondale Football Club. At back, left, cutting corners of the back and side walls, is the arched entrance, divided by a slim pillar, to the dance hall. This entrance is hung with crimson and black striped curtains; whenever these are parted the dancers can be seen swinging or gliding past the entrance if a dance be taking place at the time. Over the entrance is a scroll on which is printed: 'Up the Avondales!' The wall back has a wide, tall window which opens to the garden, in which the shrubs and some sycamore trees can be seen. It is hung with apple-green casement curtains, which are pulled to the side to allow the window to be open as it is at present. Between the entrance to hall and the window is a Roll of Honour containing the names of five members of the Club killed in the war. Underneath the Roll of Honour a wreath of laurel tied with red and black ribbon. To the front left is the fireplace. Between the fireplace and the hall entrance is a door on which is an oval white enamel disc with 'Caretaker' painted on it. To the right a long table, covered with a green cloth, on which are numerous bottles of wine and a dozen glasses. On the table, too, is a telephone. A brown carpet covers the floor. Two easy and one ordinary chairs are in the room. Hanging from the ceiling are three lanterns; the centre one is four times the length of its width, the ones at the side are less than half as long as the centre lantern and hang horizontally; the lanterns are black, with a broad red stripe running down the centre of the largest and across those hanging at each side, so that, when they are lighted, they suggest an illuminated black cross with an inner one of gleaming red. The hall is vividly decorated with many coloured lanterns, looped with coloured streamers.

When the scene is revealed the curtains are drawn, and the band can be heard playing a fox-trot. Outside in the garden, near the window, Simon and Sylvester can be seen smoking, and Teddy is walking slowly up and down the path. The band is heard playing for a few moments, then the curtains are pulled aside, and Jessie, with Barney holding her hand, comes in and walks rapidly to the table where the wine is standing. They are quickly followed by Harry, who wheels himself a little forward, then stops, watching them. The curtains part again, and Mrs. Heegan is seen watching Harry. Simon and Sylvester, outside, watch those in the room through the window. Barney wears a neat navy-blue suit, with a rather high, stiff collar and black tie. Pinned on the breast of his waistcoat are his war medals, flanked by the Victoria Cross. Harry is also wearing his medals. Jessie has on a very pretty, rather tight-fitting dance frock, with the sleeves falling widely to the elbow, and cut fairly low on her breast. All the dancers, and Harry too, wear coloured, fantastically shaped paper hats.

Jessie [*hot, excited, and uneasy, as with a rapid glance back she sees the curtains parted by Harry*]. Here he comes prowling after us again! His watching of us is pulling all the enjoyment out of the night. It makes me shiver to feel him wheeling after us.

Barney. We'll watch for a chance to shake him off, an' if he starts again we'll make him take his tangled body somewhere else. [*As Harry moves forward from the curtained entrance*] Shush, he's comin' near us. [*In a louder tone to Jessie*] Red wine, Jessie, for you, or white wine?

Harry. Red wine first, Jessie, to the passion and the power and the pain of life, an' then a drink of white wine to the melody that is in them all!

Jessie. I'm so hot.

Harry. I'm so cold; white wine for the woman warm to make her cold; red wine for the man that's cold to make him warm!

Jessie. White wine for me.

Harry. For me the red wine till I drink to men puffed up with pride of strength, for even creeping things can praise the Lord!

Barney [*gently to Harry, as he gives a glass of wine to Jessie*]. No more for you now, Harry.

Harry [*mockingly*]. Oh, please, your lusty lordship, just another, an' if I seek a second, smack me well. [*Wheeling his chair viciously against Barney*] Get out, you trimm'd-up clod. There's medals on my breast as well as yours! [*He fills a glass*].

Jessie. Let us go back to the dancing, Barney. [*Barney hesitates.*] Please, Barney, let us go back to the dancing!

Harry. To the dancing, for the day cometh when no man can play. And legs were made to dance, to run, to jump, to carry you from one place to another; but mine can neither walk, nor run, nor jump, nor feel the merry motion of a dance. But stretch me on the floor fair on my belly, and I will turn over on my back, then wriggle back again on to my belly; and that's more than a dead, dead man can do!

Barney. Jessie wants to dance, an' so we'll go, and leave you here a little.

Harry. Cram pain with pain, and pleasure cram with pleasure. I'm going too. You'd cage me in from seeing you dance, and dance, and dance, with Jessie close to you, and you so close to Jessie. Though you wouldn't think it, yes, I have — I've hammer'd out many a merry measure upon a polish'd floor with a sweet, sweet heifer. [*As Barney and Jessie are moving away he catches hold of Jessie's dress*] Her name? Oh, any name will do — we'll call her Jessie!

Jessie. Oh, let me go. [*To Barney*] Barney, make him let me go, please.

[*Barney, without a word, removes Harry's hand from Jessie's dress.*

*Jessie and Barney then go out to the dance hall through the cur-
tained entrance. After a while Mrs. Heegan slips away from the
entrance into the hall. After a moment's pause Harry follows
them into the hall. Simon and Sylvester come in from the garden,
leaving Teddy still outside smoking and walking to and fro in the
cautious manner of the blind. Simon and Sylvester sit down near
the fire and puff in silence for a few moments.*

Sylvester [*earnestly*]. I knew it. I knew it, Simon — strainin' an'
strainin' his nerves; driftin' an' driftin' towards an hallucina-
tion!

Simon. Jessie might try to let him down a little more gently, but
it would have been better, I think, if Harry hadn't come here
tonight.

Sylvester. I concur in that, Simon. What's a decoration to an
hospital is an anxiety here.

Simon. To carry life and colour to where there's nothing but the
sick and helpless is right; but to carry the sick and helpless
to where there's nothing but life and colour is wrong.

[*The telephone bell rings.*

Sylvester. There's the telephone bell ringing.

Simon. Oh, someone'll come in and answer it in a second.

Sylvester. To join a little strength to a lot of weakness is what I
call sensible; but to join a little weakness to a lot of strength is
what I call a . . .

Simon. A cod.

Sylvester. Exactly.   [*The telephone continues to ring.*

Sylvester. There's that telephone ringin' still.

Simon. Oh, someone'll come in and answer it in a second.

[*Teddy has groped his way to French window.*

Teddy. The telephone's tinklin', boys.

Sylvester. Thanks, Teddy. We hear it, thanks. [*To Simon*] When
he got the invitation from the Committay to come, wearin'

his decorations, me an' the old woman tried to persuade him that, seein' his condition, it was better to stop at home, an' let me represent him, but [*with a gesture*] no use!

> [*Teddy resumes his walk to and fro.*

Simon. It was natural he'd want to come, since he was the means of winning the Cup twice before for them, leading up to their keeping the trophy for ever by the win of a year ago.

Sylvester. To bring a boy so helpless as him, whose memory of agility an' strength time hasn't flattened down, to a place wavin' with joy an' dancin', is simply, simply ——

Simon. Devastating, I'd say.

Sylvester. Of course it is! Is that god-damn telephone goin' to keep ringin' all night?

> [*Mrs. Foran enters from hall quickly.*

Mrs. Foran. Miss Monican says that one of you is to answer the telephone, an' call her if it's anything important.

Sylvester [*nervously*]. I never handled a telephone in my life.

Simon. I chanced it once and got so hot and quivery that I couldn't hear a word, and didn't know what I was saying myself.

Mrs. Foran. Have a shot at it and see.

> [*The three of them drift over to the telephone.*

Sylvester. Chance it again, Simon, an' try to keep steady.

> [*As Simon stretches his hand to the receiver.*

Sylvester. Don't rush, don't rush, man, an' make a mess of it. Take it in your stride.

Simon [*pointing to receiver*]. When you lift this down, you're connected, I think.

Sylvester. No use of thinkin' on this job. Don't you turn the handle first?

Simon [*irritably*]. No, you don't turn no handle, man!

Mrs. Foran. Let Simon do it now; Simon knows.

> [*Simon tremblingly lifts down the receiver, almost letting it fall.*

Sylvester. Woa, woa, Simon; careful, careful!

Simon [*speaking in receiver*]. Eh, hallo! Eh, listen there. Eh, hallo! listen.

Sylvester. You listen, man, an' give the fellow at the other end a chance to speak.

Simon. If you want me to manipulate the thing, let me manipulate it in tranquillity.

Mrs. Foran [*to Sylvester*]. Oh, don't be puttin' him out, Sylvester.

Simon [*waving them back*]. Don't be crushing in on me; give me room to manipulate the thing.

[*Dead silence for some moments.*

Mrs. Foran. Are you hearin' anything from the other end?

Simon. A kind of a buzzing and a roaring noise.

[*Sylvester suddenly gives the cord a jerk and pulls the receiver out of Simon's hand.*

[*Angrily*] What the hell are you trying to do, man? You're after pulling it right out of my mit.

Sylvester [*heatedly*]. There was a knot or a twist an' a tangle in it that was keepin' the sound from travellin'.

Simon. If you want me to work the thing properly, you'll have to keep yourself from interfering. [*Resuming surlily*] Eh, hallo, listen, yes? Ha! ha! ha! ha! Yes, yes, yes. No, no, no. Cheerio! Yes. Eh, hallo, listen, eh. Hallo.

Sylvester. What is it? What're they sayin'?

Simon [*hopelessly, taking the receiver from his ear*]. I don't seem to be able to hear a damn sound.

Sylvester. An' Holy God, what are you yessin' and noin' and cheerioin' out of you for then?

Simon. You couldn't stand here like a fool and say nothing, could you?

Sylvester. Show it to me, Simon, show it to me — you're not holdin' it at the proper angle.

Mrs. Foran. Give it to Syl, Simon; it's a delicate contrivance that needs a knack in handlin'.

Sylvester [*as he is taking the receiver from Simon and carefully placing it to his ear*]. You have always to preserve an eqwee-balance between the speakin' mouth and the hearin' ear. [*Speaking into receiver*] Hallo! Anybody there at the other end of this? Eh, wha's that? Yes, yes, I've got you [*taking the receiver from his ear and speaking to Simon and Mrs. Foran*]: Something like wine, or dine, or shine, or something — an' a thing that's hummin'.

Simon. I can see no magnificent meaning jumping out of that!

Mrs. Foran. They couldn't be talkin' about bees, could they?

Sylvester [*scornfully*]. Bees! No, they couldn't be talkin' about bees! That kind of talk, Mrs. Foran, only tends to confuse matters. Bees! Dtch, dtch, dtch — the stupidity of some persons is . . . terrifyin'!

Simon. Ask them quietly what they want.

Sylvester [*indignantly*]. What the hell's the use of askin' them that, when I can hear something only like a thing that's hummin'?

Mrs. Foran. It wouldn't be, now, comin', or even bummin'?

Sylvester. It might even possibly be drummin'. Personally, Mrs. Foran, I think, since you can't help, you might try to keep from hinderin'.

Simon. Put it back, Syl, where it was, an' if it rings again, we'll only have to slip quietly out of this.

Mrs. Foran. Yes, put it back, an' say it never rang.

Sylvester. Where was it? Where do I put it back?

Simon. On that thing stickin' out there. Nice and gently now.

[*Sylvester cautiously puts receiver back. They look at the telephone for a few moments, then go back to the fire, one by one. Sylvester stands with his back to it; Simon sits in a chair, over the back of which Mrs. Foran leans.*

Mrs. Foran. Curious those at the other end of the telephone couldn't make themselves understood.

Simon. Likely they're not accustomed to it, and it's a bit difficult if you're not fully conscious of its manipulation.

Sylvester. Well, let them study an' study it then, or abide by the consequences, for we can't be wastin' time teachin' them.

[*The curtains at entrance of dance hall are pulled aside, and Teddy, who has disappeared from the garden a little time before, comes in. As he leaves the curtains apart, the dancers can be seen gliding past the entrance in the movements of a tango. Teddy comes down, looks steadily but vacantly towards the group around the fire, then goes over carefully to the table, where he moves his hand about till it touches a bottle, which he takes up in one hand, feeling it questioningly with the other.*

Simon. How goes it, Teddy?

Teddy [*with a vacant look towards them*]. Sylvester — Simon — well. What seest thou, Teddy? Thou seest not as man seeth. In the garden the trees stand up; the green things showeth themselves and fling out flowers of divers hues. In the sky the sun by day and the moon and the stars by night — nothing. In the hall the sound of dancing, the eyes of women, grey and blue and brown and black, do sparkle and dim and sparkle again. Their white breasts rise and fall, and rise again. Slender legs, from red and black, and white and green, come out, go in again — nothing. Strain as you may, it stretches from the throne of God to the end of the hearth of hell.

Simon. What?

Teddy. The darkness.

Simon [*knowing not what to say*]. Yes, oh yes.

Teddy [*holding up a bottle of wine*]. What colour, Syl? It's all the same, but I like the red the best.

Mrs. Foran [*going over to Teddy*]. Just one glass, dear, and you'll sit down quietly an' take it in sips.

[*Mrs. Foran fills a glass of wine for Teddy, leads him to a chair, puts him sitting down, and gives the glass of wine carefully to him. The band in the hall has been playing, and through the parted curtains the dancers are seen gliding past. Jessie moves by now in the arms of Barney, and in a few moments is followed along the side of the hall by Harry wheeling himself in his chair and watching them. Mrs. Foran and the two men look on and become attentive when among the dancers Susie, in the arms of Surgeon Maxwell, Jessie partnered with Barney, and Harry move past.*

Sylvester [*as Susie goes by*]. Susie Monican's lookin' game enough tonight for anything.

Simon. Hardly remindful of her one-time fear of God.

Sylvester [*as Jessie goes by followed by Harry*]. There he goes, still followin' them.

Simon. And Jessie's looking as if she was tired of her maidenhood, too.

Mrs. Foran. The thin threads holdin' her dress up sidlin' down over her shoulders, an' her catchin' them up again at the tail end of the second before it was too late.

Simon [*grinning*]. And Barney's hand inching up, inching up to pull them a little lower when they're sliding down.

Mrs. Foran. Astonishin' the way girls are advertisin' their immodesty. Whenever one of them sits down, in my heart I pity the poor men havin' to view the disedifyin' sight of the full length of one leg couched over another.

Teddy [*forgetful*]. A damn nice sight, all the same, I think.

Mrs. Foran [*indignantly*]. One would imagine such a thought would jar a man's mind that had kissed goodbye to the sight of his eyes.

Teddy. Oh, don't be tickin' off every word I say!

Mrs. Foran [*after an astonished pause, whipping the glass out of Teddy's hand*]. Damn the drop more, now, you'll get for the rest of the evenin'.

[*The band suddenly stops playing, and the couples seen just then through the doorway stop dancing and look attentively up the hall. After a slight pause, Harry in his chair, pushed by Susie, comes in through the entrance: his face is pale and drawn, his breath comes in quick faint gasps, and his head is leaning sideways on the back of the chair. Mrs. Heegan is on one side of Harry, and Surgeon Maxwell, who is in dinner-jacket style of evening dress, wearing his medals, including the D.S.O., walks on the other. Harry is wheeled over near the open window. Barney and Jessie, standing in the entrance, look on and listen.*

Maxwell. Here near the window. [*To Mrs. Heegan*] He'll be all right, Mrs. Heegan, in a second; a little faint — too much excitement. When he recovers a little, I'd get him home.

Harry [*faintly but doggedly*]. Napoo home, napoo. Not yet. I'm all right. I'll spend a little time longer in the belly of an hour bulgin' out with merriment. Carry on.

Maxwell. Better for you to go home, Heegan.

Harry. When they drink to the Club from the Cup — the Silver Tassie — that I won three times, three times for them — that first was filled to wet the lips of Jessie and of me — I'll go, but not yet. I'm all right; my name is yet only a shadow on the Roll of Honour.

Mrs. Heegan. Come home, Harry; you're gettin' your allowance only on the understandin' that you take care of yourself.

Harry. Get the Cup. I'll mind it here till you're ready to send it round to drink to the Avondales — on the table here beside me. Bring the Cup; I'll mind it here on the table beside me.

Maxwell. Get the Cup for him, someone.

[*Simon goes to the hall and returns with the Cup, which he gives to Harry.*

Harry [*holding the Cup out*]. A first drink again for me, for me alone this time, for the shell that hit me bursts for ever between Jessie and me. [*To Simon*] Go on, man, fill out the wine!

Maxwell [*to Simon*]. A little — just a glass. Won't do him any harm. [*To Harry*] Then you'll have to remain perfectly quiet, Heegan.

Harry. The wine .. fill out the wine!

Simon [*to Harry*]. Red wine or white?

Harry. Red wine, red like the faint remembrance of the fires in France; red wine like the poppies that spill their petals on the breasts of the dead men. No, white wine, white like the stillness of the millions that have removed their clamours from the crowd of life. No, red wine; red like the blood that was shed for you and for many for the commission of sin! [*He drinks the wine.*] Steady, Harry, and lift up thine eyes unto the hills. [*Roughly to those around him*] What are you all gaping at?

Maxwell. Now, now, Heegan — you must try to keep quiet.

Susie. And when you've rested and feel better, you will sing for us a Negro Spiritual, and point the melody with the ukulele.

Mrs. Heegan. Just as he used to do.

Sylvester. Behind the trenches.

Simon. In the Rest Camps.

Mrs. Foran. Out in France.

Harry. Push your sympathy away from me, for I'll have none of it. [*He wheels his chair quickly towards the dance hall.*] Go on with the dancing and keep the ball a-rolling. [*Calling loudly at the entrance*] Trumpets and drum begin! [*The band begins to play.*] Dance and dance and dance. [*He listens for a moment.*] Sink into merriment again, and sling your cares to God! [*He whirls round in the chair to the beat of the tune. Dancers are seen gliding past entrance.*] Dear God, I can't. [*He sinks sideways on his chair.*] I must, must rest. [*He quietly recites:*]

> For a spell here I will stay,
> Then pack up my body and go —
> For mine is a life on the ebb,
> Yours a full life on the flow!

[*Harry goes over to far side of window and looks out into garden. Mrs. Heegan is on his right and Teddy on his left; Simon and Sylvester a little behind, looking on. Mrs. Foran to the right of Mrs. Heegan. Surgeon Maxwell and Susie, who are a little to the front, watch for a moment, then the Surgeon puts his arm round Susie and the pair glide off into the dance hall.*

[*When Surgeon Maxwell and Susie glide in to the motions of the dance through the entrance into the dance hall, the curtains are pulled together. A few moments' pause. Teddy silently puts his hand on Harry's shoulder, and they both stare into the garden.*

Simon. The air'll do him good.

Sylvester. An' give him breath to sing his song an' play the ukulele.

Mrs. Heegan. Just as he used to do.

Sylvester. Behind the trenches.

Simon. In the Rest Camps.

Mrs. Foran. Out in France.

Harry. I can see, but I cannot dance.

Teddy. I can dance, but I cannot see.

Harry. Would that I had the strength to do the things I see.

Teddy. Would that I could see the things I've strength to do.

Harry. The Lord hath given and the Lord hath taken away.

Teddy. Blessed be the name of the Lord.

Mrs. Foran. I do love the ukulele, especially when it goes tinkle, tinkle, tinkle in the night-time.

Sylvester. Bringin' before you glistenin' bodies of blacks, coilin'
   themselves an' shufflin' an' prancin' in a great jungle dance;
   shakin' assegais an' spears to the rattle, rattle, rattle an' thud,
   thud, thud of the tom-toms.

Mrs. Foran. There's only one possible musical trimmin' to the
   air of a Negro Spiritual, an' that's the tinkle, tinkle, tinkle of
   a ukulele.

Harry. The rising sap in trees I'll never feel.

Teddy. The hues of branch or leaf I'll never see.

Harry. There's something wrong with life when men can walk.

Teddy. There's something wrong with life when men can see.

Harry. I never felt the hand that made me helpless.

Teddy. I never saw the hand that made me blind.

Harry. Life came and took away the half of life.

Teddy. Life took from me the half he left with you.

Harry. The Lord hath given and the Lord hath taken away.

Teddy. Blessed be the name of the Lord.

   [*Susie comes quickly in by entrance, goes over to the table and,
      looking at several bottles of wine, selects one. She is going
      hurriedly back, when, seeing Harry, she goes over to him.*

Susie [*kindly*]. How are you now, Harry?

Harry. All right, thank you.

Susie. That's good.

   [*Susie is about to hurry away, when Mrs. Foran stops her with a
      remark.*

Mrs. Foran [*with a meaning gesture*]. He's takin' it cushy till you're
   ready to hear him singin' his Negro Spiritual, Miss.

Susie. Oh, God, I'd nearly forgotten that. They'll be giving out
   the balloons at the next dance, and when that fox-trot's over
   he'll have to come in and sing us the Spiritual.

Mrs. Heegan. Just as he used to do.

Simon. Behind the trenches.

Sylvester. In the Rest Camps.

Mrs. Foran. Out in France.

Susie. As soon as the Balloon Dance is over, Harry, out through the garden and in by the front entrance with you, so that you'll be ready to start as they all sit down. And after the song, we'll drink to the Club from the Silver Tassie.

[*She hurries back to the hall with the bottle of wine.*

Mrs. Foran. I'm longin' to hear Harry on the ukulele.

Harry. I hope I'll be able to do justice to it.

Mrs. Heegan. Of course you will, Harry.

Harry [*nervously*]. Before a crowd. Forget a word and it's all up with you.

Simon. Try it over now, softly; the sound couldn't carry as far as the hall.

Sylvester. It'll give you confidence in yourself.

Harry [*to Simon*]. Show us the ukulele, Simon.

[*Simon gets the ukulele and gives it to Harry.*

Teddy. If I knew the ukulele it might wean me a little way from the darkness.

[*Harry pulls a few notes, tuning the ukulele, then he softly sings.*
Harry:

Swing low, sweet chariot, comin' for to carry me home,
Swing low, sweet chariot, comin' for to carry me home.
I looked over Jordan, what did I see, comin' for to carry
   me home?
A band of angels comin' after me — comin' for to carry
   me home.

[*A voice in the hall is heard shouting through a megaphone.*

Voice. Balloons will be given out now! Given out now — the balloons!

Mrs. Foran [*excitedly*]. They're goin' to send up the balloons!
    They're going to let the balloons fly now!
Harry [*singing*]:

> Swing low, sweet chariot, comin' for to carry me home.
> Swing low, sweet chariot, comin' for to carry me home.

Mrs. Foran [*as Harry is singing*]. Miss Monican wants us all to see
    the flyin' balloons.
            [*She catches Teddy's arm and runs with him into the hall.*
Simon. We must all see the flyin' balloons.
Mrs. Heegan [*running into hall*]. Red balloons and black balloons.
Simon [*following Mrs. Heegan*]. Green balloons and blue balloons.
Sylvester [*following Simon*]. Yellow balloons and puce balloons.
    [*All troop into the hall, leaving the curtains apart, and Harry alone
        with his ukulele. Through the entrance various coloured balloons
        that have been tossed into the air can be seen, mid sounds of
        merriment and excitement.*
Harry [*softly and slowly*]. Comin' for to carry me home.
    [*He throws the ukulele into an armchair, sits still for a moment, then
        goes to the table, takes up the Silver Cup, and wheels himself into
        the garden.*
    [*After a pause Barney looks in, then enters pulling Jessie by the
        hand, letting the curtains fall together again. Then he goes quickly
        to window, shuts and bolts it, drawing-to one half of the curtains,
        goes back to Jessie, catches her hand again, and tries to draw her
        towards room on the left. During the actions that follow the dance
        goes merrily on in the hall.*
Jessie [*holding up a broken shoulder-strap and pulling back towards the
    hall*]. Barney, no. God, I'd be afraid he might come in on us
    alone.
    [*Hands part the curtains and throw in coloured streamers that
        encircle Jessie and Barney.*

Barney. Damn them! . . . He's gone, I tell you, to sing the song an' play the ukulele.

Jessie [*excited and afraid*]. See, they're watching us. No, Barney. You mustn't. I'll not go! [*Barney seizes Jessie in his arms and forces her towards the door on the left.*] You wouldn't be good. I'll not go into that room.

Barney. I will be good, I tell you! I just want to be alone with you for a minute.

[*Barney loosens Jessie's other shoulder-strap, so that her dress leaves her shoulders and bosom bare.*

Jessie [*near the door left, as Barney opens it*]. You've loosened my dress — I knew you weren't going to be good. [*As she kisses him passionately*] Barney, Barney — you shouldn't be making me do what I don't want to do!

Barney [*holding her and trying to pull her into room*]. Come on, Jessie, you needn't be afraid of Barney — we'll just rest a few minutes from the dancing.

[*At that part of the window uncurtained Harry is seen peering in. He then wheels his chair back and comes on to the centre of the window-frame with a rush, bursting the catch and speeding into the room, coming to a halt, angry and savage, before Barney and Jessie.*

Harry. So you'd make merry over my helplessness in front of my face, in front of my face, you pair of cheats! You couldn't wait till I'd gone, so that my eyes wouldn't see the joy I wanted hurrying away from me over to another? Hurt her breast pulling your hand quick out of her bodice, did you? [*To Jessie*] Saved you in the nick of time, my lady, did I? [*To Barney*] Going to enjoy yourself on the same little couch where she, before you formed an image in her eye, acted the part of an amateur wife, and I acted the part of an amateur husband — the black couch with the green and crimson butterflies, in the yellow bushes, where she and me often tired of the things you're dangling after now!

Jessie. He's a liar, he's a liar, Barney! He often tried it on with coaxing first and temper afterwards, but it always ended in a halt that left him where he started.

Harry. If I had my hands on your white neck I'd leave marks there that crowds of kisses from your Barney wouldn't moisten away.

Barney. You half-baked Lazarus, I've put up with you all the evening, so don't force me now to rough-handle the bit of life the Jerries left you as a souvenir!

Harry. When I wanted to slip away from life, you brought me back with your whispered 'Think of the tears of Jess, think of the tears of Jess', but Jess has wiped away her tears in the ribbon of your Cross, and this poor crippled jest gives a flame of joy to the change; but when you get her, may you find in her the pressed-down emptiness of a whore!

Barney [*running over and seizing Harry*]. I'll tilt the leaking life out of you, you jealous, peering pimp!

Jessie [*trying to hold Barney back*]. Barney, Barney, don't! don't!

Harry [*appealingly*]. Barney, Barney! My heart — you're stopping it!

Jessie [*running to entrance and shouting in*]. Help! help! They're killing each other!

[*In the hall the dance stops. Surgeon Maxwell runs in, followed by Susie, Simon, Sylvester, Mrs. Foran, Mrs. Heegan, and lastly Teddy finding his way over to the window. Dancers gather around entrance and look on.*

[*Surgeon Maxwell, running over, separates Barney from Harry.*

Maxwell. What's this? Come, come — we can't have this sort of thing going on.

Mrs. Heegan. He was throttlin' him, throttlin' a poor helpless creature, an' if anything happens, he and that painted slug Jessie Taite'll be held accountable!

Maxwell. This can't be allowed to go on. You'll have to bring him home. Any more excitement would be dangerous.

Mrs. Heegan. This is what he gets from Jessie Taite for sittin' on the stairs through the yawnin' hours of the night, racin' her off to the play an' the pictures, an' plungin' every penny he could keep from me into presents for the consolidation of the courtship!

Maxwell. Bring the boy home, woman, bring the boy home.

Sylvester [*fiercely to Jessie*]. And money of mine in one of the gewgaws scintillatin' in her hair!

Jessie. What gewgaw? What gewgaw?

[*Coloured streamers are thrown in by those standing at entrance, which fall on and encircle some of the group around Harry.*

Sylvester. The tiarara I gave you two Christmases ago with the yellow berries and the three flutterin' crimson swallows!

Harry [*faintly and bitterly, with a hard little laugh*]. Napoo Barney Bagnal and napoo Jessie Taite. A merry heart throbs coldly in my bosom; a merry heart in a cold bosom — or is it a cold heart in a merry bosom? [*He gathers a number of the coloured streamers and winds them round himself and chair.*] Teddy! [*Harry catches Teddy by the sleeve and winds some more streamers round him.*] Sing a song, man, and show the stuff you're made of!

Maxwell [*catching hold of Mrs. Heegan's arm*]. Bring him home, woman. [*Maxwell catches Sylvester's arm.*] Get him home, man.

Harry. Dear God, this crippled form is still your child. [*To Mrs. Heegan*] Dear mother, this helpless thing is still your son. Harry Heegan, me, who, on the football field, could crash a twelve-stone flyer off his feet. For this dear Club three times I won the Cup, and grieve in reason I was just too weak this year to play again. And now, before I go, I give you all the Cup, the Silver

Tassie, to have and to hold for ever, evermore. [*From his chair he takes the Cup with the two sides hammered close together, and holds it out to them.*] Mangled and bruised as I am bruised and mangled. Hammered free from all its comely shape. Look, there is Jessie writ, and here is Harry, the one name safely separated from the other. [*He flings it on the floor.*] Treat it kindly. With care it may be opened out, for Barney there to drink to Jess, and Jessie there to drink to Barney.

Teddy. Come, Harry, home to where the air is soft. No longer can you stand upon a hill-top; these empty eyes of mine can never see from one. Our best is all behind us — what's in front we'll face like men, dear comrade of the blood-fight and the battle-front!

Harry. What's in front we'll face like men! [*Harry goes out by the window, Sylvester pushing the chair, Teddy's hand on Harry's shoulder, Mrs. Heegan slowly following. Those left in the room watch them going out through the garden, turning to the right till they are all out of sight. As he goes out of window*] The Lord hath given and man hath taken away!

Teddy [*heard from the garden*]. Blessed be the name of the Lord! [*The band in the hall begins to play again. Those in hall begin to dance.*

Maxwell. Come on, all, we've wasted too much time already.

Susie [*to Jessie, who is sitting quietly in a chair*]. Come on, Jessie — get your partner; [*roguishly*] you can have a quiet time with Barney later on.

Jessie. Poor Harry!

Susie. Oh nonsense! If you'd passed as many through your hands as I, you'd hardly notice one. [*To Jessie*] Jessie, Teddy Foran and Harry Heegan have gone to live their own way in another world. Neither I nor you can lift them out of it. No longer can they do the things we do. We can't give sight to the blind or make the lame walk. We would if we could. It is the misfortune of war. As long as wars are waged, we shall be vexed by woe; strong legs shall be made useless and bright eyes made dark. But we, who have come through the fire unharmed, must go on living. [*Pulling Jessie from the chair*] Come along, and take your part in life! [*To Barney*] Come along, Barney, and take your partner into the dance!

[*Barney comes over, puts his arm round Jessie, and they dance into the hall. Susie and Surgeon Maxwell dance together. As they dance the Waltz 'Over the Waves', some remain behind drinking. Two of these sing the song to the same tune as the dance.*

Maxwell:

> Swing into the dance,
> Take joy when it comes, ere it go;
> For the full flavour of life
> Is either a kiss or a blow.
> He to whom joy is a foe,
> Let him wrap himself up in his woe;
> For he is a life on the ebb,
> We a full life on the flow!

[*All in the hall dance away with streamers and balloons flying. Simon and Mrs. Foran sit down and watch the fun through the entrance. Mrs. Foran lights a cigarette and smokes. A pause as they look on.*

Mrs. Foran. It's a terrible pity Harry was too weak to stay an' sing his song, for there's nothing I love more than the ukulele's tinkle, tinkle in the night-time.

CURTAIN

SONGS AND CHANTS IN
THE SILVER TASSIE

1st CHANT.

Intonation

I sees the mis - sus paryd-ing a - long Wal-ham Green, Through the jewels

Mediation

an' silks on the cos - ters' carts, Em - mie a - pull - ing her skirt

Ending

an' mut - ter - ing, "A bal - loon, a bal - loon, I wants a bal - loon",

The mis-sus . . . an' your fa-ther fight-ing: You'll wait . . that's wot we wants to know!

Tabs 'll . . . for - ty-eight bat-ta-lion, The Yel-low . . . leg up on the path to glo-ry;

Now with . . . Ar-my of the Marne, An' all the time . . . two men looking after business.

The padre . . . muv-ver 'as you 'ere." An' last time . . . sep-er-y-tion mon-eys reg'-lar.

But wy - 'r we 'ere, wy - 'r we 'ere—that's wot I wants to know!

2nd CHANT.

A Brass-hat . . . world an' the Es-tam-i-nay's daugh-ter,

In a py-jam-a'd . . . an Es-tam-i-na-y cock, An' I was pinch'd . . .

with a pint of peas. And the hens . . . a place of des-o-la-tion!

3rd CHANT.

The perk-y . . . queers me. Furi-ous-ly feel-ing . . . front-line fight-ing.

In his full-blown, . . . mur-mur, "Here's a stand-fast . . . whis-per "yes-sir".

Like a bride, . . . ser-mon, From the cush-y . . . Tom-my's back-side.

4th CHANT.

Jazz-ing back to his ho-tel he now goes gai-ly, Shel-ter'd

and safe where the clock ticks tame-ly. His back-side warm-ing

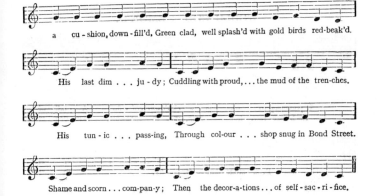

a cu - shion, down - fill'd, Green clad, well splash'd with gold birds red-beak'd.

His last dim . . . ju - dy; Cuddling with proud, . . . the mud of the tren-ches.

His tun - ic . . . pass-ing, Through col-our . . . shop snug in Bond Street.

Shame and scorn . . . com-pan-y; Then the decor-a-tions . . . of self - sac - ri - fice.

5th CHANT.

A warn-ing . . . give, To the front . . . do, to God.

God, un-chang-ing, . . . night sky To mask . . . His self-slay-ing chil-dren.

Stumbling, swiftly . . . grous-ing, Through mud . . . seek slow the front line.

Squeals of hid - den . . . wounded—Christ who bore . . . tied to a field gun.

WOULD GOD I SMOK'D.

Would God I   smok'd   and walk'd and watch'd - -   The dance of a
Would God I   smok'd   and lift - ed car - goes   From the lad - en
To   hang here   ev - en   a lit - tle lon - ger,   Loung - ing
If you creep to   rest   in a clos'd-up cof - fin,   A   tail of
Each spar - row,   hop - ping, ir - re - sponsible,   Is in - den - tur'd

gol - den Brim - stone but - ter - fly, - -   To   the
shoul - ders of Lon - don's riv - er   way; - -   Then
through   fear - swell'd, anx - ious   moments;   The
com - rades see - ing   you   safe   home; -   Or be a
in   God's migh - ty   mem - o - ry; . -   And we,

sau - cy   pipe   of a   green - finch rest - ing   In a
holi - day'd, roar - ing   out   courage and move - ment   To the
hin - der - parts   of the   god   of   bat - tles   Shading our
ker - nel lost   in a   shell   ex - plod - ing—   It's all,
more than they   all,   shall   not   be   lost   In the for-

drowsy, brambled lane in   Cumber - land.   In   Cumber - land.
mus - cled ma-chines of   Tottenham Hotspur.   Of   Tottenham Hotspur.
war   tir'd   eyes from his flam - ing face.   From his flaming face.
sure,   on - ly   in a   life - time.   A   life - time.
get - ful - ness of the Lord of   Hosts.   Of the Lord of   Hosts.

STRETCHER-BEARERS' SONG.

Oh, bear it gent - ly, car - ry it soft - ly—A bull-et or a shell said stop, stop, stop. It's had its day, and it's left the play, Since it gam - boll'd ov - er the top, top, top. It's had its day and it's left the play, Since it gam - boll'd o - - ver the top.

SONG TO THE GUN.

Hail, cool-hardened tower of steel em-boss'd With the fever'd, fig - ment thoughts of man; Guard - ian of our love and hate and fear, Speak for us to the in - ner ear of God! We be - lieve in God and we be - lieve in thee.

THE ENEMY HAS BROKEN THROUGH.

The en-em-y has brok-en through, brok-en through, brok-en through! Ev-ery

man born of wo-man to the guns, to the guns. To the

guns, to the guns, to the guns! Those at prayer, all in bed and the

swillers drinking deeply in the pubs. To the guns, to the guns. All the

bat-men, ev-ery cook, ev-ery bitch's son that hides A whiff of

cour-age in his veins, Shelter'd vig-our in his bod-y, That can

run, or can walk, ev-en crawl— . . . Dig him

out, dig him out, shove him on— . . . To the guns!

SURGEON'S SONG.

Stret - ched   on   the couch, Jess - ie   fon - dled her dress,   That

hid   all her beaut - ies just   o - ver the knee; And I won-dered and said, as I

sigh'd, "What a shame, That there's no room at   all   on the   couch there for me."

PURPLE DUST

A Wayward Comedy in Three Acts

TO

SHIVAUN

CHARACTERS IN THE PLAY

CYRIL POGES
BASIL STOKE
SOUHAUN, *Cyril's mistress*
AVRIL, *Basil's mistress*
BARNEY, *their manservant*
CLOYNE, *their maidservant*
O'KILLIGAIN, *a foreman stonemason*
1ST WORKMAN
2ND WORKMAN
3RD WORKMAN
REVEREND GEORGE CANON CHREEHEWEL,
    P.P. of Clune na Geera
POSTMASTER
YELLOW-BEARDED MAN
THE FIGURE
THE BULL

————

SCENES

ACT   I.—A room in an old Tudor mansion
           in Clune na Geera.
ACT   II.—The same.
ACT III.—The same.

TIME.—The present.

ACT I

SCENE: *A wide, deep, gloomy room that was once part of the assembly or living room of a Tudor-Elizabethan mansion. The floor is paved with broad black and dull red flagstones. The walls are timbered with oak beams, and beams of the same wood criss-cross each other, forming the roof, so that the room looks somewhat like a gigantic cage. The beams are painted, alternately, black and white so as to show they are there and to draw attention to their beauty; but the paint makes them too conspicuous and, therefore, ugly.*

On the right is a huge open fireplace, overhung by a huge hood. In the centre of the fireplace is a big iron arm with a swinging cross-piece thrust out like a crane; from this cross-piece hangs a thick chain to which a big shining copper kettle is attached. At the back are two rather narrow arched doorways, one towards the right, the other towards the left. Between these are two long, deep, mullioned windows. At the right, nearly opposite the fireplace, is a wider arched doorway leading to the entrance hall. Near the fireplace are two straight-backed seats, like infantile church pews, each big enough only to hold one person. A small Elizabethan or Jacobean table is somewhere near the centre of the room. On this table is a vase in which are a collection of violets and primroses, mostly primroses.

It is about seven o'clock of an autumn morning, fine, crisp, and fair.

Three workmen are seen in the room, two with shovels and one with a pickaxe. One with a shovel and the one with the pickaxe are standing near the archway leading to the entrance hall; the other, with a shovel, is beside the wide fireplace, looking curiously at it. The 1st Workman is a tall, lean man with a foxy face; the 2nd Workman is tall too, and strongly built; he has a dreamy look, and has a dark trim beard faintly touched with grey; the 3rd Workman is stouter than the others, and not so tall. They are all roughly dressed in soiled clothes, and wear high rubber boots.

1st Workman [*near the fireplace*]. Well, of all th' wondhers, to come to live in a house that's half down and it's wanin' over. Thrickin' th' rotten beams into a look o' sturdiness with a coat o' white and black paint, an' they for long a dismal dwellin', even for the gnawin' beetle an' th' borin' worm.

3rd Workman [*with the pickaxe*]. They like that sort of thing.

1st Workman. An' th' maid was tellin' me they're goin' to invest in hins an' cows, an' make th' place self-supportin'.

3rd Workman. An' th' two o' them business men, rollin' in money.

1st Workman. Women you're not married to cost a lot to keep; an' th' two with them'll dip deep into the oul' men's revenue. Goin' over to London done them a world o' good.

3rd Workman. Irish, too, an' not a bit ashamed o' themselves.

1st Workman. Ashamed is it? Isn't th' oulder one proclaimin' she's straight derived from th' Duke of Ormond?

3rd Workman. An' we knowin' th' two o' them well as kids with patched petticoats an' broken shoes, runnin' round th' lanes o' Killnageera.

1st Workman. God be good to her, anyway, for bringin' a bit o' th' doddherers' money to where it's needed.

3rd Workman. Th' two poor English omadhauns won't have much when th' lasses decide it's time for partin'.

2nd Workman [*who has been silently leaning on his shovel, looking dreamily ahead of him*]. That day'll hasten, for God is good. Our poets of old have said it often: time'll see th' Irish again with wine an' ale on th' table before them; an' th' English, barefoot, beggin' a crust in a lonely sthreet, an' th' weather frosty.

1st Workman. Afther a reckless life, they need th' peace o' th' country.

3rd Workman [*assuming a listening attitude*]. They're stirrin'.

[*Mr. Cyril Poges, Souhaun, and Barney come in by one entrance at the back; Avril, Basil Stoke, and Cloyne from the other; they dance in what they think to be a country style, and meet in the centre, throwing their legs about while they sing. Avril has a garland of moonfaced daisies round her neck and carries a dainty little shepherd's crook in her hand; Cyril Poges, a little wooden rake with a gaily-coloured handle; Souhaun has a little hoe, garlanded with ribbons; Cloyne, a dainty little hayfork; Barney, a little reaping-hook; and Basil Stoke, a slim-handled little spade. Each wears a white smock having on it the stylised picture of an animal; on Poges's, a pig; on Basil's, a hen; on Souhaun's, a cow; on Avril's, a duck; on Cloyne's, a sheep; on Barney's, a cock.*

[*Poges is a man of sixty-five years of age. He was, when young, a rather good-looking man, but age has altered him a lot. He is now inclined to be too stout, with a broad chest and too prominent belly; his face is a little too broad, too ruddy, and there are perceptible bags of flesh under his eyes. He has a large head; getting bald in front; though behind and over his ears the hair is long, fairly thick, and tinged with grey. He has a fussy manner, all business over little things; wants his own way at all times; and persuades himself that whatever he thinks of doing must be for the best, and expects everyone else to agree with him. He is apt to lose his temper easily, and to shout in the belief that that is the only way to make other people fall in with his opinions. He has now persuaded himself that in the country peace and goodwill are to be found; and expects that everyone else should find them there too. Under the smock he is dressed in morning clothes, and he wears a tall hat.*

[*Basil Stoke is a long, thin man of thirty, with a rather gloomy face which he thinks betokens dignity, made gloomier still by believing that he is something of a philosopher. His cheeks are thin and their upper bones are as sharp as a hatchet. He is clean-shaven, and the thin hair on his half-bald head is trimly brushed back from his forehead. His eyes are covered with a pair of large horn-rimmed glasses. Under the smock he is dressed in jacket, plus-fours, and he wears a cap.*

[*Souhaun is a woman of thirty-three years of age. She must have been a very handsome girl and she is still very good-looking, in a more matronly way. She has the fine figure of her young friend Avril, but her arms and her legs have grown a little plumper. She is still attractive enough to find attention from a good many men, when her young friend is out of the way. She wears, under the smock, what a lady would usually wear in the morning.*

[*Cloyne is a stoutly-built, fine-looking girl of twenty-six or so, and wears the servant's dress under her smock, and has a smart servant's cap on her head.*

[*Barney is a middle-aged man with a discontented face and a muttering manner. Under his smock he wears the usual dress of a butler.*

[*Avril is dressed, under her smock, in gay pyjamas.*

Poges [*singing*]:

> Rural scenes are now our joy:
> Farmer's boy,
> Milkmaid coy,
> Each like a newly-painted toy,

All:

> In the bosky countrie!

Avril [*singing*]:

> By poor little man the town was made,
> To degrade

Man and maid;
God's green thought in a little green shade
Made the bosky countrie!

All [*chorus*]:

Hey, hey, the country's here,
The country's there
It's everywhere!
We'll have it, now, last thing at night,
And the very first thing in the morning!

Basil [*singing*]:

Our music, now, is the cow's sweet moo,
The pigeon's coo,
The lark's song too,
And the cock's shrill cock-a-doodle-doo,

All:

In the bosky countrie!
                [*chorus*]
Hey, hey, the country's here,
The country's there,
It's everywhere!
We'll have it, now, last thing at night,
And the very first thing in the morning!

[*As they are singing the last lines of the chorus for the second time,
those who have come in by the left entrance go out by the right
one; and those who have come in by the right entrance go out by
the left one. The workmen stand silent for a few moments, watching
the places where the singers disappeared.*

1st Workman. Well, God help the poor omadhauns! It's a bad
sign to see people actin' like that, an' they sober.

3rd Workman. A sthrange crowd, they are, to come gallivantin'
   outa the city to a lonely an' inconsiderate place like this.

1st Workman. At home, now, they'd be sinkin' into their first
   sleep; but because they're in the counthry they think the
   thing to do is to get up at the crack o' dawn.

3rd Workman. An' they killin' themselves thryin' to look as if
   the counthry loved them all their life.

1st Workman. With the young heifer gaddin' round with next to
   nothin' on, goadin' the decency an' circumspection of the
   place.

3rd Workman. An' her eyes wiltin' when she sees what she calls
   her husband, an' widenin' wondherfully whenever they
   happen to light on O'Killigain.

1st Workman. A handsome, hefty young sthripling, with a
   big seam in his arm that he got from a bullet fired in
   Spain.

3rd Workman. For ever fillin' the place with reckless talk against
   the composure of the Church in the midst of the way things
   are now.

2nd Workman. Ay, an' right he is, if ears didn't shut when his
   mind was speakin'.

1st Workman [to 2nd Workman]. If I was you I'd be dumb as well,
   for Canon Chreehewel's mad to dhrive him outa th' place,
   with all who hear him.

2nd Workman [fervently]. There's ne'er another man to be found
   as thrue or as clever as him till you touch a city's centre; an'
   if he goes, I'll go too.

1st Workman [a little derisively]. Me brave fella.

3rd Workman. It's what but they're thryin' to be something else
   beside themselves.

1st Workman. They'd plunge through any hardship to make
   themselves believe they are what they never can become.

2nd Workman [dolorously]. An' to think of two such soilifyin'
    females bein' born in Ireland, an' denizenin' themselves here
    among decent people!

3rd Workman. Whissht; here's the boss, O'Killigain.

[O'Killigain comes in from the side entrance, with a short straight-
    edge in his hand. He is a tall, fair young man twenty-five or
    twenty-six years old. He has a rough, clearly-cut face; dogged-
    looking when he is roused, and handsome when he is in a good
    humour, which is often enough. He is clean-shaven, showing rather
    thick but finely-formed lips. His hair, though cut short, is thick
    and striking. When he speaks of something interesting him, his
    hands make graceful gestures. He has had a pretty rough life,
    which has given him a great confidence in himself; and wide
    reading has strengthened that confidence considerably. He is
    dressed in blue dungarees and wears a deep yellow muffler,
    marked with blue decoration, round his neck. He is humming a
    tune as he comes in, and goes over towards the men.

O'Killigain [lilting, as he comes in]:

    They may rail at this life, from the hour I began it,
    I found it a life full of kindness and bliss;
    And until they can show me some happier planet,
    More social and bright, I'll content me with this.

[To the men] 'Morra, boys.

All the Men. 'Morra, Jack.

O'Killigain [with a gesture pointing to where he thinks the people of
    the house may be]. Up yet?

1st Workman. Up is it? Ay, an' dancin' all about the place.

O'Killigain. Bright colours, in cloth and paint, th' ladies want,
    they say; jazz pattherns, if possible, say the two dear young
    ladies: well, they'll want pretty bright colours to cheer up this
    morgue.

3rd Workman. It's a strange thing, now, that a man with money
   would like to live in a place lonesome an' cold enough to
   send a shiver through a year-old dead man!

O'Killigain. Because they think it has what they call a history.
   Everything old is sacred in every country. Give a house a
   history, weave a legend round it, let some titled tomfool live
   or die in it — and some fool mind will see loveliness in rotten-
   ness and ruin.

1st Workman. A nephew of the Duke of Ormond, they say,
   dhrank himself to death in it, and the supernumary wife of
   the older codger says she's a direct descendant of the nephew;
   and she says they've come from the darkness an' danger of
   England to settle down in what is really their proper home.

O'Killigain. And they're goin' to have the spoons and forks an'
   knives done with what they say is the Ormond crest; Ormond's
   motto will shine out from their notepaper; and this tumble-
   down oul' shack is to be christened Ormond Manor.

2nd Workman [*savagely*]. The English gett, hurryin' off with the
   ensign privilege of an Irish gentleman!

3rd Workman. Isn't it sthrange how many'll fall for a mere
   name? Remember oul' Miss MacWilliam who used to faint
   with ecstasy the times she told the story of sittin' for a second
   in the King o' Denmark's chair; an' oul' Tom Mulligan who
   swaggered round for years afther the son o' the Earl of Skib-
   bereen had accidentally spit in his eye!

O'Killigain. Well, men, we'd better make a start.

1st Workman [*warningly*]. Shush! Here's the flower o' Finea!

   [*Avril comes in from the left entrance. She is a pretty girl of twenty-
   one or so, inclined, at times, to be a little romantic, and is very
   much aware of her good looks. She is far from being unintelligent,
   but does little and cares less about developing her natural talents.
   Her eyes are large and expressive, but sometimes sink into a*

hardened lustre. She is inclined to think that every good-looking young fellow, rich or poor, should fall for her pretty face and figure, and is a little worried if one of them doesn't. She adopts a free-and-easy and very unnatural attitude when she is talking to workmen. She is dressed now in gay scarlet trousers, widening at the ends, and very tight around her hips and bottom; low-cut black silk bodice, slashed with crimson, half hidden by a red-and-white striped scarf thrown carelessly round her shoulders — and black shoes. She trips over in a slow dancing way to where the workmen are standing, and as she comes in she lilts the first verse of The Maid of Bunclody.

Avril [*close to the workmen*]. Top o' the mornin', boys!

O'Killigain [*humouring her*]. Same to you, miss, an' many of them, each of them fairer an' finer than the finest of all that ever brought the soft light o' the dawn at the peep o' day into your openin' eyes.

Avril. It's meself that hopes you like the lovely house you're renovatin'?

O'Killigain. An' tell me who wouldn't like the lovely house we're renovatin'? It's a dark man he'd be, without a stim o' light, an' destitute o' feelin'.

1st Workman [*enthusiastically*]. Sure, miss, it's dumb with many wondhers we've all been for years that no one o' the well-to-do laid hands suddenly on the house to give it the glory again that musta been here throughout the jewel'd days of the times gone by!

Avril. When it's thoroughly restored it'll be a pleasure an' a pride to the whole district.

O'Killigain [*with just a touch of sarcasm in his voice*]. Sure, when we're done with it wouldn't it be fit for the shelther an' ayse an' comfort of Nuad of the Silver Hand, were he with us now, or of the great Fergus himself of the bright bronze chariots?

Avril. Or even the nephew of Ormond's great Duke, the warlike
    ancestor of my very own friend an' distant cousin?

O'Killigain. An' all the people here who are anything'll be mad
    with envy that they hadn't seized holt of it to make it what it'll
    soon be shown to be! [*Avril lilts a reel and dances lightly about the
    room. The 1st and 3rd Workmen join in the lilting of the air. As she
    is passing O'Killigain he catches her excitedly and whirls her
    recklessly round the room till she is breathless, while the two men
    quicken the time of the lilting. To Avril while she stands breathlessly
    before him*] Bow to your partner. [*Avril bows to him and he bows
    to her. Indicating the two men who lilted the tune of the reel*] Bow,
    bow to the bards.

    [*She bows to the two men, and when she has bent to the bow,
        O'Killigain gives her a sharp skelp on the behind. She straightens
        herself with a little squeal of pain and a sharp cry of indignation,
        and faces him angrily.*

Avril [*indignantly*]. You low fellow, what did you dare do that for!
    How dare you lay your dirty hands on a real lady! That's the
    danger of being friendly with a guttersnipe! Wait till you hear
    what Mr. Basil Stoke'll say when he hears what you've done.
    Get out of the room, get out of the house — go away, and
    never let your ugly face be seen here again!

O'Killigain [*with some mockery in his voice*] Sure, I meant no harm,
    miss; it was simply done in the excitement of the game.
    [*To 1st Workman*] Wasn't it, now, Bill?

3rd Workman. Ay was it, miss. Sure, th' poor man lost his caution
    in the gaiety and the gayer tune.

O'Killigain. I did it all in play; I thought you'd like it.

Avril [*sarcastically*]. Oh, did you? Well, I didn't like it, and I
    don't allow anyone to take advantage of any effort I make to
    treat workmen as human beings.

2nd Workman [*maliciously*]. If I was asked anything, I'd say I

saw a spark of pleasure in the flame of pain that came into her
eyes when she was hot!

Avril [*furiously — to the men*]. Be off, you, and let me speak alone
to this young man! I don't require any explanation from such
as you; so be off, and I'll deal with this fellow! [*The three
workmen slide away out of the scene. With a gentler tone in her
voice*] Never, never do a thing like that again, young man.

O'Killigain [*with mocking earnestness*]. Never again, young lady.
You looked so handsome, gay, and young that my thoughts
became as jaunty an' hilarious as your little dancin' feet.

Avril. Never again, mind you — especially when others are here
to stand and gape. [*She goes over and feels the muscle of his arm.*]
There's too much power in that arm to give a safe and gentle
blow to a poor young girl.

O'Killigain. Ashamed I am of the force that sent a hand to hit
a girl of grace, fit to find herself walkin' beside all the beauty
that ever shone before the eyes o' man since Helen herself
unbound her thresses to dance her wild an' willin' way through
the sthreets o' Throy!

Avril. It's I that know the truth is only in the shine o' the words
you shower on me, as ready to you as the wild flowers a
love-shaken, innocent girl would pick in a hurry outa the
hedges, an' she on her way to Mass.

O'Killigain. Is it afther tellin' me that you are, an' your own words
dancin' out as fair an' fine as the best o' mine?

Avril. An' why wouldn't they, now, an' me that sing me song,
first runnin' me years in, an' runnin' them out, in th' fields an'
roads that skirted the threes an' hills o' Killnageera? But is
there an Irishman goin' who hasn't a dint o' wondher in his
talkin'?

O'Killigain. I never met many who had it; but I got the touch of
makin' a song from me mother, who — [*proudly*] — once

won a grand gold medal at a Feis for a song of her own, put
together between the times of bringin' up six children an'
puttin' an odd flower on the grave of the one that died.

Avril. You must sing me a few of your songs sometime.

O'Killigain. Now, if you'd like to listen, an' you think that the
time is handy.

Avril Not now; we might be disturbed; but some evening, somewhere away from here.

O'Killigain. I will, an' welcome; some of them, too, that have
been set in a little book, lookin' gay an' grand, for all the world
to see. Come; listen — [*in a mocking whisper*] — and brave the
wrath of the gouty, doughty Basil Stoke.

Avril [*with a toss of her head*]. That thing! [*With bitter contempt*] A
toddler thricking with a woman's legs; a thief without the
power to thieve the thing he covets; a louse burrowing in a
young lioness's belly; a perjurer in passion; a gutted soldier bee
whose job is done, and still hangs on to life!

O'Killigain [*embracing her tightly*]. Tonight, or tomorrow night,
then, beside the blasted thorn three.

Avril [*with fright in her voice*]. The blasted thorn tree! Oh, not
there, not there — for evil things sit high, sit low in its
twisty branches; and lovers, long ago, who leaned against it
lost their love or died. No, no, not there: a saint himself would
shudder if he had to pass it on a dusky night, with only a sly
chit of a moon in the sky to show the way.

O'Killigain. Oh, foolish girl, there never can be evil things where
love is living. Between the evil things an' us we'll make the
sign of the rosy cross, an' it's blossomin' again the dead an'
dhry thing will be, an' fruit will follow. We are no' saints,
and so can abide by things that wither, without shudder or
sigh, let the night be dark or dusky. It is for us to make dying
things live once more, and things that wither, leaf and bloom

again. Fix your arm in mine, young and fair one, and face for life.

Avril [*after a little hesitation*]. Undher the thorn three then, with you.

[*As the sound of voices is heard he holds her tight for a few moments, kisses her several times, then lets her go. He goes over and examines a wall where a telephone is evidently being put in.*

[*Avril, all demure, stands at the other end of the room watching him.*

[*Souhaun, followed by Poges and Basil, comes into the room. She is carrying a large two-handled earthenware jug in her right hand, and two coloured cushions under her left arm. Cyril Poges is carrying a large coloured picture of himself in a gold frame; and Basil Stoke too is bearing a picture of himself in a silver frame; he has a hammer sticking out of his side pocket. Cloyne follows them in with a six-step A ladder. Poges and Stokes are wearing gum-boots reaching to their thighs, and bright scarves round their necks.*

[*Poges and Basil rest the pictures against a wall.*

Souhaun [*to Avril*]. Oh, here you are, with Mr. O'Killigain. We were wondering where you were. We've a lot to do, dear, before we can get the house comfortable, so don't keep Mr. O'Killigain from his work. [*She leaves the jug down in a corner.*] Filled with gay flowers, Cyril, this jug'll be just the thing on your quattrocento desk-bureau.

Poges. Lovely, darling. [*To O'Killigain*] We've been for a run over the fields, O'Killigain; lovely; feel as fresh as a daisy after it. [*Indicating the boots*] Great comfort, these boots, in the long damp grass. Saw a swarm of rabbits — quaint creatures.

Basil. With these and rubber hats and rubber coats, we'll be able to weather anything. I've got the hammer. Have you got the nails?

Poges. I forgot them. I'll get them now.

Basil. And I'll get the string.

[*One goes out left, and the other right.*

Souhaun [*to Cloyne*]. Hold this curtain stuff end, Cloyne, till we see its width.

[*Cloyne holds one end of the stuff while Souhaun holds the other. O'Killigain, pretending to be interested, bends over Cloyne and, stretching out a hand to handle the stuff, half puts his arm around Cloyne's neck, who is very well pleased.*

O'Killigain. Finely woven as a plover's wing, it is. No way odd it ud look as a cloak for the lovely Emer; an', if it hung from th' sturdy shouldhers of Queen Maev herself, she'd find a second glory!

Souhaun [*displeased at his covert attention to Cloyne*]. Over here, Cloyne, please; hold this end.

[*Souhaun and Cloyne change places, and O'Killigain bends over Souhaun.*

Avril [*to O'Killigain*]. I must have a chat with that man working for you who knows everything worth knowing about Ireland's past and present, Mr. O'Killigain.

O'Killigain [*very seriously*]. And please, miss, don't try to make fun of him. Touch him not with a jibe, for he's a wandherin' king holdin' th' ages be th' hand.

Souhaun. How could a common worker be a king, O'Killigain?

O'Killigain. Easier than for a king to be a common worker. Th' king o' a world that doesn't exist was a carpenter.

Avril. Where is the real world to be found, then?

O'Killigain. Where I have found it often, an' seek to find it still.

Avril. And where's that place to be found?

O'Killigain. With the bitterness an' joy blendin' in a pretty woman's hand; with the pity in her breast; in th' battlin' beauty of her claspin' arms; an' rest beside her when th' heart is tired.

Cloyne. Sure, it's only makin' fun of us all he is.

O'Killigain. Softer an' safer than St. Patrick's breastplate is a woman's breast to save a man from the slings of life. [*Singing softly, moving a little away. Slyly towards the women:*]

Come in, or go out, or just stay at the door,
With a girl on each arm an' one standin' before;
Sure, the more that I have, the more I adore,
For there's life with the lasses,
Says Rory O'More!

Oh, courtin's an illigant, gorgeous affray,
When it's done in the night, or just done in the day;
When joy has been spent, sure, there's joy still in store;
For there's life with the lasses,
Says Rory O'More!

When all has been done, though nothin's been said,
Deep in the green grass, or at home in the bed;
To ev'rey brave effort we'll yield an encore;
For there's life with the lasses,
Says Rory O'More!

[*As he ends his song, Poges and Basil return, the one with the nails, the other with the string-wire.*

Poges [*to O'Killigain — briskly*]. The garage is well in hand, isn't it, O'Killigain?

O'Killigain [*who has tapped the wall, and is shaking his head*]. Yes, well in hand.

Poges [*enthusiastically*]. Good man; when it's done I'll get a first-class artist over from London to paint and make it exactly like a little Tudor dwelling, so that it won't in any way distort the beauty of the fine old house. What do you say, O'Killigain? [*O'Killigain is silent.*] Eh?

O'Killigain. I didn't speak.

Basil [*who has moved over, and is looking ecstatically up at an end wall*]. Early Tudor, I think; yes, Early Tudor, I'll swear. A great period, a great period. Full of flow, energy, colour, power, imagination, and hilarity.

O'Killigain [*tapping the wall beside him — ironically*]. And this is Middle Tudor — not a doubt about it.

Poges [*looking ecstatically at the other end wall*]. Late Tudor this one, I'm sure. Ah, England had no equal then. Look at the Lionheart, eh? Smashed the infidel, smashed him out of Jerusalem into the desert places. What was his name, follower of the Prophet? You remember, Hegira, the white stone, or was it a black stone? — oh, what was the bounder's name?

Souhaun [*helpfully*]. Tuttuttankamen, dear?

Poges [*scornfully*]. Tuttuttankamen! My God, woman, he was only the other day!

Avril [*more helpfully*]. The Mahdi, dear?

Poges [*more scornfully*]. The Mahdi! [*Plaintively*] Is there no one here knows a line of the history of his country!

Basil [*with complacent confidence*]. Genghis Khan.

Poges [*emphatically*]. Genghis Khan! That was the name of the bounder driven from Jerusalem by the Lionhearted Richard. A warrior, a hero. And maybe he was actually in this very house. It's all very moving. [*To O'Killigain*] I imagine I hear the clank, clank, clank of armour when I walk the rooms, and see the banners and banneroles, with their quaint designs, fluttering from the walls! Don't you feel the lovely sensation of — er — er — er — old, unhappy, far-off things, and battles long ago? [*O'Killigain is silent.*] [*Insistently*] Don't you feel something of all that, O'Killigain, eh?

O'Killigain [*quietly*]. I let the dead bury their dead.

Souhaun. Oh, don't worry Mr. O'Killigain, Cyril; he's a workaday worker, and neither understands nor takes an interest in these things.

Poges. Nonsense; O'Killigain's an intelligent man, and is only too glad to learn a little about the finer things of life; and to think of great things past and gone is good — isn't that so?

O'Killigain. Occasionally, perhaps; but not to live among them. Life as it is, and will be, moves me more.

Poges. Come, come; we mustn't be always brooding upon the present and the future. Life is too much with us, O'Killigain; late and soon, getting and spending, we lay waste our powers. But you've never read good old Wordsworth, I suppose?

O'Killigain. As a matter of fact, I have.

Poges. You have? Well, that promotes a fellowship between us, eh? Great man, great man; but a greater poet, eh?

O'Killigain [*with some vehemence*]. A tired-out oul' blatherer; a tumble-down thinker; a man who made a hiding-place of his own life; a shadow parading about as the sun; a poet, sensitive to everything but man; a bladder blown that sometimes gave a note of music; a fool who thought the womb of the world was Wordsworth; a poet who jailed the striving of man in a moral lullaby; a snail to whom God gave the gleam of the glowworm; a poet singing the song of safety first!

Poges [*irritated*]. Oh! Is that the result of the new schooling? I'm afraid very few will agree with you, my friend. Well, well, we've more to do than discuss the merit of a poet; so hasten on the work of building the garage, like a good man.

O'Killigain [*bowing ironically*]. I go, sir.   [*He goes out.*

Poges [*to the others*]. Isn't that a shocking example of bad taste and ignorance? [*To Souhaun*] There's one of your fine countrymen for you, dear.

Souhaun. Well, Cyril dear, you know you were just trying to show off to him. A few little quotations, drummed into you at school, is all you know of Wordsworth. You're never tired of saying that poetry isn't your cup of tea.

Poges [*angry*]. Modern poetry, modern poetry isn't my cup of tea; and I don't care who knows it. But I don't deny the past. Tradition — that is our strength in time of trouble; tradition, follow the traditions, the only things that count in a cultured man's life. Keep as close as we can to the beauties of the past — the, the glory that was Rome and the grandeur that was Greece — Shakespeare knew what he was talking about when he said that.

Basil. Well, by living in this old historic house we're keeping close to the old traditions.

Souhaun [*dubiously*]. It's beginning to feel a little cold and damp to me.

Poges [*astonished and indignant*]. Cold? What are you talking about? Damp? Nonsense. Were it warmer, it would begin to feel uncomfortable. What do you say, Cloyne?

Cloyne [*who has been dusting the walls with a long-handled duster*]. I feel quite cosy, sir; though there is a bit of a breeze blowing down the chimney.

Poges [*shivering a little*]. Eh? Cosy, eh? Of course you do; we all do. Think, too, of the loveliness all round us: river, lake, valley, and hill. [*Lilting*] Angels, often pausing here, doubt if Eden were more fair. Here we have the peace of Eden.

Souhaun. And you must admit, dear, that we Irish are a simple, honest, and obliging people.

Basil [*enthusiastically*]. They're dears. All I've met of them are dears; so quaint and charming — they are sweet. They need control, though; they need control.

Poges. I agree. All the Irish are the same. Bit backward perhaps, like all primitive peoples, especially now, for they're missng the example and influence of the gentry; but delightful people all the same. They need control, though; oh yes, they need it badly.

Basil. We must get to really know the country; it's one thing to be sensitive about the country scene, and quite another to understand it.

Poges [*heartily*]. Quite right, Basil. We must get to know the country so that everything in it is natural to us. [*Lilting*] To plough and to sow, to reap and to mow, and to be a farmer's boy-oy-oy. The different trees, for example, to call them by their names the instant we see them.

Avril. In winter or summer.

Poges. Quite. In the summer by their fruits.

Avril. Trees don't have fruits, Cyril.

Poges. Of course not. I mean barks and branches. It will be a joy to say to some ignorant visitor from the city: That tree? Oh, that's just an oak; and that one there by the river is a — a ——

Avril. Gooseberry tree, Cyril.

Poges. A lilac, or something. [*To Avril*] Don't be funny. This is a serious matter.

Cloyne. We mustn't forget the hens, either, sir.

Poges. Hens? Yes, of course — the hens. A fine idea. Yes, we'll have to have hens; a first-class strain, though: nothing else would be of any use.

Cloyne. A first-class strain, of course.

Poges. And a cow as well.

Avril. A cow might be dangerous.

Poges. Dangerous? Nonsense; if he was, then we'd simply have to keep him in a cage. [*He sets up the step-ladder, mounts it, and holds up his picture against the wall.*] How does that look?

Souhaun [*taking no notice*]. First of all, we must get to know the nature and names of all the wild flowers of the district.

Poges [*letting the picture rest on the ground, and turning to the rest*]. Especially the wild flowers that Shakespeare loved — the —

the — er — er — [*his eye catches sight of primroses in a little vase on the table*] — the primrose, for instance; you know — the primrose by the river's brim, a yellow primrose was to him, but it was nothing more; though we all actually know all there is to be known about the little primrose.

Basil [*letting his picture rest on the ground, leaning over the top so that he at one end of the room and Poges at the other look like preachers in pulpits, panelled with their own portraits*]. That's just ignorant complacency, Cyril. Of course, if we regard, assume, or look at the plant purely as a single entity, then a primrose is a primrose, and there's nothing more to be said about it.

Poges. Well, you can't assume or regard the primrose as an elm tree, can you, old boy?

Basil [*quickly*]. Don't interrupt me for a minute, please. If we take the primrose, however, into our synthetical consideration, as a whole, or, *a priori*, as a part, with the rest of the whole of natural objects or phenomena, then there is, or may be, or can be a possibility of thinking of the flower as of above the status, or substance, or quality of a fragment; and, consequently, correlating it with the whole, so that, to a rational thinker, or logical mind, the simple primrose is, or may become, what we may venture to call a universal. See?

Poges [*bewildered*]. Eh? Oh yes, yes; no, no; yes, yes: eh, what?

Souhaun [*to Cloyne*]. Cloyne, you'd better go and look after the fires in our room.

[*Cloyne rises and goes out.*

Avril [*with mockery in her voice*]. Hush, listen all — great men are speaking!

Poges [*to Basil*]. Eh, what the devil are you trying to say, man?

Avril [*with triumphant mockery*]. Ah, Cyril, you're caught!

Poges [*indignantly*]. Caught? Who's caught? Me? Nonsense, girl.

He has simply compounded a fact with a fallacy. Can I see?
Have I eyes? Yes. Very well, then. I see a flower with a root,
leaves, and a blossom; I ask myself, What is it? I answer, A
flower; I ask, What is it called? I answer, A primrose.

Basil [*languidly*]. So you say, sir.

Poges [*vehemently*]. So everyone says, sir!

Basil [*leaning forward towards Poges*]. And what is a flower
sir?

Poges [*furiously*]. A flower? Good God, sir, a plant; a contrivance
springing out of the earth; a vegetating combination of root,
leaves, and blossom.

Souhaun. Calmly, Cyril, calmly.

Basil [*leaning back and closing his eyes wearily*]. I knew you'd just
say that, sir. Words; you're merely using words. Try to
think, sir, of a primrose, not as a primrose, but as a simple
object, and as a substance outside of yourself.

Poges [*half frantic*]. Damn it, man, don't I know that a primrose
isn't a substance inside of myself! Tell us how a man is to
think of a primrose except as a primrose. He can't think of it
as the dear little, sweet little shamrock of Ireland, can he?
It is indeed a pitiful humiliation to have to listen to a half-
educated fool!

Basil [*angry at last — setting the picture aside and taking a threatening
step towards Poges, Avril stepping in front to restrain him*]. A
fool! Do you say I am a fool, sir? Is a man versed in all the
philosophies of the world to be called a fool!

Avril. Basil, dear!

Souhaun [*getting in front of Poges*]. Cyril, darling, do remember
that we are having just a little friendly discussion about a
common country flower!

Avril [*ironically*]. Basil is only trying to share his great knowledge
with us.

Poges. He calls that knowledge, does he?

Souhaun. We must remember that Basil passed through Oxford, dear.

Poges. I don't care if he crept under it or flew over it; he's not going to punish me with what he picked up there.

Basil [*a little tearfully*]. Considering that I have read every word written by Hume, Spinoza, Aristotle, Locke, Bacon, Plato, Socrates, and Kant, among others, I think my views ought to receive some respect from an ignorant man.

Poges [*boastfully*]. I was reared any old how; and here I am today, a money'd man, able to say to almost any man, come, and he cometh, and to almost any other man, go, and he goeth — and quick too; able to shake hands with lords and earls, and call them by their Christian names. This — [*he touches his forehead*] — and these — [*he holds out his hands*] — did it all, without an inherited penny to help! [*He looks balefully at Basil.*] And that's more than some of them can say. And I never passed through Oxford!

Souhaun [*soothingly — to Basil*]. Come, now, go away for a few minutes, till he's calm again.

Basil [*tearfully and wrathfully*]. Souhaun and you can see, Avril, that the virtue of respect and ready veneration that every right-minded Englishman has for the classic colleges has gone completely out of him.

Souhaun [*soothingly*]. There now, there now; it'll all come back soon.

Basil [*almost weeping*]. Whenever he got the chance he hurried me down to Oxford to meet his professor and that doctor, itching all over to obtain a degree *honoris causa*, in any faculty of Divinity, Science, Literature, Medicine, or Law!

Poges [*scornfully*]. And most of them anxious for tips from the Stock Exchange. Go away, man, and weep in silence. [*He lifts his picture up against the wall.*] We have something else to do. Here, how does that look there?

Souhaun [*gently pushing Basil out of the room*]. There, go, dear, till you recover yourself.

Basil [*going out — loudly*]. *Quisabit grunniodem expectio procum —* what can one expect from a pig but a grunt?

Poges [*with the picture against the wall*]. There, how does that look here? [*Pityingly*] Poor fool; juvenile mind, Souhaun, juvenile mind. But snappy enough, when he likes, and I, by cunning investment, having doubled his income for him. Ingratitude. [*Impatiently*] Well, how does this look here?

Souhaun. I think the opposite wall would be more suitable, dear.

Avril. Where it is, is best, mother.

Poges. Make up your minds, make up your minds!

Souhaun. Where it is, dear.

Poges. How is it for height?

Souhaun. A little higher.

Avril. A little lower.

Poges. One of you, one of you!

Souhaun. A little to the right, now.

Avril. A little to the left, now.

Poges [*lowering the picture to the ground*]. Which is it? How is it? What is it!

[*Cloyne comes in with a newspaper in her hand.*

Cloyne [*to Poges*]. Your newspaper, sir — the *Financial Universe*. [*She leaves it on the table, and goes out again. Poges breaks open his paper, and is about to look at it when Barney appears at the left entrance. A sound of cackling is heard outside, and the loud lowing of a cow, and the crowing of cocks.*

Poges [*with the paper half spread before him*]. What the hell's that?

Barney. There's a man oustide wants to know if you want any entherprisin' hins?

Poges. Any what?

Barney. Any hins, entherprisin' hins?

Poges [*impatiently*]. What the devil would I want with hins enterprising or unenterprising?

Barney. He says it's all over the counthry that you're searchin' high an' low for entherprisin' hins.

Cloyne [*appearing at the right entrance*]. There's two men here wantin' to know if you'd buy some prime an' startlin' cocks, goin' cheap?

1st Workman [*appearing beside Barney, and shoving him aside to get in front*]. Excuse me, sir, but there's a friend o' mine just arrived with a cow that ud do any man good to see; a baste with a skin on her as shiny an' soft as the down on a first-class angel's wing; an' uddhers that'll make any man hard put to it to fetch enough pails to get the milk she gives!

Poges. Hins, cocks, and cows! [*To 1st Workman*] What the hell do you take me for — a farmer's boy, or what?

Souhaun. It's all out of what you said about having hens and a cow in the place. [*To Cloyne*] And you, you little fool, must have gossiped it all over the district!

Cloyne. The only one I mentioned it to was Mr. O'Killigain.

1st Workman [*coming over to Poges*]. Listen, sir, whisper, now: Sthrike for th' honour of St. Patrick, while the iron's hot, for the cow. An' whisper, don't, for the love o' God, have anything to do with the hins an' cocks they're thryin' to palm off on you — there isn't one o' them that isn't th' essence of a false pretendher!

Souhaun [*angrily — to Cloyne*]. I won't have you gossiping to O'Killigain, spending time with him you ought to give getting the house in shape! The idea of discussing our private affairs with O'Killigain! If you think that O'Killigain has taken a fancy to you, you never made a bigger mistake, my girl.

Cloyne [*indignantly*]. Indeed, ma'am? Well, if Mr. O'Killigain bids me the time o' day, I'll do the same, without any permission from you, ma'am!

Barney [*impatiently*]. An' what am I goin' to say to the man who's brought th' entherprisin' hins?

Poges [*shouting*]. Pack him off about his business!

[*Barney goes out.*

[*To Cloyne*] And you do the same to the man who brought the startling cocks!

Souhaun [*to Cloyne*]. And no more trespassing on the good nature of O'Killigain, either!

Cloyne [*turning and facing Souhaun swiftly as she is going out*]. There's a withering old woman, not a hundred miles from where I am, who ought to take her own advice, an' keep from thryin' her well-faded thricks of charm on poor Mr. O'Killigain herself!   [*She goes out.*

Poges [*loudly and complainingly*]. Oh, stop these unseemly disputes in a house that ought to know only peace and dignity! Can't you try to act as the *les grand dames* and the *les grander monsieurs* must have acted when they moved about here in this beautiful Tudor house. While we're in it, let us forget the vile world and all its ways. [*Angrily — to 1st Workman, who has been tugging at his sleeve for the last few moments*] What the hell do you want, man?

1st Workman [*earnestly, almost into Poges' ear*]. Listen, whisper, sir; take the bull be th' horns, an' get the cow, before she's gone. An' as for entherprisin' hins, or cocks that'll do you credit, leave it to me, sir, an' you'll go about with a hilarious look in your eyes!

Poges [*catching 1st Workman by the shoulders, in a rage, and pushing him out of the room, and down the passage*]. Get out, get out, you fool, with your hins and cocks and cows!

Souhaun [*quickly — to Avril, when Poges has disappeared round the entrance*]. Go on up, and flatter and comfort your old fool by ridiculing my old fool; and, when he's half himself again, wanting still more comfort and flattery, wheedle a cheque out of the old prattler.

Avril [*jumping up*]. Splendid idea!   [*She runs off out.*

Souhaun [*calling after her*]. A good one, mind you!

[*Poges comes back fuming, and brushing his coat where it touched the 1st Workman.*

Poges. Are we to have no peace down here where peace was born? [*He takes up the paper again and begins to read it.*] Uum. Ha, tin shares up again. Good. [*He buries his face in the paper.*] If it weren't for the damned taxes.

[*1st and 3rd Workmen peer around corner of the left entrance; then they come over quickly and smoothly to where Poges is buried in his paper, the 1st Workman standing on his left hand and the 3rd Workman on his right.*

1st Workman [*persuasively — towards Poges' paper*]. Listen, here, sir: if it's genuine poulthry you want, that lay with pride an' animation, an' not poor, insignificant fowls that set about th' business o' layin' like a member o' Doyle Eireann makin' his maiden speech, I have a sthrain o' pullets that'll give you eggs as if you were gettin' them be steam!

Poges [*angrily — glancing over the top of his paper*]. Go away, go away, man, and don't be driving me mad!

3rd Workman [*towards Poges' paper*]. Oh, the lies that some can tell to gain their own ends! Sure, sir, everyone knows that his poor hins are harmless; only venturin' to lay when heavy thundher frightens them into a hasty sign o' life! But it's meself can give you what you want, with a few lively cocks thrown in, to help them on with the work of furnishing nourishment to the whole world.

Poges. Go away; when I want poultry, I'll get into touch with the experts in the Department of Agriculture.

1st Workman [*horrified — partly to Poges and partly to Souhaun*]. Oh, listen to that, now! Didja hear that, ma'am? The Department of Agriculture, is it? Wisha, God help your innocence, sir. Sure, it's only a tiny time ago that the same Department sent down a special sthrong covey o' cocks to improve the sthrain, an' only afther a short probation, didn't they give the hins hysterics?

Poges. Hysterics? Good God!

3rd Workman. Ay, an' hadn't the frightened farmers to bring guns to bear on the cocks when they found their hins scatthered over hill an' dale, lyin' on their backs with their legs in the air, givin' their last gasp, an' glad to get outa the world they knew so well! The few mighty ones who survived were that stunned that there wasn't an egg in th' place for years!

Poges [*good-humouredly catching the men by the arm and leading them to the left entrance*]. Now, now, men, I'm busy; I've some very important business to think about and can't be bothered with hins!

1st Workman [*as they go out*]. Another time, sir; but don't think of the Department in this important matther: they'll send you hins'll paralyse the cocks, or cocks that'll paralyse the hins!

[*They go out.*

Poges [*returning, and reading the paper*]. Childlike people, the Irish, aren't they? Hysterical hins! Dr. What's-his-name, the fellow who said all man is moved by streams of thought that never enter his head — well, he'd find something to study down here. Well, it's delightful to be in a lovely house, in a lovely country, with nothing to think of but hysterical hins! [*He suddenly concentrates on something in the paper.*] I must have some of those shares. [*He runs to the telephone and joggles and shakes it.*] What

can be the matter with this Exchange? — I can't hear a sound!
[*To Souhaun*] Call one of the workmen, will you? I must get
through to London at once.

[*Souhaun runs out to call a workman. In a moment or two the
2nd Workman comes into the room.*

2nd Workman. Is it me you want, sir?

Poges. Not you especially; I just want to know if you know, or
anyone in the county knows, why I can't connect with the
Exchange?

2nd Workman. Oh, is that all, sir?

Poges [*snappily*]. Is that all! Isn't it enough, fool!

2nd Workman [*sharply*]. Who th' hell are you callin' a fool to?

Poges [*placatingly but with some impatience*]. My good man, please
let me know if you can say why the Exchange doesn't answer
my call.

2nd Workman. Ask anyone from one end o' the counthry to the
other, or even O'Killigain himself, if Philib O'Dempsey's a
fool, an' see what they'll say. A sound mind, armed with a
firm education for seven long years in a steady school, an'
now well fit to stand his ground in any argument, barrin'
th' highest philosophies of the greatest minds mendin' th'
world!

Poges. My good man, I only asked you a simple question.

2nd Workman [*ignoring the remark*]. Comin' over here, thinkin' that
all the glory an' grandeur of the world, an' all the might of
man, was stuffed into a bulgin' purse, an' stickin' their tongue
out at a race that's oldher than themselves by a little like a
thousand years, greater in their beginnin' than they are in their
prime; with us speakin' with ayse the mighty languages o' the
world when they could barely gurgle a few sounds, sayin'
the rest in the movement of their fingers.

Poges [*shouting in rage*]. Go to the devil, man, and learn manners!

2nd Workman [*going on vehemently, but moving slowly to one of the entrances*]. Hammerin' out handsome golden ornaments for flowin' cloak an' tidy tunic we were, while you were busy gatherin' dhried grass, an' dyin' it blue, to hide the consternation of your middle parts; decoratin' eminent books with glowin' colour an' audacious beauty were we, as O'Killigain himself will tell you, when you were still a hundhred score o' years away from even hearin' of the alphabet. [*Beside the entrance*]. Fool? It's yourself's the fool, I'm sayin', settlin' down in a place that's only fit for the housin' o' dead men! Settlin' here, are you? Wait till God sends the heavy rain, and the floods come!   [*He goes out.*

Poges [*to Souhaun*]. There's Erin, the tear and the smile in her eye for you! The unmannerly ruffian! Venomous, too — wanting me to wait till the floods come! Cheeking me up to my very face!

Souhaun. Well, it's not a royal face, is it? You'll have to learn to be respectful to the people if you want them to be respectful to you.

Poges [*sarcastically*]. I'll be most deferential in the future. [*Stormily — to 1st Workman appearing at the entrance*] Well, what do you want?

1st Workman. Excuse, but I sailed in, hearin' you were in a difficulty, an' I wanted to see if I could help.

Poges. Well, I want to know where's the man who is responsible for putting in this phone?

1st Workman. Why, is there anything wrong with it, sir?

Poges [*stormily*]. Everything's wrong with it, man! I can't get on to the Exchange.

1st Workman. Sure, that's aysily explained: it's not connected yet.

Poges. It was to be connected first thing this morning. When will it be connected?

1st Workman [*cautiously*]. Oh, now, that depends, sir.

Poges. Depends? Depends on what?

1st Workman. On how long it'll take to get the sthrame o' sound from here flowin' safely to whatever other end there may be fixed for it to be heard in.

Poges [*impatiently*]. Get O'Killigain, get him to come here at once.

1st Workman. Sure, that's the Postmaster's job — Mr. O'Killigain has nothing to do with it.

Poges [*shouting*]. Then get me the man that has something to do with it!

Souhaun [*who has been looking at the coloured curtain stuff and spreading it out*]. Now, Cyril, see what you think: Is the red with the green stripe or the green with the red stripe the most suitable to go with the walls?

[*The sound of horses trotting is heard outside, becoming plainer, till the sound ceases somewhere close to the house.*

Poges [*to Souhaun — with irritation*]. For goodness' sake, one thing at a time. [*To 1st Workman*] Go and get the man that's doing this job.

1st Workman. I'm afraid you'll have to thravel a long way if you want to get him, sir; you see, he had to go to pay his last respects to a dead cousin; but never fear, he won't be gone beyond a couple of hours, unless something out o' the ordinary keeps him away the whole o' the evenin' an' th' strongest part o' th' night.

[*Poges sinks down on one of the seats, silent and confounded.*

Cloyne [*appearing at back entrance*]. Th' horses are here now, sir.

Poges [*sitting up*]. Horses? What horses?

Cloyne. The horses Mr. Basil an' Miss Avril ordhered to come here.

Souhaun. Basil and Avril are going out for a little canter, Cyril.

Poges [*peevishly*]. But this is not the time to be thinking of amusement; we have to get the house into some shape. Ask O'Killigain to come here.

Souhaun [*to Cloyne*]. Yes, get O'Killigain, Cloyne; he has a good eye, and will be able to judge which of these curtain stuffs should go on the windows.

[*Cloyne goes. O'Killigain appears at the left entrance with an anxious look on his face.*

O'Killigain. Who's going to ride these horses that are outside?

Souhaun [*haughtily*]. Miss Avril and her friend Mr. Basil Stoke are going to ride them.

O'Killigain. I suppose you know these horses are mettlesome creatures, and need riders at home in the saddle?

Souhaun [*more haughtily still*]. Miss Avril and her friend learned the art in a London riding-school, and exercised frequently in Richmond Park; so your kind solicitude is unnecessary, sir.

O'Killigain [*viciously*]. Richmond Park isn't Clune na Geera, ma'am. The horses there are animals; the horses here are horses. [*Avril comes tripping in, dressed in jersey and jodhpurs, and is followed by Basil, dressed in a dark-green kind of hunting coat, buckskin breeches, and big gleaming top-boots with spurs; he carries a whip in his hand, and a high, handsome, shining tall hat on his head. With a frightened look at Basil*] Good God!

[*He turns on his heel and walks out again.*

Basil [*with complacent conceit — to Souhaun*]. The old ways coming back again to the old house, Souhaun.

Souhaun [*rapturously*]. Isn't it grand, dear? Don't forget to go through the village.

Avril [*joyously*]. Basil has been so kind, Souhaun, dear; he has given me a grand cheque.

Souhaun [*giving Basil a kiss and winking at Avril*]. Basil, you're a darling!

Poges [*grumpily*]. Be careful how you handle those horses.

Basil [*haughtily — to Poges*]. Did you say anything, sir?

Poges [*with some heat*]. I said be careful how you handle those horses!

Basil [*with a mocking bow*]. Thank you, sir; we'll do our best. [*To Avril*] Come, darling.

[*Avril trips out, and Basil follows her in a way that he deems to be stately.*

Poges. I hope they'll do no damage, now.

Souhaun. Oh, never fear; Basil sits the saddle like a centaur.

[*The movement of horses' hooves is heard, then a trot, getting fainter till it dies away.*

Poges [*exasperated*]. God send he doesn't frighten the horse. More decent of him had he remained here to get this telephone going. They all seem to be determined here to keep us away from every semblance of civilisation! [*To Souhaun — stormily*] Will you, for God's sake, try to get O'Killigain to do something to get this thing in order? [*He goes over to where Souhaun is busy with the curtains and pulls the curtains out of her hands, then flings them on the floor.*] D'ye hear, d'ye hear what I'm saying to you, woman?

Souhaun [*losing patience and seizing him, and shaking him roughly*]. What d'ye think you're doing, you old dim-eyed, old half-dead old fool! I'll disconnect you as well as the telephone i you don't learn to behave yourself! You settled on coming here, and you'll put up with the annoyances!

Poges [*protestingly*]. Eh, eh, there! It was you who persuaded me to come to this god-forsaken hole!

Souhaun [*shaking him more fiercely*]. You're a liar, I didn't! It was you yourself who were always pining to see the little squirrels jigging about on the trees, and see the violets and primroses dreaming in the budding stir of spring! [*She pushes*

him violently from her.] Another snarly sound out of you, and
I'm off to live alone.

Poges [*gloomily*]. You can well afford to be independent now,
since, like a fool, I settled five hundred a year on you.

[*During this contest Cloyne has appeared at the left entrance and
now gives a judicious cough.*

Souhaun [*quickly — to cover dispute from Cloyne*]. We'll decide
on this stuff, then, for the curtains, Cyril dear.

Poges. It'll look delightful, darling. [*Pretending to see Cloyne for
the first time.*] Oh, what do you want?

Cloyne. Canon Chreehewel's outside an' would like to have a
few words with you, if you're not too busy.

Poges [*showing irritation*]. Oh, these priests, these priests! Thick
as weeds in this poor country. Opposed to every decent thought
that happens not to have come from them. Ever on guard to
keep the people from growing out of infancy. No one should
give them the slightest encouragement. Oh, if the misguided
people would only go back to the veneration of the old Celtic
gods, what a stir we'd have here! To the delightful, if legendary,
loveliness of — er — er — er — what's his name, what's her
name, what's their name? I have so often said it, so often in
my mind, the chief, or one of the chief gods of the ancient
Celts?

Souhaun. Was it Gog or Magog, dear?

Poges [*with fierce scorn*]. Oh, no, no, no; try to think a little, if
you really want to assist me. Can't you remember that Gog
and Magog were two Philistinian giants killed by David, or
Jonathan, or Joshua, or Joab, or Samson, or someone? It's the
old Celtic god I have in mind the one — what was his name?

Souhaun. Gulliver?

Poges. Oh no; not Gulliver!

Souhaun. Well, I don't know the hell who it was.

Poges [*slapping his thigh exultantly*]. Brobdingnag! That was the
   fellow — the fellow that ate the nine nuts — or was it seven?
   — plucked from the tree hanging over the well near the world's
   end.

Cloyne. What am I to say to the Canon, sir?

Poges. What does he want; did you ask him what he wants?

Cloyne. He says he just wants to drop a word or two of thanks
   for the fifty pounds you sent him.

   [*A murmur of voices is heard outside. It comes nearer and the
      sound seems excited.*

Poges [*listening*]. What's that, now?

1st Workman's Voice [*outside*]. Keep his head up.

3rd Workman's Voice [*outside*]. You're home, sir, you're home
   now.

   [*They come in supporting Basil by the arms, followed by the 2nd
      Workman, holding Basil's coat-tail. Basil is pale, and has a
      frightened look on his face. His lovely coat is spattered with mud
      and, in some places, torn. The 1st Workman is carrying the tall
      hat, now looking like a battered concertina.*

Poges [*anxiously*]. What's this; what's happened?

1st Workman [*soothingly*]. He's all right, sir; just a little shock.
   We seen him crawling towards the house an' went to his help.
   His horse flung him. [*Whispering to Poges*] He shouldn't
   be let on anything more mettlesome than a rocking-horse,
   sir.

Souhaun [*running to Basil*]. Are you much hurt, Basil, dear?

Basil [*brokenly*]. Bruised, bruised from head to foot.

Poges [*with irritation*]. Well, why the hell didn't you stay here and
   help me to get the telephone fixed?

Basil. Why didn't you hold me back by force? Oh, why did you
   let me go!

Souhaun [*anxiously*]. Where's Avril?

Basil [*ignoring her query*]. Oh, I should never have ventured upon an Irish horse! Irresponsible, irresponsible, like the people. When he wouldn't go, I gave him just a little jab with the spur — [*moaningly*] — and the brute behaved like a wild animal, just like a wild animal!

1st Workman [*soothingly — to Souhaun*]. He's not hurt much, ma'am; came down in th' grass on his poor bum.

Souhaun. But where's Avril? [*Shaking Basil's shoulder*] Where's Avril?

Basil. Gone!

Souhaun. Gone?

Basil. Away with O'Killigain. He came bounding up to help Avril and abused me for falling off. Then they cantered away together. [*Loudly and a little shrilly*] Naked and unashamed, the vixen went away with O'Killigain!

[*Plaster falls and a hole appears in the ceiling, almost directly over the fireplace; then a thin rope, with a bulb attached to its end, comes dangling down, followed by the face of a heavily Yellow-bearded Man, who thrusts his head as far as it can go through the hole.*

Yellow-bearded Man [*to those below*]. Hay, hay there; is this where yous want the light to go?

Poges [*with a vexatious yell when he sees where the rope hangs*]. No it isn't, no it isn't, you fool! [*Indicating a place near the centre and towards the back*] There, there's where it's wanted! Where my desk will be! Oh, they're knocking down more than they're building up!

Yellow-bearded Man [*soothingly*]. Don't worry; just a little mistake in measurement, sir. Never fear, we'll hit th' right spot one o' these days! The one thing to do, sir, is to keep cool.

[*He takes his head out of the hole and disappears, leaving Poges furious.*

Poges [*shouting up at the hole*]. Who are you to order me to keep
   cool? I won't keep cool. I refuse to keep cool!

Souhaun [*to Poges*]. Here, help me in with poor Basil till he
   drinks some brandy and lies down for a little.

   [*Poges takes one arm, Souhaun takes the other, and they lead
      Basil out of the room.*

Poges [*to Basil — helping him out*]. I hope you realise the sterling
   trouble you give people by your damned refusal to recognise
   your limitations!

Basil [*petulantly*]. Carry me out, man; carry me out!

Cloyne [*as they pass*]. What am I to do with the Canon, sir?

Poges [*ferociously*]. Tell him I'll give him another cheque if he
   gets the telephone fixed for me before the night is out!

   [*Basil, Souhaun, and Poges go out by the left entrance; Cloyne by
      that on the right, leaving the men standing together in a corner
      of the room.*

2nd Workman [*pensively*]. Th' spirit of th' Grey o' Macha's in our
   Irish horses yet!

1st Workman [*excitedly*]. Did yous hear that, eh? Did yous hear
   what he just let dhrop? That the lassie o' th' house went off with
   O'Killigain riding naked through the locality!

2nd Workman. Stark naked she was, too. Didn't I know well be
   th' cut of her jib that she was a hop, step, an' lep of a lassie!
   An' right well she looked too!

1st Workman. Th' sight near left me eyes when I seen her go
   prancin' out without as much as a garther on her to keep her
   modesty from catchin' cold.

3rd Workman. This'll denude the disthrict of all its self-denyin'
   decency.

1st Workman [*excitedly jumping upon a seat to get nearer to the hole
   in the ceiling*]. Cornelius, eh, there, Cornelius!

Yellow-bearded Man. What's up?

1st Workman. Didja hear th' terrible thing that's afther happenin'?

Yellow-bearded Man. No; what terrible thing?

1st Workman. The lassie o' th' house's gone careerin' all over th' counthry on horseback with only her skin as a coverin'!

Yellow-bearded Man [*horrified*]. G'way!

3rd Workman [*up to him*]. An' th' poor men workin' in th' fields had to flee to th' ditches to save th' sight of their eyes from th' shock o' seein' her!

Yellow-bearded Man [*with aggravated anguish in his voice*]. Oh, isn't it like me to be up here outa sight o' th' world, an' great things happenin !

CURTAIN

ACT II

The same as in the preceding Act.

The two portraits, one of Stoke, the other of Poges, are now hanging on the wall at back, between the windows. Bright-green curtains, broadly striped with red, are on the windows. A Jacobean armchair has been added to the two stiff pew-like seats beside the fireplace. The table is to the left, so that two mattresses, one beside the other, can be seen, with their heads against the wall and their feet towards the front. On these, wrapped round with rugs and blankets, are Poges and Stoke. Some thick rolled-up floor rugs are lying against the wall. A bunch of pampas grass is in the earthenware jug standing on the table. The rejected crimson curtain stuff is lying over one of the pew-like seats. A walking-stick — Basil's — is leaning against the wall, near to where he is lying.

It is about half-past seven on a cold and misty morning. A few misty beams of sunlight are coming in through the windows, paling the light of a lighted lantern standing between the two beds.

The two men are twisting about uneasily on the mattresses; when Poges twists to the right, Basil twists to the left, and vice versa. Then Poges, wearing a blue beret with a black bow at the side, lifts his head a little and glances over at Basil. He is in that drowsy state felt by a man who has spent long hours of the night trying to get to sleep and failing to do so.

Before the scene is disclosed, the hooting of owls is heard first; then the faint lowing of cattle, grunting of swine, crowing of cocks, bleating of sheep; then, vigorously from various directions the whistling of the chorus of The Farmer's Boy.

Poges [*after he has twisted about several times — half to himself, half to Basil*]. Good God, isn't it cold! [*Basil is silent.*] Eh, Basil, are you awake? How d'ye feel now?

Basil [*with a faint groan*]. Stiff as hell still! It's a mercy I'm alive. And, on the top of it, Avril to make a laughing-stock of me by enjoying herself with O'Killigain.

Poges [*sympathetically*]. It was damned mean of her, Basil. She's inclined that way, I'm afraid. You'll have to keep a strong hand over her, my boy.

Basil [*with a deep groan*]. I can't — now.

Poges. Why can't you, man?

Basil. A month before we came here I did a very foolish thing.

Poges. Oh?

Basil [*mournfully*]. Settled five hundred a year on her for life.

Poges. Oh! [*A fairly long pause.*] Basil, Basil, I did the same to Souhaun!

Basil. We're done for, Cyril.

Poges [*in a sprightly way*]. No, no; a month in the country'll make us young again. We'll be as lively as goats in no time. Besides we can always cautiously hint at an increase in the settlement.

Basil [*gloomily*]. With the workers always striking for higher wages, it'll have to remain a hint.

Poges [*as gloomily*]. It's damnable, Basil. If much more is given to them, how's a poor man to live? [*He sinks back on the mattress and pulls the clothes over his head. Outside a cock crows loudly, followed by the call of a cuckoo. Clicking his tongue exasperatedly — from under the clothes.*] Dtch, dtch, dtch! Isn't it a good thing those birds aren't in the house! [*The cock crows again, much louder this time, and the cuckoo calls again. Popping his head from under the clothes.*] Damn that cock and cuckoo! Did you hear that cock crowing, Basil, and the cuckoo calling?

Basil. Deafening, aren't they! And the owls, too, all the night. Jungle noises!

Poges. The country's not going to be so quiet as I thought. Still, I'm glad we came.

Basil. So am I, really. These sounds are just part of the country's attractions — pleasant and homely.

Poges. And stimulating, Basil, stimulating. Look at the sunlight coming in through the windows — another dawn, Basil; another life. Every day in the country brings another chance of living a new life.

Basil [*enthusiastically*]. And we're going to live it, eh, what, Cyril?

Poges [*enthusiastically*]. Oh, boy, ay!

[*Souhaun appears at the back entrance, left, and Avril at entrance to the right. Both are wearing fur coats over their night-dresses, and shiver a little.*

Souhaun [*plaintively*]. For goodness' sake, will you two men get up and do something. Cloyne's fallen down in a dark passage and hurt her wrist, and she can't do much.

Poges. Oh?

Avril. And something will have to be done to heat the rooms — we were almost frozen last night.

Poges. Ah! Well, we weren't scorched with the heat either.

Souhaun. Well, stir yourselves, and you'll soon get warm. O'Killigain and his men are already at work, and will want to be coming in and out of here.

[*The cock crows louder than ever, and is joined by many more, a few of them at a great distance, so that the sounds are heard but faintly; these are mingled with the barking of dogs, the lowing of cattle, the bleating of sheep, the twittering of birds, the grunting of pigs, and the cackling of hens.*

Avril. There, you hear; everything's alive but you two.

Poges. Well, we'll be in the midst of them all in a second.

[*The two women withdraw. Basil and Poges, with the clothes wrapped round them, sit up, and dive down again. After a second or two they sit bolt-upright again, and again dive down.*

Poges [*shivering*]. Ooooh, Basil, cold!

Basil [*shivering*]. Bitter, bitter! What would I not give now for a cosy flat; a cosier bed; and a blazing hot-water bottle!

[*They lie quiet for a short time.*

Poges. There's nothing for it but to plunge out of the summer into the black and bitter winter.

Basil. You say the word.

Poges. Ready! Steady! Go!

[*They climb laboriously out of the beds. When they get out, it can be seen that they have been fully dressed, even to their heavy topcoats and scarves wound round their necks.*

Poges [*blowing on to his hands and rubbing them*]. Ooooh, crisp, isn't it? Healthy, though. Ooooh! Where the hell's that Barney, that he hasn't a fire lighted for us? Ooooh! One would want to be on his tail all day. [*Shouting*] Barney, Barney! [*Barney comes in holding some logs in the crook of his right arm, and a lantern in his left hand. Cloyne follows, with some paper and a bellows. Her left wrist is bandaged. Barney is wearing a topcoat, and has a muffler round his neck. Cloyne, too, is wearing a heavy coat. They both go over to the fireplace. As they come in*] Ah, here we are. Bit nippy, Barney; sharp, but beneficial. [*To Cloyne*] You'll have to be more careful with the steps and passages. Mind your feet coming in, mind your head going out. Oooooh! [*To Basil*] You better slip off, and give the others any help you can. [*As Basil is going*] What about your walking-stick?

Basil [*moving stiffly*]. I must try to do without it — about the house, anyway.

[*He takes the lantern that is beside his bed, and goes out, limping a little.*

Poges [*to the other two*]. Well, what do the pair of you think of the country, eh? And the house? Better than any your old Kings of Tarara had, eh?

Cloyne [*effusively*]. I'm sure it'll be lovely, sir, when we settle down.

[*Poges has been jerking his arms about in an effort to drive the cold from his body. Cloyne begins to fold the clothes on the beds, and tidy them up.*

Poges. Of course it will. We'll enjoy it all; we'll feel younger; we will *be* younger. The air, fresh air, pure air, exhilarating air, will be able to get at us. [*He sucks in his breath and blows it out again.*] Ooooh! Soon we won't know ourselves. We'll eat better, sleep better; flabby muscles will become firm, and we'll realise that we are alive, alive, alive-O. Think of the walks we'll have; so much to see, so much to hear, so much to smell; and then to come back, nicely tired, to such a lovely house. A life for the gods!

Cloyne. Wondherful, wondherful, sir.

Poges. Now I must be off to swallow down a cup of tea, for there's a lot to be done, a lot to be done yet.

[*He hurries off out of the room.*

Cloyne. The poor oul' codger!

Barney. Comin' down to this back o' God-speed place for rest an' quietness! Afther all that science has thried to do for us, goin' back to lanterns an' candles. Th' only electric light he'll allow in a Tudor house is one over his own desk! Runnin' in the face o' God Almighty's goodness — that's what it is.

Cloyne. They'll get tired of it before us.

Barney. I can tell you, I'm tired of it already. Looka the place we're livin' in: doors everywhere shaped like doors o' dun-

geons; passages dark as hell when it was first formed; crackin'
your head when you're goin' in, and breakin' your toe when
you're goin' out; an' I'm tellin' you, it's only beginnin'.

Cloyne. It might be worse.

Barney [*striking a match to light the paper*]. We're goin' to be worse,
I'm tellin' you.

Cloyne. We can't be worse than we are.

Barney [*as the flames of the paper die down*]. There's no chance o'
kindlin' here. Why did you say, then, that we might be worse?

Cloyne. Well, so, indeed, an' we might.

Barney. How can we be worse, woman, when we're as bad
as we can be?

Cloyne. Simply be bein' worse than we were.

Barney. How can we be worse than we were, when we're as bad
as we can be, now.

Cloyne. You'll see we'll be worse before we're betther.

Barney. Damn these logs! Isn't that what I'm sthrivin' to dhrive
into your head?

Cloyne. What are you sthrivin' to dhrive into me head?

Barney. That we'll be worse than we were before we're as bad
as we are now, an' in a week's time we'll be lookin' back with
a sigh to a time, bad as it could be then, that was betther than
the worst that was on top of us now.

[*Poges bustles in again. The heavy topcoat is gone and he is now
dressed in bright-blue shorts, emerald-green jersey, brown shoes,
and the scarf is still round his neck. He has a cup of tea in his
hand, and he is sipping it as he comes into the room. He is miser-
ably cold, but he puts on a brisk air, sorting it out in his mind
that to be cold in the country is natural, to be ignored as far as
possible, and to be countered by a smiling face, a brisk manner,
and the wearing of brilliant clothes denoting freedom of movement
and utter disregard of the common rules of convention. He is*

feeling far from comfortable, but thinks this shouldn't be shown;
for the colder you are, and the more uncomfortable you feel, the
brisker you must be, and the hardier you'll get.

Poges. Here we are again! Ready for anything now. [*Losing his*
gay attitude when he sees that the fire isn't lighted.] Isn't the fire
lighted yet? What are you doing, Barney? Being in the
country's no reason why we should be frozen to death.

Barney. I can't get a spark out of it, afther all me sthrivin'.

Poges [*testily*]. You can't light logs with a bit of paper, man.
Oh, use your brains, Barney, use your brains.

Barney. An' what else have I got to light them with?

Poges. Small sticks, man; put some small sticks under them.

Barney. An' will you tell me where I'm goin' to get the small
sticks? Isn't the nearest shop a dozen miles away?

Poges. Well, if there's no sticks, sprinkle a little paraffin on them.

Barney [*sarcastically*]. An' where am I goin' to get the paraffin?
There's no oil wells knockin' about here.

Poges [*severely*]. Don't be funny. You've got to remember you're
in the country now.

Barney. Isn't it meself that's gettin' to know it well!

Poges. We've got to do things for ourselves: there's no chance
of pushing a button to get things done here.

Barney. Sure, I'm beginnin' to think you're right.

Poges. Can't you see that those logs are too big?

Barney. I think I do, unless me sight's goin' curious.

Poges [*hotly*]. Well, then, why don't you do it!

Barney. Arra, do what?

Poges [*loudly*]. Make them smaller, man!

Barney [*calmly and sarcastically*]. An' how?

Poges. And how? Why, with an axe, of course.

Barney [*losing his temper — loudly*]. An' where's the axe, an'
where's the axe?

Poges. There must be an axe knocking about somewhere.

Barney. There's nothin' knockin' about here but a bitther breeze whirlin' through the passages that ud make the very legs of a nun numb!

Cloyne [*trying to mollify things*]. Sure, the poor man's back broken an' heart-broken thryin' to kindle it, sir.

Poges [*who has been waving his arms and stamping his feet while his teeth chatter — turning fiercely on Cloyne*]. You mind your own business, girl! [*Seeing her putting the mattresses by the wall.*] Have we got to sleep down here again tonight?

Cloyne. Ay, an' yous have. Th' other rooms are too damp still. Sure, Mr. O'Killigain says that it'll take a month of fierce fires to dhry them out.

Poges [*testily*]. Mr. O'Killigain says this, and Mr. O'Killigain says that! I'm getting tired of what Mr. O'Killigain says. If we have to sleep here, you or Barney'll have to stay up all night keeping the fire going, or we'll be frozen in our sleep. [*His eye catches sight of the telephone. He goes over to it and lifts the receiver.*] Not a sound! No, oh no; not a bit of a hurry. [*Angrily to Cloyne*] Go out, girl, and send in the boy who's working at this telephone. [*With a low moan*] Ireland!

[*Cloyne goes out by the doorway on the right leading to the entrance hall. After a few seconds the loud lowing of a cow is heard, followed by a scream from Cloyne, who rushes frantically back into the room, pale and tembling.*

Cloyne [*breathlessly rushing back into the room, falling on the floor, and catching Poges wildly by the legs*]. Save me! Stuck his head into me face, th' minute I opened the door. Mother o' God, I'll never see th' light of another day with th' fright I got!

Poges [*alarmed*]. What is it, what is it, woman?

Cloyne [*almost incoherent*]. A bull, a wild bull, out in th' enthrance hall!

Barney [*frantically*]. A wild bull! We're all desthroyed.

Poges [*trying to release himself from Cloyne's hold*]. Let me go, girl! Let me go, or I can't defend myself. If he comes in here, the whole of us'll be horned!

Cloyne [*frantically*]. My legs have given undher me. Let me hold on to you, sir — it's me only hope!

Poges [*to Barney*]. Put the table to the doorway, man, and help to bar him out — quick, quick, man! And a mattress. [*To Cloyne while Barney is pushing the table and a mattress to the door*] Why didn't you clap the door in his face, you fool?

Cloyne. Wasn't he half into the hall before I'd the door half open! Oh, sir, what are we goin' to do? Oh, please go, sir, an' thry an' shove him out!

                    [*The bellow of the animal is heard outside in the hall.*

Poges [*half dead with panic*]. My God, woman, you can't shove bullocks about! [*Shouting*] Souhaun, there's a wild bull in the house! Help, O'Killigain, help. [*To Barney*] Run, run, man, and get Mr. Stoke to bring down the gun. Oh, go quick, man! An' keep well out of range. [*Barney runs off. Shouting*] O'Killigain, help! Can't you let me go, girl?

Cloyne [*still clinging to him*]. Carry me off, sir, please. Don't leave me here to die alone! Maybe he won't be able to climb the stairs afther us. Oh, when I came to th' counthry, I never thought there'd be wild animals on th' door-step!

[*Basil appears at one of the entrances at the back; he moves forward stealthily and extends a gun to Poges.*

Basil [*nervous*]. What is it, what is it?

Poges. A bull, out in the hall.

Basil. Who let him in? Damn it, such carelessness! You must be on guard in the country, you know. Here, take the gun, man.

Poges [*angrily — to Basil*]. Come out, come out in the open, man, and be ready to use the gun if he comes into the room!

[*Shoving the gun from him.*] You use it, man; weren't you an A.R.P. man?

Basil [*indignantly*]. I never did anything more than clay-pigeon shooting! Let whoever let the damned animal in, let the damned animal out! [*He pokes Poges with the gun.*] Here, take this, and down him — you're nearer the bull than I am.

Poges [*angrily*]. I'm not a toreador, am I? And don't point, don't point the gun at me! Lower the barrel, man; oh, lower the barrel! D'ye want me to die two deaths at once? What's the advantage of your passing through Oxford if you can't face a bull with a gun in your hand? Be a man, man, and not a mouse.

Basil [*keeping well in the passage, and only showing his nose*]. Telephone the police, the fire brigade, or something.

Poges [*violently*]. Don't you know the kind of a country we're in! There's no police, no fire brigade, no telephone! Come here, if you won't use the gun, and help me carry this girl away out of danger.

[*The cow puts a stylised head, with long curving horns, over the barricade and lets out a loud bellow. Cloyne spasmodically tugs the legs of Poges, making him lose his balance so that he topples to the floor, after a frantic effort to save himself.*

Cloyne. Oooh, sir, save me!

Poges [*with a wild shout as he is falling*]. My God, he's on top of us! We're done for! Help!

[*Basil throws the gun into the room and runs for his life.*

Barney [*in the far distance*]. Sing out, sir, if you want any assistance!

[*Someone is heard stirring outside where the animal is; this stir is followed by the voice of the 1st Workman shooing the cow out of the hall. After a few moments, Poges slowly sits up and listens.*

1st Workman [*shouting outside*]. Eh, oick, oick, eh, yeh gett; ay, ay, oick oick!

[*Poges gets up on to his feet, shaking a little, and going over, picks up the gun and, steadying himself on it, stands over the prostrate Cloyne, who is almost in a faint, bundled up on the floor, with her face hidden in her hands. Shortly after, the 1st Workman appears at the entrance with a bucket of coal and some sticks. He looks over the table, astonished to see the prostrate Cloyne, and Poges standing near with a gun in his hand.*

Poges [*stormily*]. Where the hell did that bull come from? who owns her? who let that bull come tearing into a private house?

1st Workman. Bull, sir? Oh, that wasn't a bull, sir. [*He pushes the table back to its place.*] Jest a harmless innocent cow, sir. Frightened the poor girl, now, did it? [*Cunningly*] But I see it didn't frighten you, sir.

Poges [*flattered*]. No, no, not me. [*To Cloyne*] Here, girl, get up on your feet. [*Loudly*] It wasn't a bull; I knew it couldn't be a bull! and it's gone, so get up. [*Putting down the gun.*] Get up! [*With the help of the 1st Workman and Poges, Cloyne gets up on her feet.*] There now, be off with you. Get Miss Avril to give you a stiff glass of whiskey, and you'll be all right. And take this gun back to Mr. Basil.

[*He picks up the gun and hands it to the shaking Cloyne.*

Cloyne. Oh, sir, this place is worse than a jungle in th' desert!

Poges. Go on, go on! I thought you Irish were a brave people. [*He is shaky himself, but he stiffens himself to conceal the tremors.*

Cloyne [*going out with the gun*]. For ages now, it's bulls I'll be dhreamin' of, an' there's ne-er a lock on me door either!

Poges. Fainting, shouting, screaming, and running about for nothing! No nerves, no nerves, no spirit; no coolness in a crisis.

1st Workman [*craftily*]. An' did they all think it was a bull, sir? An' you stood your ground. Looka that now. Prepared for anything, sir.

Poges [*taking it all in*]. The other fellow, Mr. Basil, ran for his life; think of that — ran for his life!

1st Workman. Did he, now?

Poges. British, too, think of that; surprising and disappointing, very. [*Briskly and a little anxiously*] Still, I must acquaint the police. I can't have cows or bulls wandering about the rooms of Ormond Manor.

1st Workman [*who has started to light the fire*]. One o' th' ladies sent me in to light a fire for you. [*Placatingly*] Sure, sir, she was only the cow me friend brought this mornin' so that, when you had a minute, you could run out an' look her over. A fine animal, sir. She got loose an' wandhered in when she found th' door open. She's betther than th' best that was in th' cattle raid o' Cooley.

[*Souhaun comes in by a back entrance followed by Avril. She is carrying a black vase, striped with blue, and has a jazzy overall on one of her arms. Avril carries a blue bowl, striped with black. They are carrying them very carefully, as if they were very precious indeed.*

Souhaun. What's all this commotion about a bull? We had to stop Basil from trying to throw himself out of a window!

Avril. And Barney got out on top of the roof.

Poges. Oh, nothing, nothing at all; a stray cow in the garden mooed, and Basil lost his head and Cloyne lost her feet.

Avril. But Barney, when he was rushing past, said that you were out here roaring for help!

1st Workman. Roarin' for help, is it? Indeed an' he wasn't, for I can testify to that, but standin' here, cool as you like, he was, waitin' for the worst.

Souhaun. Well, if we're to stay in the country, we'll have to get used to all kinds of animals, big and small.

Poges [*shaking his head*]. I'm convinced now that poor Basil can't be wholly English. There's a weak joint somewhere.

Souhaun [*leaving the overall on a seat*]. There's your overall, dear, to wear when you're working, and we're taking your precious Annamese vase and Cambodian bowl to our room for safety, till everything's straight.

Poges. Oh, that's right, if anything happened to either of them, I'd pass out. Lift the vase up, dear, till I see it a second. [*She lifts it up.*] Oh, Lord, isn't it lovely? [*To Avril*] The Cambodian bowl too. [*She lifts it over her head.*] A little too high, dear; just go down on one knee. [*She does so.*] Aaah! Precious, precious! The chaste form, the tender planes, the refined colouring; the exquisite design, the *tout ensemble* — they go down into the undiscoverable deeps of the heart!

1st Workman. Arra, be God, indeed an' they do, sir.

Avril [*languishingly*]. A background of eau-de-nil would set them off to their full advantage.

Souhaun [*cocking her eye at them*]. Oh no, Avril; Chinese white's the pure and proper background for them.

Avril. Eau-de-nil.

Souhaun. Chinese white, dear.

Poges. Neither. Chrome yellow's the tone. A warm and pure cloak, as it were, for the chaste bodies of the vase and the bowl. [*He goes over and touches them tenderly.*] My darling treasures! Take them off, and lay them down with circumspection. Mind the step going out.

[*Souhaun and Avril go slowly and stately out, carrying the vase and the bowl as if they were precious relics.*

1st Workman [*to Poges who has come over to the fireplace where a fine fire is blazing now*]. There y'are, sir; a fire that'll warm y' up an' make your mind easy.

Poges [*stretching out his hands to the fire*]. Good, great, grand! Are you the workman who knows all the stories and legends of Ireland since the world began?

1st Workman. No, no, not me, sir; it's Philib you mean — th'

powerful man with th' powerful beard. [*Touching his forehead.*]
Some say he isn't all there, but a wondherful man, ay, indeed,
is Philib. Does a man good to talk to him.

Poges. I'll have a chat with him, the first chance I get.

1st Workman [*looking round the room with a ravishing air*]. This is a
wondherful house, so it is. It's an honour to be workin' in it.
Afther hundhreds o' years standin' in frost, rain, an' snow,
frontin' th' winds o' the world, it's a marvel it isn't flat on its
face, furnishin' only an odd shelther for a sthray fox; but here
it stands, an' we all waitin' for a windy winther ud stagger it
an' send it tottherin' down.

Poges [*indignantly*]. Tottherin' down! What d'ye mean, tottherin'
down? The place is as firm as a lighthouse. Tottherin' down,
indeed!

1st Workman [*repelling the idea that he thought of such a thing*].
Tottherin' down, is it? Now who, in th' name o' God, save
a sure an' safe fool ud think it was tottherin' down? Not me,
now; oh no, not me. Tottherin' down me neck! Isn't the grand
oul' house goin' to show, soon an' sudden, a sign of what a fine
residence it was when the quality harnessed their horses for a
hunt be the risin' rim o' th' dawn, or sat down in their silks
an' satins to their evenin' meal in the shadowy shine o' th'
gold candles!

Poges. Purple nights and golden days, my friend. [*He sighs.*] Aah!

1st Workman [*with a long, deep, imitative sigh*]. Aah! We'll never
set eyes on the like o' them again, sir; th' sparklin' carriages
comin' an' goin', th' steeds throttin' nicely an' neatly, or movin'
at a gallop, always elegant, on a visit to me lord here, or me lady
there, with th' sky above in a fair swoon o' pride for th' fine
things movin' about below; an' they full o' grace, an' decked
out in the grandeur o' th' West Indies an' th' East Indies, sobered
down a thrifle for use in a Christian counthry, the women's

bosoms asway with jewels, like a tendher evenin' sky, alive
with stars. An' th' gentlemen, just a dim step down, but elegant
too, in finery fair, with ruffles an' lace, with cutaway coats an'
vests embroidhered, each holdin' a cane to keep them steady,
an' all halo'd with scents to ring them round from th' smell o'
th' poor an' dingier world at work or play!

Poges [*enthusiastically*]. Those were handsome days. [*He fixes a
plume of pampas grass in his beret.*] When shall we look upon their
like again? [*He folds the crimson curtain stuff round him as if it
were a cavalier's cloak.*] The lawns and ramparts still are here,
and we shall be the men! [*He snatches up Basil's walking-stick.*]
The plume in the hat, the velvet cloak over the shoulder, the
tapering rapier in the hand! [*He makes a vicious lunge at the 1st
Workman, who narrowly dodges the pass.*] Die, varlet!

1st Workman [*remonstratively*]. Eh, eh, there; careful, sir, be careful!
Be careful how yeh prod!

Poges [*leaning on the stick as if it were a sword — sorrowfully*].
Where are the kings and queens and warriors now? Gone with
all their glory! The present day and present men? Paltry,
mean, tight, and tedious. [*Disgustedly*] Bah!

1st Workman. What are we now, what are we all, but a tired
thribe thryin' to do nothin' in th' shortest possible time?
Worn away we are, I'm sayin', to shreds and shaddas mouldin'
machines to do everything for us. Tired, is it? Ay, tired an'
thremblin' towards th' edge of th' end of a life hardly worth
livin'!

Poges [*gloomily pacing up and down*]. Not worth living, not worth
living.

1st Workman [*with greater energy*]. Time ago, an' we gave a ready
ear to one speakin' his faith in God an' his neighbour; but
now, there's so many gabbers goin' that there's hardly a
listener left. Sure, that in itself is as sharp a punishment as a

lease o' hell for a long vacation. It's meself is sayin' ourselves
came late, but soon enough to see the finery fade to purple dust,
an' the glow o' th' quality turn to murmurin' ashes.

Poges [*striking the attitude of a clumsy cavalier*]. We won't let them
perish completely! We'll keep the stern old walls standing.
We'll walk where they walked, sit where they sat, and sleep
where they slept!

1st Workman. An' talk as they talked too.

Poges [*wildly*]. Our pride shall be their pride, our elegance their
elegance, and the banner of the Ormonds shall fly from the
battlements again! The King, the King, God bless him!

1st Workman [*warningly*]. I wouldn't say too much about the
King, sir; we're a little touchy about kings down here in
Clune na Geera.

[*From outside is heard a scream from Souhaun and a squeal from
Avril; then the sound of running feet, and the crash of breaking
chinaware. After a moment or so, Souhaun pitches into the room
from the left entrance at back, and Avril from the right one.
Souhaun is holding the top rim of the vase in her hand, and
Avril the butt of the bowl. When he sees the damage, the 1st
Workman slinks off.*

Poges [*furiously*]. What the hell's all this?

Avril [*breathlessly*]. Rats!

Souhaun [*breathlessly*]. Gigantic creatures!

Avril. Here.

Souhaun. There.

Both [*together*]. Everywhere!

Poges [*in anguish*]. Oh, look at what's left of my Annamese vase
and Cambodian bowl! A hundred pounds of the best for
each, and then only when I happened to catch the cunning
Keeper drunk in the Bazaar of Singapore. What the hell
were the pair of you thinking of?

Souhaun. Rats.

Avril. Here, there, and everywhere.

Poges [*wildly*]. You evil-handed dolts to destroy my two best treasures! You'll pay for them, you'll pay for them!

Avril [*scornfully*]. We'd look well thinking of them, and we running for our lives.

Souhaun. You can imagine what it was when Basil is up there now on guard with the gun.

Poges [*mockingly*]. Oh, he's the boy to shoot down wild animals. [*Imploringly*] For God's sake go up and take the gun off him or he'll send a bullet through the body of some human being! And for the future, you and your friend keep your awkward hands off any treasures I may have left.

Souhaun [*scornfully*]. Treasures! Who told you that the Annamese vase and your old Cambodian bowl were treasures?

Poges. Everyone who saw them, woman!

Souhaun. Ay, to humour you. Well, let me tell you they weren't more valuable than a second-hand vase or bowl bought at a Woolworth sale. That's the fact, and it's best to know it.

Poges [*with quiet emphasis*]. And who gave you that information?

Avril. Couldn't anyone, not a fool, see what they were the minute they saw them?

Souhaun. The minute Mr. O'Killigain set eyes on them, he said that they went from Derby in thousands to Singapore and Saigon for suckers to buy them!

Poges [*with furious scorn*]. Oh, indeed, did he? Oh, an authority on what kind of art d'ye call it in Clune na Geera? I'll test them. I'll send them to the Curator of the Wallace Collection. We'll see. Mr. O'Killigain — good God!

[*He takes the pieces from Avril and Souhaun and puts them on the table. Cloyne appears at an entrance at back with a troubled look on her face.*

Cloyne. Here, they've gone and dumped the garden tools an'
the roller right in front of the hall door! And the roller's so
close that when you want to go out or come in you have to
climb over it.

Poges. Tell whoever brought them to bring them to the back
and put them in the shed, fool!

Cloyne. How can I tell him when him an' the lorry's gone?

Poges [*furiously*]. And why didn't you tell him before he went?

Cloyne. An' didn't I now? He just said that the back was threnched
be the workmen an' he hadn't time to build pontoon bridges.

Poges. What a country! What a people! [*Viciously — to Souhaun*]
And you encourage them, because you and your friend Avril
are Irish too!

Souhaun. If you ask me, you're not such a shining paragon of
goodness yourself.

Poges [*explosively*]. I believe in efficiency! I demand efficiency
from myself, from everyone. Do the thing thoroughly and
do it well: that's English. The word given, and the word kept:
that's English. [*Roaring*] And I'm an Englishman!

Souhaun. You are indeed, God help you!

Cloyne. An' what are we goin' to do about the garden tools an'
th' roller?

Souhaun [*in a bustling and dominant way, catching up the jazz-
patterned overall and putting it on Poges*]. Here, if we waste any
more time talking, the house will never be ready to live in. Put
this on, and go and bring the roller from the front door through
here, out of the way, to the back. When you've done that,
bring the garden tools to the back too, and let us see your
grand English efficiency at work while I and Avril do some of
the hundred things remaining to be done.

[*She gives him a push from her, and she and Avril hurry away out
by one of the back entrances.*

Cloyne [*warningly*]. It seems a heavy roller, sir, so mind you don't sthrain yourself when you're pullin' it.

Poges [*testily*]. Go away, go away, girl; I'm not an invalid. [*Cloyne goes. Poges moves over to the blazing fire and stretches out his hands to the flame. The 2nd Workman comes in by left entrance at back wheeling a barrow filled with bricks. He is a powerful man of fifty, with gleaming eyes and wide and strong beard. As he comes nearer, Poges turns to give him greeting. Warmly*] Good day, good sir; it's a cold day that's in it, surely.

2nd Workman [*eyeing Poges curiously*]. Ay is it, for them who has to brave it, an' can't stand all day in front of a sturdy fire like a kingly Pharaoh.

Poges [*a little nonplussed*]. Quite, yes, yes, quite. Everyone tells me the place round here is a rich storehouse of history, legend, and myth?

2nd Workman [*with a little scorn in his voice*]. It's a little they know an' little they care about those things. But the place has her share o' histhory an' her share o' wondhers.

Poges [*flatteringly*]. And I'm told you have a rare stock of them yourself.

2nd Workman. Ay, indeed, I have me share o' wondhers, new an' old.

Poges [*trying to be Irish*]. Looka that, now. Arra, whisht, an' amn't I told it's strange stories you do be tellin' of the noble things done by your fathers in their days, and in the old time before them.

2nd Workman [*sinking into a meditative mood*]. When less than a score of the Fianna brought back the King of England prisoner, invaded Hindostan, an' fixed as subjects the men of all counthries between our Bay o' Dublin and the holy river that gave to holy John the holy wather to baptize our Lord.

Poges [*astonished*]. I never heard that one before.

2nd Workman [*with murmuring scorn*]. An' where would th' like o' you hear it, man? That was in the days o' Finn Mac Coole, before his hair was scarred with a hint o' grey; the mighty Finn, I'm sayin,' who stood as still as a stone in th' heart of a hill to hear the cry of a curlew over th' cliffs o' Erris, the song of the blackbird, the cry o' the hounds hotfoot afther a boundin' deer, the steady wail o' the waves tumblin' in on a lonely shore; the mighty Finn who'd surrendher an emperor's pomp for a place with the bards, and the gold o' the King o' Greece for a night asleep be the sthream of Assaroe!

Poges [*solemnly*]. A great man, a great man, surely; a great man gone for ever.

2nd Workman [*sharply*]. He's here for ever! His halloo can be heard on the hills outside; his spear can be seen with its point in the stars; but not with an eye that can see no further than the well-fashioned edge of a golden coin.

Poges [*moving back a step — a little awed*]. You see these things, do you?

2nd Workman. I hear sthrange things be day, an' see sthrange things be night when I'm touched be the feel of the touch of the long-handed Lugh. When the Dagda makes a gong o' the moon, an' the' Sword o' Light shows the way to all who see it.

Poges. Aah!

2nd Workman. Then every rib o' grass grows into a burnished fighter that throws a spear, or waves a sword, an' flings a shield before him. Then Ireland crinkles into a camp, an' kings an' sages, queens an' heroes, saints an' harpers stare me in the face, an' bow, an' pass, an' cry out blessing an' vict'ry too, for Heber's children, with the branch of greatness waving in their hands!

Poges [*sadly*]. And there it ends!

2nd Workman [*giving Poges a drowsy glance*]. I'm thinkin' it might have been well for some if the end an' all was there; but it sthretches out to the sight of a big dim ship with a followin' fleet in the great dim distance, with a stern-fac'd man in the blue-gold coat of the French Armee, standin' alone on th' bridge of the big dim ship, his eyes fixed fast on the shore that was fallin' undher the high-headed, rough-tumblin' waves o' the sea!

Poges [*awed into interest — murmuringly*]. A big dim ship and a following fleet, carrying a man in the blue-gold coat of the French Armee — who was he, and when was that, now?

2nd Workman. Th' man was Wolfe Tone, and the time was yestherday.

Poges. Yesterday!

2nd Workman. The man was there, but the fleet was a golden dhream, always comin' in an' ever goin' out o' th' Bay o' Banthry!

[*O'Killigain has come in at the commencement of the 2nd Workman's musing, unnoticed by the dreaming worker, and barely noticed by the interested Poges, listening intently to what is being said, and a little awed by the influence of the 2nd Workman. O'Killigain comes softly over, and stands a little behind but close to the dreaming workman.*]

Poges [*bending towards the 2nd Workman*]. And who was the man in the blue-gold coat of the French Armee?

2nd Workman. He was a great Irish soldier and a great Irish friend to the people of no property in Ireland.

O'Killigain [*very softly*]. And there are others.

2nd Workman [*softly too, but not so softly*]. And there are others; for through the roads of the four green fields goes Shane the Proud, with his fine head hidden, waving away his more venturesome friends from the horns of a bull, the hoofs of a horse, the snarl of a dog, an' th' smile of an Englishman.

Poges [*going back a step*]. The smile of an Englishman!

2nd Workman [*unheeding the interruption*]. An' in the midst of them all is Parnell standing still; unheeding he stands with a hand on his breast, his white faced fixed on the East, with his wine-coloured eyes flashin' hathred to England!

O'Killigain [*very softly*]. And there are others.

2nd Workman [*with a glance at O'Killigain*]. They came later, an' haven't wandhered fully back to where they cleared a way for a gropin' people, but they will come, an' stare us into the will to take our own again.

Poges [*detaching himself from the spell*]. And do none other of those you know, good man, see the things that you see?

2nd Workman. Barrin' a few an' O'Killigain there, they see these things only as a little cloud o' purple dust blown before the wind.

Poges. That's very sad.

2nd Workman. Barrin' O'Killigain there an' a few, what is it all now but a bitther noise of cadgin' mercy from heaven, an' a sour handlin' o' life for a cushion'd seat in a corner? There is no shout in it; no sound of a slap of a spear in a body; no song; no sturdy winecup in a sturdy hand; no liftin' of a mighty arm to push back the tumblin' waters from a ship just sthrikin' a storm. Them that fight now fight in a daze o' thradin'; for buyin' an' sellin', for whores an' holiness, for th' image o' God on a golden coin; while th' men o' peace are little men now, writin' dead words with their tiny pens, seekin' a tidy an' tendher way to the end. Respectable lodgers with life they are, behind solid doors with knockers on them, an' curtained glass to keep the stars from starin'!

[*The 2nd Workman stoops, lifts the shafts of the barrow, and is about to go out.*

Poges [*to 2nd Workman — placatingly*]. My own great-grandfather was Irish, I'm told, and my grandmother was a kind of a Scotswoman.

2nd Workman [*going out with the barrow slowly*]. That's not such a lot, an' you're not sure of any of it either.

Poges. What a strange, odd man! I couldn't get half of what he was trying to say. Are there many like him?

O'Killigain. Millions of them, though few of them have tongues so musical.

Poges. He rather took to me, I think, and looks upon me as a friend.

O'Killigain [*ironically*]. He looks upon you, and all Englishmen, as a rascal, a thief, and a big-pulsed hypocrite.

Poges [*indignantly*]. Good God, but that's pure ignorance. Where would the world be without us?

O'Killigain. The giddy globe would wobble, slow down, stand still, and death would come quick to us all.

Poges [*a little puzzled by this remark*]. Eh? Quite. Well, no, not so bad as that, you know, but near it, damned near it.

[*Souhaun runs in with a look of dark annoyance on her face.*

Souhaun. Oh, look at you standing here still, and so much to be done — [*her voice rises*] — so much to be done, so much to be done! I asked you to get the roller away from the door an hour ago, and here's Barney after twisting his wrist trying to climb over it standing in the same old place! [*She catches him by the overall.*] Come, for God's sake, and take the damn thing out of the way!

Poges [*pulling her hand away from the overall — angrily*]. Oh, have some decency, order, and dignity, woman! Can't you see I'm having a serious discussion with O'Killigain? [*He turns swiftly on O'Killigain.*] We, sir, are a liberty-loving people, and have always striven to preserve perfect — perfect, mind you — freedom of thought, not only in our own land, but throughout

the whole world; but that anyone should be permitted to hold
opinions such as are held by that lunatic just gone out, and are
apparently held by you, sir, too, is a perfect scandal and disgrace!

Souhaun. Oh, there's no use of you trying to ride your high horse
here in Clune na Geera!

Poges [*stormily*]. I'm not trying to ride my high horse here in
Clune na Geera! What is said in Clune na Geera is a matter of
very little importance indeed. But every right-minded man
the world over knows, or ought to know, that wherever we
have gone, progress, civilisation, truth, justice, honour, human-
ity, righteousness, and peace have followed at our heels. In the
Press, in the Parliament, in the pulpit, or on the battlefield, no
lie has ever been uttered by us, no false claim made, no right
of man infringed, no law of God ignored, no human law,
national or international, broken.

O'Killigain [*very quietly*]. Oh, for God's sake, man, don't be
pratin' like a pantaloon priest!

Souhaun [*trying to push Poges from the room — impatiently*]. Go
out and get the garden roller!

Poges [*loudly*]. I say, sir, that Justice is England's old nurse;
Righteousness and Peace sit together in her common-room, and
the porter at her gate is Truth!

O'Killigain [*quietly, but sarcastically*]. An' God Himself is England's
butler!

Poges [*roaring with rage*]. That's a vile slander, sir!

O'Killigain. Whether it is or no doesn't matter much, for in a
generation or so the English Empire will be remembered only
as a half-forgotten nursery rhyme!

Poges [*fiercely as Souhaun is pushing him out*]. An opinion like that
deserves the jail!

Souhaun [*giving him a last strong push out into one of the back
entrances*]. Oh, go on! [*She goes over towards O'Killigain and*

stands looking shyly and a little archly at him.] What a naughty
  man you are to provoke him into such a tantrum!

O'Killigain. Why doesn't he spend his time, money, and energy
  in building something new, something showing a new idea
  leading our eyes to the future?

Souhaun. Oh, I don't know. You like your job here anyhow.

O'Killigain. A little.

Souhaun. A lot, because Avril is here.

O'Killigain. Just as O'Dempsey likes it because you are here.
  [*As he is about to go, O'Dempsey, the 2nd Workman, appears and
  speaks to O'Killigain while his gaze is fixed on Souhaun.*

2nd Workman. You're wanted on the roof, Jack.

O'Killigain [*with a laconic laugh*]. More mending — like slappin'
  the back of a dyin' man!
  [*He goes out while the 2nd Workman continues to look shyly but
  firmly at Souhaun. O'Killigain comes back in far enough to
  push O'Dempsey into the room.*

Souhaun [*busying herself at the desk. She picks up a brush*]. Well,
  Mr. Man, do you find me pleasant to look at?

2nd Workman. Yes, you are a fine-lookin' woman, and a fine-
  lookin' woman shows me a sign that God is smilin'.

Souhaun [*a little bitterly*]. It's Avril you have in mind, good man,
  and not me.

2nd Workman. When I look at you close, I see you a week or
  two oldher than your younger friend, and when you go as
  bright about the house, an' dress as gay as she does, you look
  like an earlier summer kissin' a tardier spring goodbye.

Souhaun. It's ridiculous for me to be with Poges. It's like a young
  bird I feel that has just got command of its wings. [*She pauses
  a moment and picks up a rag to clean the brush.*] You do think me
  as a woman worthy to be looked on — you're not just teasing
  me, are you?

2nd Workman. Not I. You are one of the fine sights of the world.
  [*He lilts:*]

> There are many fair things in this world as it goes,
> Th' blue skies of summer, the flushin' red rose;
> But of all th' fair blossomin' things that men see,
> A comely-built lass is the nearest to me!
> A comely-built lass is the dearest to me!
> And you are a comely lass.

Souhaun [*coming close to him*]. What's your name?
2nd Workman. Me name? [*He moves away.*] Why, O'Dempsey, of
  course.
Souhaun [*following him*]. No, no; your more familiar name;
  the name your girl would call you by?
2nd Workman. Philib.
Souhaun [*lingering over it*]. Philib! What a dear name. What a
  dear name! [*She suddenly leans towards him and kisses his cheek.*]
  Philib! [*She is backing away from him, a little frightened at what she
  has done, when she bumps into Poges laboriously pulling a gigantic
  roller as high as he is tall. The heavy iron side discs are vividly painted
  in panels of red, white, green and yellow. The 1st Workman is
  pushing the roller from behind, and is followed by O'Killigain
  gazing with laughing amazement at the ponderous machine.*
Poges [*angrily, as Souhaun bumps into him*]. Eh, eh, there, look
  where you are going, can't you?
Souhaun [*amazed at the size of the roller*]. God bless us, Cyril,
  what on earth's that you're carting into the house?
Poges [*petulantly*]. Can't you see what it is? The roller you told
  me to bring through here to the back. The roller, the roller I
  bought to roll the lawn.
Souhaun. But it's too big, man.

Poges. No, it isn't too big. The man who sold it to me said that the bigger it was, the more effective it would be.

Souhaun. But you'll never be able to pull a mighty thing like that.

Poges. And what's to prevent me from pulling it? Amn't I pulling it now? A child of ten could pull it, the man said; well-balanced, you know, the man said. Easy to pull, and easier to propel, the man said.

Souhaun. You've just been taken in, Cyril. The thing's altogether too big. [*To the 1st Workman*] Isn't it?

1st Workman. It looks a size too large to me, ma'am.

Poges. The grass in this district needed a special big roller to level it, the man said, and this was the roller to level it.

1st Workman. Sure, that roller ud level a hill.

O'Killigain. The grass'll give way undher that, right enough.

Souhaun. The cheek of declaring that a child of ten could pull it like a toy.

1st Workman. G'way, ma'am, an' did he really say that now?

Poges. One pull over the lawn with that roller would be enough for the season, the man said.

O'Killigain. An', faith, so it would, an' for every season afther too.

1st Workman. Sure, an' wouldn't a specially powerful horse himself wilt undher a thing like that! Whoever gave you that, man, musta taken it off an oul' steam-roller.

[*The 3rd Workman appears at entrance to right and proceeds to take an enjoyable interest in what is happening.*

3rd Workman. Mother o' God, looka what he's after buyin' be th' name of a roller! Isn't it a shame, now, to have imposed on a poor, simple, inoffensive man with a vehicle like that!

Poges [*defiantly*]. It's a bargain, I know it's a bargain; the man said it's a bargain.

Souhaun [*mockingly*]. The man said, the man said — ay, and you swallowed everything the man said.

O'Killigain [*to 1st Workman*]. Give Mr. Poges a hand to take this machine out of the sight of mortal men.

Poges [*obstinately*]. I'll take it myself, thank you all. Once you got the knack of balancing it, the man said, you could turn it with your little finger, and I believe what the man said.

O'Killigain [*to 3rd Workman*]. Here, you go on back to your work; go on, off you go!

[*He follows the 3rd Workman out of the room. Poges gives a mighty push to the roller, propelling it slowly to one of the entrances at the back. The 1st Workman goes over and helps him to push it.*

Poges [*fiercely — to 1st Workman*]. Let go, you! I'll manœuvre it myself. Let go, I tell you!

1st Workman [*as fiercely — to Poges*]. Can't you see, man, the declivity runnin' down the passage that'll lead you, if the roller once gets outa hand, into God knows where?

Poges [*with a roar into the face of the 1st Workman*]. Let go! [*The 1st Workman, startled, suddenly lets go his hold on the roller and the roller shoots forward down the declivity, Poges going with it, like a flash of lightning. Heard as he is careering down the passage — with anguish in his voice*] Help!

[*There is a pause of a few moments, then a thud is heard, followed by a rumbling crash of falling bricks and mortar; then silence again.*

Souhaun [*with vehement rage — running out*]. The blasted fool! He has rocked the house and killed himself and hasn't made his will!

1st Workman [*staring down the passage*]. Right through the wall he's gone! [*He runs to where the hole is in the ceiling, gets a seat and stands on it. Calling up to the hole*] Eh, Cornelius, eh, quick! [*The face of the Yellow-bearded Man appears at the hole, and he thrusts down his head as far as it will go.*

Yellow-bearded Man. Well, what's up now?

1st Workman [*excitedly*]. The oul' man, the oul' fool, has gone

right through the wall with the roller, an' shook the house —
bang!

Yellow-bearded Man. Didn't I think it was an earthquake!
[*Testily*] An' don't be tellin' me these things while I'm up here.
Can't you wait till I'm down in th' world o' men, and can
enjoy these things happenin'!

[*He angrily takes his head out of the hole. The 1st Workman gets
down from the seat and runs out by entrance on right.*

1st Workman [*running out*]. Mr. O'Killigain, Jack, eh, Jack!

[*Souhaun returns, followed by Cloyne and Barney leading in the
frightened Poges, powdered with the dust of the falling mortar.
Souhaun arranges a mattress for him on which he squats, supported
by pillows.*

Souhaun. You were warned, you were warned, and you would
have your own way. It's fortunate you are, indeed, that none
of your bones is broken.

Poges [*moaningly*]. Brandy, get me some brandy. [*Barney goes
out and comes back with a glass, brandy, and soda-water. He fills
out a glassful and gives it to Poges. After he has drunk the brandy —
to Cloyne and Barney*] Go away, you two, and don't stand there
gaping at me! [*They go. Musingly*] What a rascal that man
must be who sold me the roller! In this simple country, among
a simple people, where the very air is redolent with fairy lore,
that such a dangerous and materialistic mind should be lurking!

Souhaun. For God's sake, man, talk sense.

Poges [*shaking his head sorrowfully*]. A gay and charming people,
but irresponsible, utterly irresponsible.

[*O'Killigain appears at the right entrance with a cloudy look on his
face.*

O'Killigain. Look here, that Basil of yours is goin' about the
grounds carrying a fully-cocked gun at a dangerous angle.
He'll do harm. Send someone to take it off him, or I'll twist it

out of his hands myself! And you'll want to be more careful yourself, or you'll have th' oul' house down!

Poges [*indignantly*]. Oh, what a conceited fool that fellow is — going about to do dangerous damage for want of a little common sense and caution. I don't believe he ever fired a gun in his life. [*To Souhaun*] Go out, dear, and take it off him, before he shoots somebody — and go quick! [*Souhaun runs out by the entrance on the right, and O'Killigain is following her when Poges speaks to him, and halts him at the entrance.*] Oh yes, Mr. O'Killigain, a word please. [*He drinks some more brandy.*] Er, just a word. People are saying — there's a rumour going about that you and — and Miss Avril are — are, well, seen together at times.

O'Killigain. Well?

Poges. Well? Damn it, man, she's a lady, Mr. Stoke's a gentleman, and you're only a — a tradesman!

O'Killigain. Well?

Poges. Well? Oh, don't be welling me! The week she was away from here was bad enough, and very suspicious. She had the damned cheek to say she was with you.

O'Killigain. So she was.

Poges. So she was, was she? Well, it's dishonourable, and it will have to stop.

O'Killigain. And who'll stop it?

Poges [*firmly*]. I and Mr. Stoke will stop it.

O'Killigain [*quietly*]. You pair of miserable, old, hypocritical, wizened old getts, I'd like to see you trying!

Poges [*choking with rage*]. Get out of the house, and come here no more! I'll write to your parish priest! I'll — [*A shot rings out in the grounds outside.*] Good God, the fool has shot somebody! [*O'Killigain goes off in a hurry. There is a pause. Then the yellow-bearded face is thrust through the hole in the ceiling as far as it can go, and shouts down at Poges sitting like Buddha on the mattress:*

Yellow-bearded Man [*down to Poges*]. He's shot her, shot her dead, the poor little innocent creature! Th' charmin' little thing full o' gaiety an' go!

Poges [*very frightened, up to the Yellow-bearded Man*]. Shot who, shot who, man? Is it the young lass?

Yellow-bearded Man. Without warnin' he done it, without a flicker of an eyelid he sent her into the unknown!

Poges [*murmuring in agony*]. Avril! Oh, my God, little Avril. The curse of the Irish thorn-tree is on us! The little lass gone. [*Near swooning*] Cut down like a coloured bubble! The fairies must be manœuvring, and they'll get me next, maybe. Sweet little Avril the first to go!

Yellow-bearded Man [*savagely*]. Twenty-five pounds, an' not a penny less, he'll pay for it, or I'll have the heavy law on him. I'd ha' let you have her at first for the twenty, but in some compensation for th' agony of seein' the poor thing sink down into death, I'll have to get the other five, or I'll have the heavy law on him!

Poges [*sitting up suddenly*]. What are you talking about, man? What's shot, who's killed?

Yellow-bearded Man. Be th' way, you don't know that that lean, skulkin' friend o' yours has shot dead me poor little innocent, poor little cow! [*Sarcastically*] He thought it was a bull!

Poges [*bewildered*]. Oh, what a terrible country to have anything to do with! My precious vase is gone, my beautiful bowl is broken; a wall's demolished, and an innocent animal's shot dead: what an awful country to be living in! A no-man's land; a waste land; a wilderness!

CURTAIN

ACT III

Before the room appears, the sounds of falling rain and swishing winds are heard; and these go on, at intervals, throughout the scene.

The same as in the preceding Act; but some more articles of furniture have been added to the room. Between the entrance to the right at the back, and the right wall, stands what is said to be a Jacobean china-cabinet, filled with old pieces of china. At each side of the larger entrance on the right stands an armoured figure, comical-looking things, with long sharp points protruding where the man's nose (if a man were inside the suit) would certainly be; each figure, standing stiff, holds a long halberd well out from his body. Over these are, crossed, pennons, green and blue, fixed on the wall.

A blazing fire is in the fireplace. No one is in the room. After a moment Poges, dressed in his jazz-patterned overall, with a paper in his hand, runs in and rushes over to the telephone.

Poges [*into the mouthpiece — hurriedly*]. Get me — Oh, good evening, good evening. This is Mr. Poges, Ormond Manor. Get me St. Paul, London: 123. The house is getting on all right, thank you. Be quick, please. [*Warmly*] There's no — seems — in it; I am in a hurry. Oh, the ladies are quite well, sir. No, no, no; I don't want to go to an all-night dance to hear Irish songs sung! I want St. Paul! Eh? No, St. Peter won't do; please don't try to be funny; I am on very serious business. Get me the number I want at once! [*He takes the mouthpiece from his mouth and gives vent to a roaring growl of anger.*] Whether it won't matter a hundred years from now

187

isn't the point, sir. [*Shouting*] Damn it, get me St. Paul! [*Bursting with rage*] No wonder I use bad language. Is this the way business is done here? No wonder this country's as it is. What's wrong with it? [*Roaring*] Everything's wrong with it! You what? You hope my stay here will help to civilise me a little! [*He looks stupefied; then he slams the receiver on the hook. Almost instantly the 'phone rings. He whips off the receiver again and puts it to his ear.*] What the hell does this — Eh? Who are you? St Paul? Good God! This is Poges, Bradford. Oh, it's an awful place. People helpless, superstitious, and ignorant. I want you to get me five hundred shares in the Welldonian Cement Co.; shares are bound to jump, the minute the bombing starts seriously. They have jumped? Ah. What, a fiver a share, now? Well, get me two fifty. What? Not one to be had? [*Clicking his tongue*] Dtch, dtch. Run on them, eh? One wouldn't imagine there'd be so many trying to cash in on splintered bodies. The world, the world, Bradford! Yes, yes, of course; if there's any going, snap them up. Righto. Goodbye.

[*He hangs up the receiver. Barney appears at the entrance on the right.*

Barney. Canon Chreehewel would like to speak to you, sir.

Poges. Right; send the Canon in to me.

[*Barney goes; and, in a second or so, the Canon comes in. He is inclined to be portly, has rather a hard face, head bald at the front, with bushy greying hair at the back of his head and over his ears. He is wearing a soft hat, sodden with rain, which he puts on the end of the table when he comes in; and a long dark cloak, glistening with rain too. He comes over eager — to Poges, with a smile on his face, and outstretched hand.*

Canon. Ah, my dear friend, I'm so glad to have a chance of a word with you. How are you liking Clune na Geera?

Poges. Splendid, though the weather has been cold and very wet. Take your cloak off.

Canon [*taking off his cloak. When his cloak is off, it can be seen that his clothes fit nicely*]. Isn't it a nuisance; and we're in for more of it, by all accounts. If it goes on much more, the district will be a dismal swamp.

Poges [*indicating a seat*]. Sit down, Canon, sit down. Glass of sherry?

[*The Canon sits, and Poges sits too, opposite the Canon.*

Canon. No, thanks. I drink rarely. [*Apologetically*] Good example, you know. Well, welcome, my dear sir, to our district. You have a very beautiful house here. An old house, but a fine one. It is almost a sacred thing to keep an old thing from dying, sir; for whatsoever things are just, whatsoever things are honest, whatsoever things are pure, whatsoever things are lovely and of good report, are invariably found close to, and, sometimes, intimately enclosed in the life and being of ages that have passed, and in the life of men and women who have gone away before us.

Poges [*gratified*]. I wholeheartedly agree with you, reverend sir. I feel it, I know it.

Canon. With all its frills, its frivolities, its studied ceremonial, however gaily-coloured its leisure may have been, the past had in it the core of virtue; while the present swirl of young life, I'm saying, with its feverish sthrut of pretended bravery, its tawdry carelessness about the relation and rule of religion to man, with all its frantic sthretching of pleasure into every second of life, contains within it a tawny core of fear that is turning darker with every chime of the passing hours!

[*The rain and wind are plainly heard.*

Poges [*leaning towards the Canon — eagerly*]. We must lengthen our arm back to the past and pluck back some of the good things that haven't gone away as far from us as the dead who knew them.

Canon. A worthy enterprise, dear sir, and I hope you and your good people will be a help to us here to bring some of the slow movement of the past into the reckless and Godless speed of the present. [*He leans over towards Poges till their heads nearly touch.*] You and yours can do much to assist the clergy to keep a sensible check on the lower inclinations of the people, a work which should be near the heart of every sensible and responsible man with a stake in the country.

Poges. I'll do all I can. [*Leans back with an air of business importance.*] From the practical point of view, how am I to help?

Canon [*dropping a little into the idiom of the district*]. Help us to curtail th' damned activity of the devilish dance halls! Open a dance hall, and in a month or less the innocent disthrict becomes worse than your Leicester Square in London when the night has fallen. If the dance halls are allowed to go ahead without the conthrol of the clergy an' responsible people, God will go from Clune na Geera!

Poges [*shocked*]. Good God! Such a condition of things among a simple, charming, and pastoral people amazes me.

Canon [*warming to it*]. Arra, wouldn't it sicken you, when the hot days come, to see fools of oul' men an' fools of oul' women too, settin' a bad example, goin' about nearly naked, in their coloured shorts, an' brazen-fac'd lasses mixed among them in low-cut bodices, defiant short skirts, or shorter trousers, murdherin' modesty with a restless an' a reckless hand!

Poges. A lamentable state of affairs entirely, sir.

Canon [*rising and going over close to Poges — intensely*]. An' like Eden, sir, we've a snake in our garden too!

Poges. Oh!

Canon. O'Killigain!

Poges. Ah!   [*The wind and the rain are plainly heard.*

Canon. Guard your womenfolk from him, for no woman is safe
with that man. He publicly defends the wearing of low-
necked blouses by brazen hussies; he stands be the practice of
courting couples walking the highways and byways be night.
Why, one moonlight night, meetin' my curate dhrivin' home
a lasciviously-minded girl, O'Killigain tore the stick from the
curate's hand an' smashed it into pieces! A dangerous man,
my dear sir, a most dangerous man.

Poges [*a little nervously*]. I'm what you'd call a foreigner down
here, and so couldn't interfere with O'Killigain personally;
but what I can do to help you, I certainly will, in any other way.

Canon. Thank you — I guessed you would. Your fifty pounds
have helped a lot already. And now I've taken up a lot of your
time and must go. [*He takes up his hat.*] By the way, how's
the workman I sent you getting along?

Poges. Which one?

Canon. The one doing your electric light — a yellow-bearded
fellow.

Poges [*emphatically*]. Oh, he's getting along splendidly!

Canon. I'm glad to hear it. A good fellow — a Knight of St.
Columbus.

Poges. Well, now, I never knew Columbus was a saint.

Canon [*smiling indulgently*]. Oh yes indeed; a great Irish saint.

Poges. I always thought he was an American.

Canon. An American; who?

Poges. Christopher Columbus.

Canon [*smiling*]. Oh, there were two Columbuses, one Irish and
the other — er — American.

[*As the Canon is about to move away, Avril, followed by Souhaun,
dances into the room from an entrance at the back. She is dressed
in a low-cut blouse, short tailor-made skirt, and soft leather high
boots moulded to her calves and reaching to just below her knees;*

and looks, indeed, a very tempting and desirable young hussy.
She has a mackintosh over her arm. Souhaun, too, is dressed in
very short shorts of a vivid crimson and a black V-necked jersey,
looking as enticing, in a more mature way, as young Avril
herself. Poges is a little embarrassed, but the good Canon does
not flicker an eyelid. Souhaun whips off Poges' overall and shows
him in a green jersey and brown shorts.

Souhaun. You mustn't receive the Canon, dear, in an overall!

Avril. I say, Cyril, old boy, when are we going to get that
damned bathroom? It's a bit thick trying to have a bath in a
basin.

[*She sees the Canon and stops to gaze at him.*

Poges [*introducing her*]. Mr. Stoke's — er — wife — Miss Avril,
Canon. [*Introducing Souhaun*] My — er — wife, Miss Souhaun.

Canon [*bowing graciously — to Avril*]. My dear young lady. [*To
Souhaun*] Madam, I'm very pleased to know you.

Avril [*nodding to Canon — to Poges*]. Well, when are we going to
have a decent bathroom, old cock o' th' walk?

Poges [*deprecatingly*]. The Canon's here, Avril.

Canon [*jovially*]. Youthful spirits, sir, youthful spirits.

Poges. We'll have a bathroom if we can fit one in without in-
juring the harmony of the old house. The Tudor period never
saw a bathroom. This generation's getting soft, Canon; we want
hardening.

Avril. Bunkum!

Poges [*indignantly*]. It's anything but bunkum! Shakespeare had
to do without one.

Souhaun. But surely, dear, you must know that the Tudor people
knew nothing about the use of steam?

[*Basil now appears at an entrance at the back, and when he sees the*
company, he stays there and listens. He is dressed in a yellow jersey
and black shorts. No one notices him.

Poges [*petulantly*]. Steam! We stand here, in the centre, not of a house, but of a great civilisation, and you mention steam!

Souhaun. In the centre of a hot bath, dear, I can remain in the centre of your civilisation.

Basil [*joining in — looking like a statue in the doorway*]. Not precisely, Souhaun, for it would require, or at least postulate, a full and concentrated retirement through the avenues of thought back to the time of which the visible surroundings are vividly, but quiescently reminiscent. The conception of the conscious thoughts, interrelating with the — with the outward and inward action and reaction of all — or most of the bodily senses, incorporating the outward vision of sight with the inward vision of the inward conception of the — of the fragmentary stumuli — er — stimuli, into a perfect and harmonious whole; a thing, if I may be allowed to say so, if not impossible, is at least improbable, sitting down, or indeed even standing up, in the middle of a hot bath.

Avril [*with mock enthusiasm*]. Hooray!

Poges [*to the Canon*]. Mr. Stoke, Canon; cousin to the uncle of a K.G., and passed through Oxford.

Canon. Really? Well, well, remarkable connections. [*In the far distance a faint clap of thunder is heard; the Canon cocks his ear to listen.*] I must be off. Bad sign. The soft rain that's falling may change to a downpour, and I've a long way to go.

[*Canon puts on his cloak. Barney and Cloyne come in carrying a heavy Jacobean chair between them.*

Souhaun. Ah, the Jacobin chair. [*Indicating the way*] Out in the entrance hall, Barney.

Poges. Let's look at it a second. [*Barney and Cloyne pause.*] Ah, Canon, old things take a lot of beating.

Canon. They do, they do, sir. Well, I must go now.

Poges [*halting him*]. One second, sir. [*He goes to the table, writes a cheque, and hands it to the Canon.*] Another little trifle to keep things going, Canon.

Canon. Twenty-five pounds! Oh, thank you, and God bless you, my very dear sir.

Souhaun. You must come to dinner one night.

Canon. I will, I will, with pleasure; goodbye all.

          [*Midst a murmur of goodbyes the Canon goes out.*

Poges [*indignantly*]. Never showed the slightest interest in the Jacobin chair. Ignorance; Irish ignorance! [*Angrily — to Cloyne and Barney, who are holding the chair like a salesman displaying a piece of silk*] Bring the damned thing into the entrance hall, will you, and don't stand there like fools!

    [*Cloyne, in her hurry, jerks the chair from Barney's hold and it bumps to the floor.*

Poges. Oh, butter-fingers, d'ye want to destroy it? That's a Jacobin chair, man, a Jacobin chair!

Barney [*with a yell as he carries out the chair with Cloyne*]. Well, if I let a damned chair fall, I didn't knock a wall down!

Poges. Impudent rascal. The more you do for them the less they think of you! [*He bustles into his overall again.*] Now to business. What'll we do first? The rugs?

Souhaun. There's no use in trying the rugs till you get your quattrocento bureau in position. Then we'll be able to see if the colour of the rugs suits the bureau.

    [*Avril has put on her mackintosh and sidled over to the entrance on right, leading to the hall, and is about to slip out when Basil darts to her side and catches her arm.*

Basil. Where are you slipping off to?

Avril. I'm going for a brisk walk along the bank of the brimming river. I'm fed-up carrying things about to get this foolish old house in order.

Poges. In this weather? Nonsense!

Basil. A good idea; I'll go with you, darling.

Avril [*with a malevolent look at him*]. Wouldn't you like to, eh? Take my advice and don't! [*To Poges*] Ay, in this weather.

[*She goes quickly, leaving Basil, undecided, looking after her.*

Basil [*bitterly*]. She's going to go with O'Killigain!

Souhaun. Nonsense. She can't be out of your sight for a minute but you imagine the girl's with O'Killigain. The rain'll soon send her back. [*To Poges*] You see about locking the bureau, while I get the men to carry it in for you.

[*Poges goes by one of the entrances at the back.*

Basil [*going towards entrance at back*]. I tell you the jade's gone after O'Killigain.

Souhaun [*warningly*]. If I were you, Basil, I shouldn't press hard after little Avril; you are a little too consequential to please her always.

Basil [*maliciously — as he goes out*]. And you, me lady, are a lot too old to please O'Killigain at any time!

[*Souhaun stands stiff for a few moments; then she goes quickly to the entrance to the hall and is seen beckoning for one of the workmen.*

Souhaun [*calling*]. One of you, come here, please.

[*The 2nd Workman comes into the room and stands near the entrance, looking quietly at Souhaun.*

Souhaun. Send Mr. O'Killigain in to me, please.

2nd Workman. He's gone to the station to see afther a wagon-load o' bricks.

Souhaun [*slowly, after a pause*]. By himself?

2nd Workman [*after a pause*]. With th' handsome young woman. [*A pause.*] You're a handsome woman yourself; you're Irish too; an' y'ought to be sensible.

Souhaun [*slowly — a little surprised*]. Am I not sensible, good man?

2nd Workman [*earnestly*]. Your shinin' eyes can always say you are; an' soon you'll tire o' nestin' in a dusty nook with the hills outside an' th' roads for walkin'.

Souhaun. I will, will I?

2nd Workman [*with his eyes looking steadily in hers*]. Ay will you, an' dance away from a smoky bragger who thinks th' world spins round on th' rim of a coin; you'll hurry away from him, I'm sayin', an' it's a glad heart'll lighten th' journey to a one'll find a place for your little hand in th' white clouds, an' a place for your saucy head in th' blue o' th' sky.

Souhaun [*with a touch of mockery*]. Yourself, for instance?

2nd Workman. It's waitin' warm, he'll be, to please you, highly, an' show you wondhers of a manly manner.

Souhaun [*laughing, with a little catch in the laugh*]. A daughter of the Ormond with a workman!

2nd Workman [*raising his head proudly and looking steadily at her*]. An oldher name is an O'Dempsey, an' an oldher glory's in the name than the honour thrown to th' Earl o' Ormond when he crouched for favour at the English feet!

[*The 2nd Workman looks at Souhaun and Souhaun looks at the 2nd Workman for a moment, then she turns and goes slowly out by right entrance at back.*

3rd Workman [*appearing at the back left entrance*]. Here, Philib, what'r you doin'? You're to give us a hand to get in the oul' codger's bureau.

[*The two of them go out by the entrance to the left at back. After a second or two, the sound of scuffling and of voices are heard just outside the narrow entrance through which the two men have gone out, then Poges comes in with an anxious look on his face, turns and concentrates his gaze on the entrance. Presently the end of a big gilded desk-bureau comes in sight round the corner, with the three workmen puffing, pulling, pushing, and scuffling it along,*

*each giving orders to the other two, to the concern of poor old
Poges. When the bureau comes to the entrance, it can be seen to
be a very tight fit.*

1st Workman. A little to the ayste, there, a little more to the
ayste, can't yous!

2nd Workman. No, west, west; can't yous see it'll jam if yous
cant it to the ayste? To th' west, I'm tellin' yous!

Poges [*anxiously*]. Easy, boys, easy, now; take care, take great care;
that's a thing you won't meet every day, you know. I had an
anxious time while it was coming over.

3rd Workman [*taking no notice of Poges*]. Where th' hell are yous
shovin'? Are yous blind, or wha'? No squirming'll get it in
that way. [*Recklessly*] Here, throw th' thing up on its hind
legs an' let her go!

Poges [*loudly and anxiously*]. Eh, there, eh; steady, steady. Careful
how you handle that. It's not a thing to throw up on its hind
legs. I can't have a precious thing like that scratched and
mangled. That's a quattrocento piece of furniture, and there
isn't another piece like it in the world.

1st Workman [*to the others*]. Hear what the gentleman's sayin' to
yous! Amn't I tired tellin' yous yous ud look long before
yous ud find such a piece o' furniture in th' whole o' Clune
na Geera? Yous can't fling a thing like this about the way you'd
fling about an oul' kitchen chair. [*To Poges*]Amn't I right, sir?

Poges. Yes, yes; quite right, my man. Thousands of people
would give a fortune to possess a thing like that bureau. So
gently, boys, gently. The slightest scratch will do irreparable
damage.

1st Workman. See, boys, it's a quattrocento lump o' furniture, an'
so needs gentle handlin'. [*To 2nd Workman*] You, Philib,
there, give it a sudden swing to the ayste, an' while she's
swingin' we'll shoot her ahead.

2nd Workman [*angrily*]. How am I goin' to give her a sudden swing to the ayste when there's no purchase to get a grip of her? Squattrocento or nottorcento, I'm not goin' to let it whip a slice outa my hand!

3rd Workman [*thoughtfully*]. Th' only way to get it in proper is to get a sledge-hammer an' knock down some o' th' archway.

Poges [*indignantly*]. Knock down some of the archway! You'll do no such thing! You'll be suggesting that the house should be knocked down next. There's no sledge-hammer to be brought within sight of this precious bureau. [*Leaning over towards the men*] Listen: this is a piece of quattrocento — understand that, the whole of you, please!

1st Workman [*to the others*]. There, now, what did I tell yous? Yous hear what the gentleman says.

Poges. It ought to go in easily, if you knew your job. The driver of the furniture van looked at this entrance and told me not to worry, that the bureau would slide in without the slightest trouble.

1st Workman [*scornfully*]. Is it Larry Lunigan said that, now, did he? Don't mind anything Larry Lunigan says, sir. If your head was split he'd say it was only a scratch, to keep your heart up.

3rd Workman. Even if you were dead he'd tell your wife to wait, an' say you never could be sure of anything. An' we're not furniture shifters, sir.

Poges. Well, I'm sure of one thing: that bureau is coming into this room, and coming in without a scratch.

3rd Workman. 'Course it is.

1st Workman. Time an' patience'll do it.

Poges [*looking closely at the bureau — in anguish*]. Oh, my God, there's the stone wall eating into its edge! Get it away, pull it out, shove it in, you fools! [*As they shove*] Wait, wait!

1st Workman [*soothingly*]. I shouldn't worry, sir; a shavin' or two off is th' worst that can happen to it.

Poges Wait, wait a second. I'll go and get some cushions and pillows to guard the sides from the wall.

[*He runs out by the adjoining entrance for the cushions.*

1st Workman. J'ever see such an oul' fustherer in your life? You'd think the thing was on its way to the kingdom of heaven th' way he's cryin' over it.

3rd Workman. With a look on his ugly oul' gob like the tune th' oul' cow died of.

1st Workman. A quattrocento, mind you, says he.

3rd Workman. Seven hundred years an' more old, says he. Well, it's near time it met its death anyhow.

1st Workman. Here, let's get it in before he comes back billowin' with cushions. It's well able to take a knock or two.

2nd Workman. Here's th' crowbar he wouldn't let us use. [*He lifts up a big crowbar.*] We'll inch it in be main strength. Now, boys, get your shoulders to the quattrocento while I heave with th' bar! [*To the 1st Workman*] Start a shanty, Bill, to give us encouragement.

1st Workman [*chanting quickly, while they all brace themselves*]:

> What shall we do with th' dhrunken sailor,
> What shall we do with th' dhrunken sailor,
> What shall we do with th' dhrunken sailor,
> Early in th' mornin'?

All [*together — shoving and tugging vehemently*]:

> Pull away, an' up she rises,
> Pull away, an' up she rises,
> Pull away, an' up she rises,
> Early in th' mornin'!

[*Poges rushes in with some cushions in his arms. He is frantic when he sees what the men are doing. As he rushes in he is accompanied by a peal of thunder, louder than the last, but still fairly faint. As he comes to a halt near the bureau the peal ends.*

Poges [*enraged*]. What, in the devil's name, are you trying to do? Do you want to burst it to bits? Oh, why did I ever bring my poor quattrocento to a country like this! Shove it from the wall, shove it from the wall till I put a cushion in!

1st Workman. Sure, it won't go far enough away from the wall to fit a cushion, man.

Poges [*frantically*]. Do what you're told, do what you're told. [*He drops the cushions, seizes the edge of the bureau and tries to pull it from the wall.*] Here, somebody, help me!

[*Before he is aware of it, the 1st Workman leaps on to the top of the bureau to cross over to him, his heavy hobnailed boots scraping the top of it.*

Poges [*shouting at him*]. Get down, get down, man!

1st Workman [*astonished*]. Amn't I only comin' across to help you.

Poges [*yelling at him*]. That's a quattrocento, that's a quattrocento, man!

1st Workman. Sure, I know it is.

Poges. Then get off it, get off it — sticking your hobnailed boots through and through it!

1st Workman [*lifting up a foot so that the sole of the boot can be seen*] Is it that, sir? Sure, th' nails are worn so soft an' smooth they wouldn't mark th' wing of a butterfly.

Poges [*roaring*]. Get down, get down at once!

[*The 1st Workman jumps off the bureau back among his mates.*

2nd Workman [*muttering loudly*]. It ud be a godsend to some I know if they opened their eyes to th' signs an' wondhers showin'.

Poges. Now, no talk; and don't do anything till I give the order.

Men. All right, sir; go ahead; we're waitin'.

Poges. When I say go, you swing it to the right, while I swing it to the left. Are you all ready?

1st Workman. Ready an' waitin' an' willin'.

Poges. Go!

[*They all swing to the left, and Poges's foot is caught between the bureau and the archway. He lets a squeal out of him.*

Poges [*in anguish*]. Release my foot, my foot's caught! Why did you all swing left? Don't you know right from left?

3rd Workman. You should have said ayste, sir.

Poges. Shove it off, shove it from my foot!

1st Workman [*placing the crowbar between archway, against the column, and the bureau*]. Now, boys, all together — heave yo-ho! [*There is a mighty heave from them, one with the bar, the others with their shoulders. The bureau moves slowly; a crack is heard; the column snaps with the push of the bar against it and falls over the bureau, which suddenly shoots forward right into the middle of the room, the men stumbling after it. The men look triumphantly at the bureau, the 1st Workman leaning on the crowbar like a warrior leaning on his spear. Poges rubs his foot and contemplates the damage to the bureau and the entrance.*] There she is for you now, sir; right where you want her to be.

3rd Workman. I knew well patience ud do it in the end.

Poges. Oh, look at the bureau and look at the entrance!

1st Workman [*confidently*]. Oh, a spot o' cement an' a lick o' white paint'll make th' entrance look as young as ever again.

[*Souhaun comes in, followed by Cloyne and Barney, who are carrying a rug between them. They leave it on the floor. Basil is wearing very wide plus-fours.*

Souhaun. We're getting the house into some kind of order at last. [*She sees the damage.*] Oh, who's caused all the wreckage?

Poges [*sarcastically*]. Your very clever countrymen, dear.

Basil [*mockingly*]. And the high opinion they have of themselves.

2nd Workman. There is sweet music in the land, but not for th' deaf; there is wisdom too, but it is not in a desk it is, but out in th' hills, an' in the life of all things rovin' round, undher th' blue sky.

Poges [*angrily and despairingly*]. Take this broken column away and be off to your work again. Leave us, leave us, before the house falls!

[*The workmen take away the column and go out by entrance leading to the hall.*

Souhaun. Let us try the rugs, for God's sake! I can't go out o' th' room but there's damage done. [*Cloyne and Barney spread on the floor a rug scattered over with brightly-coloured geometrical patterns. Cloyne and Barney then go out; the rest stare at the rug.*] Rather gay-looking for the floor of a Tudor house, dear.

Basil [*decidedly*]. Too bright and too modern.

Poges. Where? how? why?

Basil. The Tudors, my dear sir, were a sensible and sober people, and wouldn't tolerate anything that was vulgar or, shall I say, conspicuous.

Souhaun [*with some mockery*]. You see, darling, it was taste, and not steam, that was everything in those days.

Basil. Quite, Souhaun; taste was the Tudor — er — er — *monumentum aere perennius.*

Poges. I don't know everything, my dear sir; but I do know something about the period that this house — er — exemplifies; in fact, the period was so riotous in colour that the men's breeches had one leg blue, the other leg red, or vice versa.

Basil [*with a patronising laugh*]. Ah, old boy, that wasn't the Tudor period.

Poges. What period was it then?

Souhaun. The Hiawatha period.

Poges [*indignantly — to Souhaun*]. This is no joke, please. [*To Basil*] What period was it, then?

Basil [*airily*]. Not the Tudor period, certainly; no, certainly not, old boy.

Poges [*contemptuously*]. Pshaw! You don't know it yourself.

[*From the entrance at back the 2nd Workman appears wheeling a barrow filled with bricks. Passing by the disputants, on his way to the hall entrance, he wheels the barrow over a rug.*

Poges [*shouting at him*]. Where the hell are you going with your dirty barrow?

2nd Workman [*dropping the shafts of the barrow and turning to answer Poges*]. I'm bringin' a barrow o' bricks to O'Killigain, sir.

Basil. Oh, he's back, is he?

Poges. What the hell do you think you're doing, man?

2nd Workman. Amn't I after tellin' you, I'm bringin' a barrow o' bricks to O'Killigain?

Poges. What d'ye mean, trundling your dirty barrow over a handsome rug laid out for inspection?

2nd Workman. What d'ye want me to do? Take th' barrow o' bricks up in me arms an' fly over it?

Basil [*with great dignity*]. Take it away at once, sir, and don't show impertinence to your betters.

2nd Workman [*eyeing Basil with scorn*]. Jasus, looka what calls itself a betther man than me!

[*O'Killigain appears at the entrance leading to the hall.*

Poges [*earnestly — to the 2nd Workman*]. My man, you're cheeking a cousin of a K.G. whose family goes back to — to — [*turning to Basil*] — William the Conqueror, isn't it?

Basil [*stiffening — with proud complacency*]. Further back, old boy — Alfred; the last man of the last family fell at the battle of Hastings.

Poges [*impressively*]. There, you see.

Souhaun [*with a sign of mockery in her voice*]. And the ancient gentleman passed through Oxford, too.

O'Killigain [*from the archway*]. The city of dissolute might!

2nd Workman [*with mock deference*]. D'ye tell me that, now? Why didn't you make me aware of all that glory before I began to speak? Isn't it an alarmin' thing to hear of the ancientology of a being that I took to be an ordinary man! An' what might be the ancient gentleman's ancient name?

Poges. Basil Horatio Nelson Kaiser Stoke.

2nd Workman. A right worthy name. It mayn't have a musical sound, but it has a steady one. There's no flightiness in that name. An' now, would you like to know mine?

Poges [*amusedly*]. Here, be off with you to your work; as if your name mattered much.

2nd Workman. Me name's O'Dempsey, of the clan that were lords of Offaly ere his ancient highness here was a thousand years from bein' born; a clan that sthretches back as far as the time before an Englishman thought of buildin' a weedy shelther; an' further back to a day or two afther th' one when the sun herself was called upon to shine.

[*He takes hold of the shafts of the barrow preparatory to starting off.*

Poges [*contemptuously*]. You don't look it, my poor man!

2nd Workman [*as he wheels the barrow out*]. I feel it; an' th' river's risin'.

Poges [*severely — to O'Killigain*]. You really oughtn't to allow, much more encourage, this silly, ignorant, and superstitious conceit among your men; it is something close to scandalous!

O'Killigain [*quoting*]. They go their own gait: looking carelessly in the faces of presidents and governors, as to say, *Who are you?*

Poges [*imperatively*]. Well, it's not going to be heard in this house! The bobtag and ragtail must be made to keep their free-and-easy manners at a distance. Dignity reigns here.

[*A louder peal of thunder is heard in the distance, and the room
  darkens a little.*

O'Killigain. It's raining.

Poges. Eh?

O'Killigain. It's raining hard.

Souhaun [*shivering*]. And growing cold.

O'Killigain. And old things are perishing.

2nd Workman [*appearing at entrance*]. We're knocking off, O'Killigain, for the rain is heavier an' the winds are keen.

O'Killigain. You do well to knock off, for it is waste of time to
 try to butthress up a tumbling house.

Souhaun [*over to the 2nd Workman*]. The house'll be lonesome
 without you.

2nd Workman. Come, then, an' abide with the men o' th' wide
 wathers, who can go off in a tiny curragh o' thought to the
 New Island with th' outgoin' tide, an' come back be th' same
 tide sweepin' in again!

Poges [*mockingly — to Souhaun, clapping her on the back*]. There's
 a high and hearty invitation to you, me lady!

       [*Avril comes in and dances over to Basil.*

Souhaun [*gleefully poking Poges in the ribs — to 2nd Workman*]. A
 long sail on the widening waters, no less; what gift is offered
 when the tide returns, good man?

2nd Workman. With firm-fed men an' comely, cordial women
 there'll be laughter round a red fire when the mists are risin',
 when th' roads an' fields are frosty, an' when th' nights is still.

Souhaun [*in a mocking voice — to Poges*]. There now, dear, is
 there anything more in the world than these that you can give?

Poges [*with pretended dismay*]. He has me beaten; what am I going
 to do at all, at all?

2nd Workman. A portion, too, with them who, ruddy-faced, were
 first in battle, with crimson cloak, white coat, an' silver belt

studded with splendour by a cunning hand; a portion, too, with them of paler faces an' dhressed in dimmer clothes, who, fearless, stepped a straight way to th' gallows, silent an' darin' in the' midst of a yelled-out Sassenach song!

Souhaun [*trying to speak mockingly, but developing a slight catch in her voice; for she has been moved by the 2nd Workman's words*]. Where is the lady who would be slow to give a man with such a coaxing way an invitation to her pillow?

Avril [*who sees her friend is affected. She comes closer to her, and touches her on the arm*]. Souhaun, Souhaun, come an' show me your newest dhresses, an' don't stay listenin' to his thrancin' talk. Don't leave me alone with them.

Souhaun [*shaking off Avril's hand. Falling into the Irish idiom*]. Let me be, girl, for it's right an' lovely listenin' to a voice that's makin' gold embroidery out o' dancin' words.

Poges [*angry and a little nervous*]. It's time to put an end to all this nonsense!

O'Killigain [*ignoring Poges's angry exclamation — to Avril*]. An' you, young girl, sweet bud of an out-spreading three, graft yourself on to the living, and don't stay hidden any longer here. Come where the rain is heavy, where the frost frets, and where the sun is warm. Avril, pulse of me heart, listen to me, an' let longin' flood into your heart for the call of life. The young thorn-three withered away now, can awaken again, an' spread its fragrance around us. Spit out what's here, an' come where love is fierce an' fond an' fruitful. Come, lass, where there's things to say an' things to do an' love at the endings!

2nd Workman. Jack has spoken fair, an' there's no handsome hindrance near to stop yous. What's here but a creakin' grandeur an' poor witherin' talk; salt food without a dhrink to go with it; an' a purple dhryness turnin' timidly to dust!

O'Killigain [*coming close to Avril*]. Aren't my words a star in your ear, lass? Haven't you heard them? They've hit your young breast, lass. Come with me, I say; come away from where rich ignorance is a blessing, an' foolishness a gift from God! Come to th' house on th' hill: the door is open, the fire's alight on the hearth, and the table's laid with a clean white cloth.

Avril. Let another go in by the door; let another eat at the table; let another sit by the fire. Why didn't you come for me, O'Killigain, before the young thorn-tree had shed its blossom, and before the stems began to die?

O'Killigain. I'd other things to do. While you were livin' your lesser life, an' singin' your dowdy songs, I was fightin' in Spain that you might go on singin' in safety an' peace. [*He grips her arm*] I've come for you, now, me love.

Avril [*emotionally and anxious*]. I cannot go where things are said and things are done, for love has had no voice in the beginning of them! [*She tries to free her arm*] Oh, Jack, let me go — you're hurting me!

O'Killigain. It's O'Killigain gives the pressure of comfort and of care. D'ye mind th' hurt when th' hurt's th' hurt of love?

Avril [*passionately*]. Yes, I do! Oh, no, no; I don't, O'Killigain! I don't, I don't! Your pressure on my arm presses on my heart, too. Oh, go away an' leave me lonely!

[*She breaks away and runs to Souhaun, who puts an arm around her.*

O'Killigain. Avril, come out of th' guttherin' candlelight here to where th' wind puts a flush on the face, ruffles th' hair, and brings a catch to the breath; come to th' one you want; come to th' man who needs you!

2nd Workman [*to Souhaun*]. An' you, Souhaun, sturdy lily o' Clune na Geera, come into the love that can fix or flutther th' stars o' th' sky an' change th' shinin' moon into a lamp for two. Come to th' one you need; come to th' man who wants you!

Souhaun [*half joking, all in earnest*]. If you only had a horse handy,
    I'd ride away with you!

2nd Workman [*quietly*]. He's outside waitin'. A loan from Mr.
    O'Killigain. An animal can gallop glorious the livelong day
    undher th' sound of a steady voice an' th' touch of a steady hand.

Souhaun [*greatly moved*]. N-no!

2nd Workman [*firmly*]. Yes.

Basil [*rising out of astonishment — to Poges, angrily*]. How long are
    you ready to stick this, man? Send these impudent fellows away!

Poges [*as if awaking from a stupor — furiously to the two men*]. Get
    out, the two of you! We haven't lived long enough here to be
    touched with your insanity! Get out!

Souhaun [*to 2nd Workman — gently*]. I'll see; I'll do whatever
    Avril advises. [*To Avril*] Come, dear, till we think out a won-
    derful answer.

O'Killigain [*to Avril as she is going out*]. Be ready: I'll call, and
    come to take you when the river rises!

[*He goes out.*

2nd Workman [*to Souhaun as she is going out after Avril*]. I'll wait
    outside be th' good gallopin' horse till th' snowy-breasted
    pearl comes to shimmer on me shouldher.

[*He goes out after O'Killigain.*

Poges [*furious and mocking*]. When the river rises! Come with me
    and be my love! Come into the garden, Maud. Were ever
    fools so foolish!

Basil [*in angry glee*]. And the fellow with the galloping horse out-
    side! Boot, saddle, and away! I never expected to see and hear
    the like, even in this odd country. [*Slapping Poges on the back —
    jokingly*] You'd better watch out for the sound of the galloping
    horse!

Poges [*slapping Basil on the back*]. And you keep an ear open for
    O'Killigain's call when the river rises!

Basil [*in a mock tragical voice*]. Beware the sound of a galloping horse!

Poges [*in the same manner*]. Beware of O'Killigain's call!

[*Poges goes over to the bureau, opens a drawer, takes some papers out of it, and looks at them; then he sits down at the bureau, and arranges things in order to write a letter.*

Basil. And, for God's sake, did you hear that vulgar fellow chatting about making the moon do something or other?

Poges [*arranging things on the bureau*]. Poor crazy fool. They're all a bit demented. Must be the climate. Most amusing.

Basil [*gloomily*]. Yes, amusing up to a point, but hardly reassuring; no. [*He comes nearer to Poges.*] I don't like it, Poges.

Poges [*a little startled*]. Eh?

Basil. Well, it isn't exactly comfortable to be living in a community of crazy people, is it? It may even become dangerous.

Poges [*sitting up straight*]. That's a serious thought, Stoke. Now that you mention it, I do feel the insidious influence of the place. We might become demented too.

Basil. If they allowed us to live long enough.

Poges. Good God, what a thought! I must have a talk with you about this when I finish this letter.

Basil. You saw for yourself how this influence is even affecting the girls.

Poges [*emphatically*]. The girls? There you are wrong, Stoke. No, no, not the girls, man. They were just humbugging the poor fools. Nonsense; not the girls.

Basil [*about to go out*]. You watch. Come up to our room when you've finished the letter, will you?

Poges. At once. [*Basil goes out. Poges takes some paper, and writes the date on the top right corner. Then he pauses, and evidently begins to think of what has happened. Shaking his head slowly from side to side — musingly*]. Erin, the tear and the smile in thine eye.

[*He clears his throat with a cough, and settles down to write. The room becomes darker. He has hardly been writing a minute when a curious face appears round the corner of the entrance leading to the hall. It is the stout little face of a little man dressed in neat black clothes covered with a saturated fawn-coloured mackintosh. Big spectacles cover his eyes. A huge fiery-red beard spreads over his chest like a breastplate, reaching to his belly, and extending out from his body like a fan turned downwards. He wears a black jerry hat. When he speaks he is found to have a little voice. He carries a blackthorn stick in his hand. As he peeps round he sees Poges at the bureau, and pulls in his head again. He thrusts it forward again, steps out, and comes into full view. He pulls his coat straight with a jerk and smoothes his trousers, and then comes with a trot into the room, right over to Poges, bends over towards him, and greets him in a hearty manner. He is the Postmaster of the village.*]

Postmaster. An honour it is, sir, to meet the owner of such a fine house. A house with a histhory. A house where the genthry joined themselves to merriment and danced th' stars to sleep! [*He dances clumsily round the room, singing*] See me dance the polka, see me dance the polka, see me dance the polka, as I have done before. [*He suddenly stops and comes close to Poges.*] I hope I see you well, sir? I bear a message from the Postmaster.

Poges [*amazed*]. I am well, thank you; and what is your message from the Postmaster?

Postmaster. When I was outside, an' heard you coughin', it's well I knew be th' sound of th' cough that the cough was th' cough of a gentleman.

Poges [*impatiently*]. Yes, yes; but what is your message?

Postmaster. Well, as genuine gentleman, you'll be th' first to agree that a Postmaster with a small wife an' a large family, an' hardly any salary — I near forgot to mention that — hardly any salary at all, if the thruth was told, as a thrue gentleman, you'll agree that a man like that is handicapped, an' has a claim on a gentleman's sympathy.

Poges. But I can't make his wife bigger or his family smaller, can I?

Postmaster. Sure, I know you can't, an' that's not what the Postmaster's complainin' about. [*He leans over Poges.*] But th' poor man needs sleep, he needs his share o' sleep.

Poges [*humouring him — thinking his visitor is out of his mind*]. Yes, yes; of course, the poor man needs sleep. We all need sleep. That's a fine stick you have in your hand, sir; can I see it?

Postmaster [*holding up the stick and stretching it away from Poges*]. Ay, ay, a fine blackthorn. There y'are; look at it as long as you like — [*warningly*] — but don't lay a finger on it. There's a stick could give a man a crack a man ud remember!

Poges [*nervous*]. Oh? I can't see it well from here; let me take it in my hand for a moment.

Postmaster. Sorra a second you're goin' to have it in your hand. That stick has never been outa me father's hand an' it has never been outa mine. D'ye know why?

Poges. No, friend, I don't.

Postmaster. Guess, now, guess.

Poges [*smiling sweetly*]. I haven't the slightest idea, friend; I couldn't guess.

Postmaster. This's th' very stick that me oul' fellow made a swipe at Parnell with — th' scandaliser of Ireland's holy name, a swipe that, had it got home, ud a laid Parnell up for a month o' Sundays! Now, as a thrue gentleman, wouldn't you say I was right?

Poges. Yes, yes; quite right.

Postmaster. Well, havin' settled that, let's settle th' other: amn't I right in sayin' that every man should have his share o' sleep?

Poges. Yes, yes; of course.

Postmaster. Well, then, amn't I right in sayin' that th' poor Postmaster should have his share o' sleep too?

Poges. To be sure. [*Rising from his seat*] Now, I must be going. [*A fairly loud clap of thunder is heard, followed by the sound, first of a trotting horse, then of one going off at a gallop. They listen till the sounds die in the distance.*] A horse going off at a gallop. [*He makes a move away*] I must go to see what's wrong.

Postmaster [*waving him back with the stick*]. Wait a minute — I'm not done yet. You've just said the poor Postmaster should have his share o' sleep — didn't you?

Poges [*impatiently*]. Yes, yes, friend.

Postmaster. I knew you'd say that. [*He stretches out his hand to Poges.*] Lave it there. [*He shakes hands with Poges.*] Now I won't have to be keepin' one eye open an' me ear glued to the bell, for fear of a toll call or a thrunk call, afther ten o'clock at night, an' I settlin' down for a cosy sleep.

Poges [*the truth dawning on him*]. Oh, so you're the Postmaster, are you? So it was you who delayed me when I wanted St. Paul?

Postmaster. Didn't you know that?

Poges. The telephonic system here is an all-night one, isn't it?

Postmaster. 'Course it is, but that says nothin'.

Poges [*decidedly*]. Look here, my man; I'm a business man, and have to make calls at all hours of the night; I can't be thinking of every man having an honest night's sleep.

Postmaster. 'Course you can't; it's only the poor Postmaster that you've got to keep in mind.

Poges [*severely*]. Look here, my man, as long as I pay for the service, the service will have to be supplied. Good day.

Postmaster. There isn't a gentleman in th' whole disthrict ud think, except in th' case o' sudden death or disasther, of givin' a tinkle afther th' hand o' th' clock had passed the figure of half-past nine o' night.

Poges. Take yourself and your stick away out of the house, man!

Postmaster [*mimicking him*]. Take yourself and your stick away outa the house, man. Is it comin' down here to teach us good manners an' feelin' y'are, an' you puttin' a surly gob on you when you're asked to fall in with the sensible an' thried institutions of the neighbourhood?

[*While they have been talking together, the room has darkened still more, and Poges sharply tugs the string that puts on the light; the wind has risen and can be heard occasionally blowing through the trees outside, and even shaking the old house.*

Poges [*in a rage*]. Go on, get out!

[*As he says this, a long, loud peal of thunder is heard.*

Postmaster. D'ye hear that? There won't be many thrunk calls goin' for a while, an' th' poor Postmaster'll have a sweeter night's sleep than some I know. [*He bends towards Poges.*] When — the river — rises!

[*The room has darkened; the wind rises; the one light in the room flickers. The Postmaster and Poges watch it. Then the Postmaster turns to go, but halts when a Figure of a man is seen standing at the entrance leading to the hall. He is dressed from head to foot in gleaming black oilskins, hooded over his head, just giving a glimpse of a blue mask, all illumined by the rays of flickering lightning, so that The Figure seems to look like the spirit of the turbulent waters of the rising river. The Postmaster goes back, startled, till he is beside Poges, and the two men stand and stare at the ominous Figure. Basil, Barney, and Cloyne appear at the entrances at back, each holding a lighted lantern in his and her hand. They are very frightened. They too hold up their lanterns and stare at The Figure.*

Basil. The river is rising!

Barney. Risin' high!

Cloyne. An' will overwhelm us all!

The Figure [*in a deep voice*]. The river has broken her banks and is rising high; high enough to come tumbling in on top of you. Cattle, sheep, and swine are moaning in the whirling flood. Trees of an ancient heritage, that looked down on all below them, are torn from the power of the place they were born in, and are tossing about in the foaming energy of the waters. Those who have lifted their eyes unto the hills are firm of foot, for in the hills is safety; but a trembling perch in the highest place on the highest house shall be the portion of those who dwell in the valleys below!

[*The lightning ceases for a moment; the entrance becomes dark, and The Figure disappears.*

Poges [*frantic*]. What shall we do? what must we do? what can we do?

Basil [*in anguish*]. We're lost!

Cloyne [*sinking down on her knees*]. King o' th' Angels, save us!

Barney [*clasping his hands*]. Amen! A nice pass we've come to when we have to call for help in a Tudor house! [*To Basil and Poges*] It's the evil livin' of you two buckos that has brought this disaster upon us!

Poges [*bawling*]. Souhaun, Souhaun! O'Killigain, help!

Basil [*roaring at Poges*]. You made us come down here!

Poges [*roaring at Basil*]. You're a liar, it was you!

Postmaster [*bringing down the blackthorn stick with a bang on the quattrocento bureau*]. Eh, order, order, law an' order there; steady! Measures o' safety to be taken. [*Thrusting his stick towards Poges — sharply*] Has the highest room in the house a way to the roof — quick!

Poges [*answering at once*]. Yes.

Cloyne [*in anguish*]. Th' roof — oh, my God!

Postmaster [*rapidly*]. Up with us all with bread and wine, with firewood and coal, and an axe. Up!

Poges. An axe?

Postmaster. To hack whatever suitable furniture we can get into a raft if we're swirled off th' roof. [*Driving Cloyne and Barney before him*] Up!

Poges [*loudly*]. Souhaun, Souhaun, where's Souhaun?

Basil [*impatiently*]. Come on, and come up.

    [*Avril comes in from one of the back entrances. She is covered with a green mackintosh, and a coloured scarf, peasant-wise, is over her head. She carries a small case. She passes between the two men without a word, and stands still near the entrance leading to the hall, looking out before her.*

Poges [*staring at her*]. What are you doing here? What are you watching? [*Avril stands still and silent.*] Where's Souhaun, where's Souhaun?

Avril [*quietly — without looking round*]. She's gone.

Poges. Gone? How? Where?

Avril [*quietly — still not moving*]. Gone with the wind; gone with the waters; gone with the one man who alone saw something in her!

Poges [*raging*]. What, with that loud-mouthed, ignorant, superstitious, low-born, half-mad Irishman! Oh, she's nicely rooked me! She was with him on the galloping horse that galloped away, was she? Oh, she's nicely rooked a simple, honest, loving-hearted, foolish man! She's gone, is she?

Avril. An' well it would be if I was with her.

Poges. You damned slut, are you in your mind as bad as she is?

Avril [*indicating Basil*]. The mind that went with him is as bad as the mind that went with you.

Basil [*sneeringly*]. You lost the chance you had to get away from it.

Avril. He said he'd come when the river rises.

O'Killigain [*outside — loudly*]. Avril!

Avril [*with a start of joy*]. O'Killigain! O'Killigain!

[*O'Killigain appears, his trench coat drenched and his hair soaking, at the entrance.*

O'Killigain. My barque is waiting, love; come!

[*Avril picks up the case and runs to O'Killigain.*

Basil. Honest, decent woman, she carries the booty of her friends in her pack!

Avril [*quietly*]. I gave more than I got, you gilded monkey. It's winnowed of every touch of life I'd be if I stayed with th' waste of your mind much longer. [*She taps the case.*] Th' thrinkets I wormed out of you are all here, an' here they stay, for th' wages were low for what was done for you.

Poges [*sneering*]. And gentleman O'Killigain will happier be with a harlot's fortune!

O'Killigain [*good-humouredly*]. Of course he will. Th' good things of this life are good for all, an' a pretty girl looks handsomer in arms that are fit and fond to hold her. You have had your day, like every dog. Your Tudors have had their day, and they are gone; and th' little heap o' purple dust they left behind them will vanish away in th' flow of the river. [*To Avril*] Come, love, to my little house up on th' hill.

[*He goes out with Avril. After a moment the sound of oars are heard splashing the waters, and O'Killigain is heard singing.*

O'Killigain [*singing: other voices, outside, join in the chorus*]:

Come from the dyin' an' fly from th' dead,
Far away O!
An' now, with th' quick, make your home an' your bed,
With a will an' a way, away O!

Then away, love, away,
Far away O!
To live any life that is looming ahead,
With a will an' a way, away O!

Away from all mouldherin' ashes we row,
Far away O!
Takin' th' splendour of livin' in tow,
With a will an' a way, away O!

Then away, love, away,
Far away O!
Where th' lightning of life flashes vivid we go,
With a will an' a way, away O!

[*Poges stands still, listening till the song fades away in the distance. Suddenly Basil clutches his arm.*

Basil [*frantically*]. Look, the waters are tumbling towards us! Run, man!

      [*He tears up the passage while Poges follows more slowly.*

Poges [*going out*]. My poor little quattrocento, the waters are about to cover thee! My comfort's gone, and my house of pride is straining towards a fall. Would to God I were in England, now that winter's here!

[*He disappears down the passage as the green waters tumble into the room through the entrance from the hall.*

CURTAIN

COME FROM THE DYIN'

Come from the dy-in' an' fly from the dead

Far__ a-way O!__ An' now, with the quick, make your

home an' your bed, With a will and a way a-way

O! Then a-way, love__, a - way,

Far__ a-way O!__ To live an-y life that is

looming a-head, With a will an' a way a-way O!

THE MAID OF BUNCLODY

Oh__ were I at the moss house, Where the

birds do in - crease, At the foot of Mount

Lein-ster Or__ some si - lent__ place, By the

streams of Bun-clo-dy Where all

plea-sures do_ meet, And_ all I would

ask is One kiss from you, sweet.

O'KILLIGAIN'S LILT

They may rail at this life, from the hour I be-gan it, I

found it a life full of kind-ness and bliss; And un-

-til they can show me some hap-pi-er pla-net, More

so-cial and bright, I'll con-tent me with this.

THERE ARE MANY FAIR THINGS IN THIS WORLD

There are ma-ny fair things in this world as it goes, The

blue skies of_ sum-mer, the flush-ing red rose, But of

all the fair blossom-ing things that men see, A-

come-ly-built lass is the near-est to me, A

come-ly-built lass is the dear-est to me.

HEY, HEY, THE COUNTRY'S HERE

Ru-ral scenes are now our joy, Farm-er's boy,

Milk-maid coy, Each like a new-ly paint-ed toy

CHORUS

In the bosk-y coun-try. Hey, hey, the country's here, The

country's there, It's ev-'ry where, We'll have it, now, last

thing at night, And the ve-ry first thing in the morn-ing!

THERE'S LIFE WITH TH' LASSES

Come in or go out or just stay at the door, With a

girl on each arm an' one stand-ing be-fore, Sure, the

more that I have, the more I a-dore, For there's
much slower

life with the lass-es, says Ro-ry O' More!

RED ROSES FOR ME

A Play in Four Acts

CHARACTERS IN THE PLAY

MRS. BREYDON
AYAMONN BREYDON, *her son*
EEADA
DYMPNA } *Mrs. Breydon's neighbours in the house*
FINNOOLA
SHEILA MOORNEEN, *Ayamonn's sweetheart*
BRENNAN O' THE MOOR, *owner of a few oul' houses*
A SINGER, *a young man with a good voice*
ROORY O'BALACAUN, *a zealous Irish Irelander*
MULLCANNY, *a mocker of sacred things*
REV. E. CLINTON, *Rector of St. Burnupus*
SAMUEL, *verger to the church*
INSPECTOR FINGLAS, *of the Mounted Police, and the Rector's churchwarden*
1ST MAN
2ND MAN } *neighbours in the next house to Breydons'*
3RD MAN
DOWZARD } *members of St. Burnupus' Select Vestry*
FOSTER
A LAMPLIGHTER
1ST RAILWAYMAN
2ND RAILWAYMAN

SCENES

ACT I.—Two-roomed home of the Breydons.
ACT II.—The same.
ACT III.—A Dublin street, beside a bridge over the river Liffey.
ACT IV.—Part of the grounds round the Protestant Church of St. Burnupus. In this Act the curtain is lowered for a few minutes to denote the passing of a few hours.

TIME.—A little while ago.

ACT I

The front one of two rather dilapidated rooms in a poor working-class locality. The walls, whitewashed, are dwindling into a rusty yellowish tinge. The main door, leading to the hall, is at the back, a little towards the right. The fireplace is in the right-hand wall, and a brilliant fire is burning in the large, old-fashioned grate. In the centre of the room is an old ebony-hued table on which stands a one-wick oil-lamp, its chimney a little smoky from the bad oil in the reservoir. Some books lie on the table, some paper, coloured chalks, a pen, and a small bottle of ink. In the left wall, up towards the back, is the door leading to the second room. Below this door is a horsehair sofa showing signs of old age. On it, to the head, is a neatly folded bundle of sheets and blankets, showing that it is used as a bed during the night. To the left of the main door at the back is a large basket used by actors when on tour. On the other side of this door is an ordinary kitchen dresser on which some of the crockery is on the ledge, for the upper shelf is filled with a row of books, by the look of them second-hand. Over the basket, on the wall, is tacked a childlike brightly-coloured pastel of what is meant to be a copy of one of Fra Angelico's angels blowing a curved and golden trumpet; and beside it is a small coloured reproduction of Constable's 'Cornfield'. In the same wall, towards the back, is a large, tall window, nearly reaching the ceiling, and, when one is in front of it, the top of a railway signal, with transverse arms, showing green and red lights, can be seen. Under this window, on a roughly made bench, stand three biscuit tins. In the first grows a geranium, in the second, musk, and in the third, a fuchsia. The disks of the geranium are extremely large and glowing; the tubular blooms of the golden musk, broad, gay, and rich; and the purple bells of the fuchsia, surrounded by their long white waxy sepals, seem to be as big as arum lilies. These crimson, gold, and purple flowers give regal tint to the poor room. Occasionally in the distance can be heard the whistle of an engine, followed by its strenuous puffing as it pulls at a heavy rake of goods wagons. A chair or two stand about the room.

It is towards the evening of a mid-spring day, and the hour would make it dusk, but it is darker than that, for the sky is cloudy and rain is falling heavily over the city.

Ayamonn and his mother are in the room when the scene shows itself. He is tall, well built, twenty-two or so, with deep brown eyes, fair hair, rather bushy, but tidily kept, and his face would remind an interested observer of a rather handsome, firm-minded, thoughtful, and good-humoured bulldog. His mother is coming up to fifty, her face brownish, dark eyes with a fine glint in them, and she bears on her cheeks and brow the marks of struggle and hard work. She is dressed in a black jacket, fitting close, marred by several patches, done very neatly, dark-blue skirt, a little faded, and rather heavily-soled boots. At the moment this is all covered with a rich blue velvet cloak, broidered with silver lace, and she is sitting on a kitchen chair covered with a dark-red, rather ragged cloth.

Ayamonn wears a bright-green silk doublet over which is a crimson velvet armless cloak bordered with white fur. The back part of the cloak is padded so as to form a big hump between his shoulders. Across his chest is a dark-green baldric from which hangs a scabbard. A cross-hilted sword is in his hand. On his head he has a black felt hat with narrow turned-up rims. A black band goes round the hat, and a crimson feather sticks up from it. His legs are in heavy, black, working corduroy trousers, and he wears heavy hobnailed boots. She and he are in an intensely listening attitude.

Mrs. Breydon [*whispering over to Ayamonn*]. She's gone; wanted

to borra something else, I suppose. They're feverish with bor-
rowing in this blessed house!

Ayamonn. Damn her for a troublesome fool! Where's this I was
when the knock came?

Mrs. Breydon. I was just goin' to say

> Ay, an' for much more slaughter after this,
> O God! forgive my sins, and pardon thee!

Ayamonn [*looking at the floor*]. Oh yes! [*He recites*] —

> What, will th' aspiring blood of Lancaster
> Sink to the ground? I thought it would have mounted.
>   [*He holds the sword aloft, and stares at it*]
> See how my sword weeps for the poor king's death!
> O, may such purple tears be always shed
> For those that wish the downfall of our house!
> If any spark of life be yet remaining,
>
> [*He stabs at the floor*] Down, down to hell;
>   and say I sent thee hither!

[*A knuckle-knock is heard at the door. Ayamonn and Mrs. Breydon
    stiffen into a silent listening attitude. A fine baritone voice,
    husky with age, is heard speaking outside.*

Voice. Is anyone in or out or what? [*Louder raps are given as
Ayamonn steals over, and places his back to the door.*] Eh, in there —
is there anyone movin', or is the oul' shack empty?

Mrs. Breydon [*in a whisper*]. Oul' Brennan on the Moor. He was
here before, today. He's got his rent for his oul' houses, an' he
wants to be told again that the Bank of Ireland's a safe place to
put it.

Ayamonn [*warningly*]. Ssshush!

Voice. No answer, eh? An' me afther seein' a light in th' window.

Maybe they are out. For their own sakes, I hope they are; for it's hardly an honourable thing to gainsay a neighbour's knock.

[*The sound of feet shuffling away is heard outside, and then there is silence for a few moments.*

Mrs. Breydon. He's gone. He's always a bit lively the day he gets his rents. How a man, with his money, can go on livin' in two rooms in a house an' sthreet only a narrow way betther than this, I don't know. What was he but an oul' painter an' paperhanger, starvin' to save, an' usin' his cunnin' to buy up a few oul' houses, give them a lick o' paint, and charge the highest rent for th' inconvenience of livin' in them!

Ayamonn. I wish he'd keep himself and his throubles far away from me now. I've higher things to think of and greater things to do than to be attached to the agony of an old fool for ever afraid a fistful of money'll be snatched away from him. Still, he isn't a miser, for he gives kids toys at Christmas, and never puts less than half a crown on the plate in church on Sundays.

Mrs. Breydon. So well he may!

Ayamonn. What was he sayin' when he was here before?

Mrs. Breydon. Oh, th' usual question of askin' me what I thought about the Bank of Ireland; mutterin' about somebody not payin' th' rent; and that his birthday's due tomorrow.

Ayamonn [*looking at the chair*]. I'll have to get a loan of a chair with arms on, and someway make them golden to do the thing proper in the Temperance Hall; and I'll paint for the back of it, on thin cardboard, a cunning design of the House of Lancaster, the red rose, so that it'll look like a kingly seat.

Mrs. Breydon. Th' killin' o' th' king be th' Duke o' Gloster should go down well, an' th' whole thing should look sumptuous.

Ayamonn. So it will. It's only that they're afraid of Shakespeare out of all that's been said of him. They think he's beyond them, while all the time he's part of the kingdom of heaven in the nature of everyman. Before I'm done, I'll have him drinking in th' pubs with them!

Mrs. Breydon. I don't know that he'll go well with a Minstrel Show.

Ayamonn. He'll have to go well. If only King Henry doesn't rant too much, saw the air with his hands, and tear his passion to tatthers. The old fool saw someone do it that way, and thinks it must be right. [*With a sigh.*] I daren't attempt to recite my part now, for Oul' Brennan on the Moor's waitin' and listenin' somewhere down below; so I'll just get it off by heart. How old does he say he'll be tomorrow?

Mrs. Breydon. Only seventy-six, he says, an' feelin' as if he was lookin' forward to his twenty-first birthday.

Ayamonn. Well, he won't have long to wait.

Mrs. Breydon [*slyly*]. He was muttherin', too, about some air or other on the oul' piano he has at home.

Ayamonn [*springing up from where he has been sitting*]. It's one o' mine he's put an air to! [*He rushes from the room and returns in a few moments.*] He's not there; gone home, I suppose. [*Irritably*] I wish you'd told me that at first.

Mrs. Breydon. I'd thry to rest a little, Ayamonn, before you go to work. You're overdoing it. Less than two hours' sleep today, and a long night's work before you. Sketchin', readin', makin' songs, an' learnin' Shakespeare: if you had a piano, you'd be thryin' to learn music. Why don't you stick at one thing, an' leave the others alone?

Ayamonn. They are all lovely, and my life needs them all.

Mrs. Breydon. I managed to get on well enough without them. [*She goes over to the window and tenderly touches the fuchsia.*]

There's this sorryful sthrike, too, about to come down on top of us.

Ayamonn [*sitting in the red-covered chair and reading Shakespeare — quietly and confidently*]. There'll be no strike. The bosses won't fight. They'll grant the extra shilling a week demanded.

Mrs. Breydon [*now fingering the musk*]. I thought this Minstrel Show was being run to gather funds together?

Ayamonn [*impatiently*]. So it is, so it is; but only in case the strike may have to take place. I haven't much to do with it, anyway. I'm with the men, spoke at a meeting in favour of the demand, and that's all.

Mrs. Breydon. You'll undhermine your health with all you're doin', tearin' away what's left of your time be runnin' afther —— [*She checks herself, and becomes silent.*

Ayamonn [*lowering his book to his lap — angrily*]. Go on — finish what you started to say: runnin' afther who?

Mrs. Breydon. Nobody, nobody.

Ayamonn. Runnin' afther Sheila Moorneen — that's what was in your mind to say, wasn't it?

Mrs. Breydon. If it was aself; is there a new law out that a body's not to think of her own thoughts.

Ayamonn [*sharply*]. What have you got against the girl?

Mrs. Breydon. Nothing. As a girl, I'd say she's a fine coloured silken shawl among a crowd of cotton ones. A girl I'd say could step away from the shadowy hedges where others slink along, tiltin' her head as she takes the centre of the road for the entherprisin' light o' day to show her off to everyone. Still——

[*She stops speaking again.*

Ayamonn. Ay, but still what? You've a maddenin' way of never finishing some of your sentences.

Mrs. Breydon [*braving it out*]. She's a Roman Catholic; steeped

in it, too, the way she'd never forgive a one for venturin' to
test the Pope's pronouncement.

Ayamonn. And who wants to test the Pope's pronouncement?
Life and all her vital changes'll go on testing everything, even
to the Pope's pronouncement. D'ye think I've laboured as I
have, and am labourin' now, to furnish myself with some of
the greatness of the mighty minds of the past, just to sink down
into passive acceptance of the Pope's pronouncement? Let
the girl believe what she may, reverence what she can: it's
her own use of her own mind. That she is fair to look upon,
charming to talk with, and a dear companion, is well and away
enough for me, were she even a believer in Mumbo Jumbo, and
had a totem pole in her front garden.

Mrs. Breydon. There's worse still than that in it.

Ayamonn. Worse, is there? An' what may that be?

Mrs. Breydon. She's th' child of a sergeant in the Royal Irish
Constabulary, isn't she?

Ayamonn. Well, she can't help it, can she?

Mrs. Breydon. I know that; but many have murmured again' a
son of mine goin' with the child of a man crouchin' close to
their enemy.

Ayamonn. Everything, it seems, is against her, save herself. I
like herself, and not her faith; I want herself, and not her
father.

Mrs. Breydon. The bigger half of Ireland would say that a man's
way with a maid must be regulated by his faith an' hers, an'
the other half by the way her father makes his livin'.

Ayamonn. And let the whole world join them! Fair she is, and
her little ear's open to hear all that I thry to say, so, were
she the child of darkness aself, I'd catch her hand and lead her
out and show her off to all men.

Mrs. Breydon. She wouldn't be a lot to look at afther she'd wended her way through poverty with you for a year an' a day.

Ayamonn. She gives no honour to gold; neither does her warm heart pine for silks and satins from China and Japan, or the spicy isles of Eastern Asia. A sober black shawl on her shoulders, a simple petticoat, and naked feet would fail to find her craving finer things that envious women love.

Mrs. Breydon. Ah, go on with you, Ayamonn, for a kingly fool. I'm tellin' you th' hearts of all proper girls glow with the dhream of fine things; an' I'm tellin' you, too, that the sword jinglin' on th' hip of Inspector Finglas, the red plume hangin' from his menacin' helmet, an' th' frosty silver sparklin' on his uniform, are a dazzle o' light between her tantalised eyes an' whatever she may happen to see in you.

Ayamonn. Tell me something else to add to my hope.

Mrs. Breydon. Go on readin', an' don't bother to listen to your mother.

Ayamonn [*going over and gently putting his hands on her shoulders*]. I do listen, but I am drifting away from you, Mother, a dim shape now, in a gold canoe, dipping over a far horizon.

Mrs. Breydon [*with a catch in her voice*]. I did an' dared a lot for you, Ayamonn, my son, in my time, when jeerin' death hurried your father off to Heaven.

Ayamonn. It's I who know that well: when it was dark, you always carried the sun in your hand for me; when you suffered me to starve rather than thrive towards death in an Institution, you gave me life to play with as a richer child is given a coloured ball. [*He gently lifts up her face by putting a hand under her chin.*] The face, the dear face that once was smooth is wrinkled now; the eyes, brown still, that once were bright, have now been dimmed by a sthrained stare into the future; the sturdy back that stood so straight, is bending. A well-tried leaf, bronzed

with beauty, waiting for a far-off winter wind to shake it
from the tree.

Mrs. Breydon [*gently removing his hand from her chin*]. I have a
tight hold still. My back can still bear many a heavy burden;
and my eyes, dimmer now than once they were, can still see
far enough. Well, I better take this fancy robe from off me,
lest it give me gorgeous notions.

[*She takes off her robe, and leaves it carefully folded on the basket,
then goes over and arranges the fire. Ayamonn looks thoughtfully
out of the window, then takes off cloak, sword, and hat, leaving
them carefully on the basket.*

Ayamonn [*musingly*]. He'll hardly come tonight in this rain. If he
does, I'll get him to read the King's part, and do mine over again.

Mrs. Breydon. Who's to come tonight?

Ayamonn. Mullcanny: he's searching Dublin for a book he
wants to give me; and, if he got it, he was to bring it tonight —
The Riddle of the Universe.

Mrs. Breydon. That's another one I wouldn't see too much of, for
he has the whole neighbourhood up in arms against his
reckless disregard of God, an' his mockery of everything
solemn, set down as sacred.

Ayamonn. Oh, Tim is all right. The people are sensible enough
to take all he says in good part; and a black flame stands out in
a brightly-coloured world.

Mrs. Breydon. You don't know them, if you say that; he'll meet
with a mishap, some day, if he doesn't keep his mouth shut.

Ayamonn. Nonsense.

[*She has quietly slipped a shawl around her, and is moving to the
door so silently as to seem to want to prevent Ayamonn from
noticing her movements, when the door opens and Eeada, Dympna,
Finnoola, and several men, appear there. The three women come
a little way into the room; the men stay around the door. All their*

faces are stiff and mask-like, holding tight an expression of dumb resignation; and are traversed with seams of poverty and a hard life. The face of Eeada is that of an old woman; that of Dympna, one coming up to middle age; and that of Finnoola, one of a young girl. Each shows the difference of age by more or less furrows, but each has the same expressionless stare out on life.

[Dympna is carrying a statue of the Blessed Virgin, more than two feet high, in her arms. The figure was once a glory of purest white, sparkling blue, and luscious gilding; but the colours have faded, the gilt is gone, save for a spot or two of dull gold still lingering on the crown. She is wearing a crown that, instead of being domed, is castellated like a city's tower, resembling those of Dublin; and the pale face of the Virgin is sadly soiled by the grime of the house. The men are dressed in drab brown, the women in a chill grey, each suit or dress having a patch of faded blue, red, green, or purple somewhere about them.

Eeada [to Mrs. Breydon]. Could you spare a pinch or two of your Hudson's soap, Mrs. Breydon, dear, to give the Blessed Virgin a bit of a wash? [To all in general] Though I've often said it's th' washin' that's done away with the bonnie blue of th' robe an' th' braver gold of its bordhers an' th' most o' th' royalty outa th' crown. Little Ursula below's savin' up her odd pennies to bring Her where She'll find a new blue robe, an' where they'll make the royalty of th' gilt glow again; though whenever she's a shillin' up, it's needed for food an' firin'; but we never yet found Our Lady of Eblana averse to sellin' Her crown an' Her blue robe to provide for Her people's need. [Mrs. Breydon gives half a packet of soap powder. Gratefully] Thank you, ma'am, an' though y'are of a different persuasion, Our Blessed Lady of Eblana's poor'll bless you an' your fine son for this little tribute to Her honour and circumspect appearance before the world.

The Rest [*murmuring*]. Ay will She, an' that's a sure thing.

> [*They open a way for Eeada to pass out, with Dympna carrying the statue, following in a kind of simple procession. Mrs. Breydon is moving slowly after them.*

Ayamonn [*who has noticed her under his eyes*]. You're not going out again, surely — on a night like this, too?

Mrs. Breydon. Not really; only down the road to Mrs. Cashmore's. She's not too well; I promised I'd dhrop in, and see to a hot dhrink or something for her before she wandhered off to sleep.

Ayamonn [*irritably*]. You think more of other homes than you do of your own! Every night for the past week you've been going out on one silly mission or another like an imitation sisther of charity.

Mrs. Breydon. I couldn't sit quiet knowin' the poor woman needed me. I'd hear her voice all through the night complainin' I never came to give her a hot dhrink, settle her bed soft, an' make her safe for th' lonely hours of th' slow-movin' night.

Ayamonn. A lot they'd do for you if you happened to need help from them.

Mrs. Breydon. Ah, we don't know. A body shouldn't think of that, for such a belief would dismay an' dismantle everything done outside of our own advantage. No harm to use an idle hour to help another in need.

Ayamonn. An' wear yourself out in the process?

Mrs. Breydon [*with a sigh*]. I'll wear out, anyway, sometime, an' a tired ould body can, at least, go to its long rest without any excuse.

> [*As she opens the door to go out, Sheila appears on the threshold. She is a girl of about twenty-three, fairly tall, a fine figure, carrying herself with a sturdiness never ceasing to be graceful. She has large, sympathetic brown eyes that dim, now and again, with a cloud of timidity. Her mouth is rather large but sweetly made;*

her hair is brown and long, though now it is gathered up into a thick coil that rests on the nape of her neck. She is dressed in a tailor-made suit of rich brown tweed, golden-brown blouse, and a bright-blue hat. These are now covered with a fawn-coloured mackintosh, darkened with heavy rain, and a hastily folded umbrella is dripping on to the floor. She comes in shyly, evidently conscious of Mrs. Breydon's presence; but fighting her timidity with a breezy and jovial demeanour. Mrs. Breydon tries, but can't keep a little stiffness out of her greeting.

Sheila. Oh! good evening, Mrs. Breydon. What a night! I'm nearly blown to bits; and the rain — oh, the wind and the weather!

Mrs. Breydon. You must be perished. Take off your mac, and come over to the fire. Get Ayamonn to make you a cup o' tea, and bring you back to life again.

Sheila. No, really; I'm burning — the battle with the wind and the rain has made me warm and lively.

Ayamonn. Hey ho, the wind and the rain, for the rain it raineth every day. Sit down and take the weight off your legs.

Sheila. Not worth while, for I can't stop long. [*To Mrs. Breydon*] Going out on a night like this, Mrs. Breydon?

Ayamonn [*hastily*]. She has to go: got an urgent call from a poor sick neighbour.

Sheila [*hesitatingly*]. What is it? Could . . . could I do it for you?

Ayamonn [*decidedly*]. No, no, you couldn't. The woman knows my mother. It's only to see her safe and warm in bed for the night; Mother won't be long.

Mrs. Breydon. Good night, Miss Sheila; perhaps you'll be here when I come back.

Sheila. I don't think so. I must go almost at once.

Mrs. Breydon. Well, good night, then.

[*She goes out, and Ayamonn goes over to Sheila, kisses her, and helps her off with the mac.*

Sheila. You shouldn't let your mother go out on a night like this — she's no longer a young woman.

Ayamonn. I don't like to interfere with her need to give help to a neighbour. She likes it, and it does her good.

Sheila. But the rain's coming down in sheets, and she's got but a thin shawl round her shoulders.

Ayamonn [*impatiently*]. Oh, she hasn't very far to go. Let's think of greater things than the pouring rain and an old woman on her way to smooth pillows on a sick bed. Look! — [*he feels her skirt*] — the hem's wringing. Better dry it at the fire. Turn round and I'll unfasten it for you.

Sheila [*forcing his hand away*]. It's nothing — you are thinking now of your own pleasure. You weren't so eager to see me when I was knocking at the door a while ago.

Ayamonn. You! But it was Old Brennan o' the Moor that was there.

Sheila. Before him, I was there. He hammered at the door too.

Ayamonn [*angry with himself*]. And I thinking the rapping was that of a pestering neighbour! I might have guessed it wasn't, it was so gentle.

Sheila. After trying to slip in unnoticed, there I was left with the whole house knowing I was at the door, and when I ran down, I heard them yelling that the stylish-dressed pusher was trying to get into Breydon's again! A nice time I'll have with my people when they hear it.

Ayamonn. I was doing my Shakespeare part, and didn't want disturbance, so there I was, standing stiff and breathless like a heron in a pond, keeping my dear one away from me! [*Going over and taking her in his arms*] Well, it's all over now, and here you are in my arms, safe and sure and lovely.

Sheila [*struggling away from him*]. No, it's not all over; and don't press me so hard; don't ruffle me tonight, for I feel a little tired.

Ayamonn [*peevishly*]. Tired again? Well, so am I, more than a little tired; but never too tired to put a sparkle into a welcome for a loved one.

Sheila. Oh, Ayamonn, I do want you to be serious for one night.

Ayamonn. Very well, very well, Sheila. [*He moves away from her, and stands at the other side of the fire.*] Let us plan, then, of how we can spin joy into every moment of tomorrow's day.

Sheila. That's why I hurried here to see you — I can't be with you tomorrow.   [*There is a long pause.*

Ayamonn. Why can't you be with me tomorrow?

Sheila. The Daughters of St. Frigid begin a retreat tomorrow, to give the Saint a warm devotion, and Mother insists I go.

Ayamonn. And I insist that you go with me. Is the Saint Frigid more to you than the sinner Ayamonn? Would you rather go to the meeting than come to see me? [*A pause.*] Would you, would you, Sheila?

Sheila [*in a hesitant whisper*]. God forgive me, I'd rather come to see you.

Ayamonn. Come then; God will be sure to forgive you.

Sheila. I daren't. My mother would be at me for ever if I failed to go. I've told you how she hates me to be near you. She chatters red-lined warnings and black-bordered appeals into my ears night and day, and when they dwindle for lack of breath, my father shakes them out of their drowsiness and sends them dancing round more lively still, dressed richly up in deadly black and gleaming scarlet.

Ayamonn. Sheila, Sheila, on the one day of the month when I'm free, you must be with me. I wouldn't go to a workers' meeting so that I might be with you.

Sheila. There's another thing, Ayamonn — the threatened strike. Oh, why do you meddle with those sort of things!

Ayamonn. Oh, never mind that, now. Don't be like a timid little girl ensconced in a clear space in a thicket of thorns — safe from a scratch if she doesn't stir, but unable to get to the green grass or the open road unless she risks the tears the thorns can give.

Sheila. Oh, Ayamonn, for my sake, if you love me, do try to be serious.

Ayamonn [*a little wildly*]. Oh, Sheila, our time is not yet come to be serious in the way of our elders. Soon enough to browse with wisdom when Time's grey finger puts a warning speck on the crimson rose of youth. Let no damned frosty prayer chill the sunny sighs that dread the joy of love.

Sheila [*wildly*]. I won't listen, Ayamonn, I won't listen! We must look well ahead on the road to the future. You lead your life through too many paths instead of treading the one way of making it possible for us to live together.

Ayamonn. We live together now; live in the light of the burning bush. I tell you life is not one thing, but many things, a wide branching flame, grand and good to see and feel, dazzling to the eye of no-one living it. I am not one to carry fear about with me as a priest carries the Host. Let the timid tiptoe through the way where the paler blossoms grow; my feet shall be where the redder roses grow, though they bear long thorns, sharp and piercing, thick among them!

Sheila [*rising from the chair — vehemently*]. I'll listen no more; I'll go. You want to make me a spark in a mere illusion. I'll go.

Ayamonn. Rather a spark from the althar of God, me girl; a spark that flames on a new path for a bubbling moment of life, or burns a song into the heart of a poet.

Sheila. I came here as a last chance to talk things quiet with you, but you won't let me; so I'll go. [*As he seizes her in his arms*] Let me go! [*Pleadingly*] Please, Ayamonn, let me go!

Ayamonn. I tell you it is a gay sight for God to see joy shine for a moment on the faces of His much-troubled children.

Sheila [*fearfully*]. Oh, don't bring God's name into this, for it will mean trouble to the pair of us. And your love for me lasts only while I'm here. When I'm gone, you think more of your poor painting, your poor oul' Ireland, your songs, and your workers' union than you think of Sheila.

Ayamonn. You're part of them all, in them all, and through them all; joyous, graceful, and a dearer vision; a bonnie rose, delectable and red. [*He draws her to him, presses her hard, lifts her on to his lap, and kisses her.*] Sheila, darling, you couldn't set aside the joy that makes the moon a golden berry in a hidden tree. You cannot close your ear to the sweet sound of the silver bell that strikes but once and never strikes again!

[*The door opens, and the head of Brennan o' the Moor looks into the room. It is a bald one, the dome highly polished; the face is wrinkled a lot, but the eyes are bright and peering. A long white beard gives him a far-away likeness to St. Jerome. He is dressed in a shabby-genteel way, and wears a long rain-soaked mackintosh. A faded bowler hat is on his head.*

Brennan. Oh, dear, dear, dear me!

[*He comes into the room showing that his back is well bent, though he still has a sturdy look about him. A strap around his body holds a melodeon on his back. Sheila and Ayamonn separate; he rises to meet the old man, while she stares, embarrassed, into the fire.*

Ayamonn. Now what th' hell do you want?

Brennan [*taking no notice of Ayamonn's remark — taking off his hat in a sweeping bow*]. Ah, me two sweet, snowy-breasted Dublin doves! Me woe it is to come ramblin' in through marjoram moments scentin' the serious hilarity of a genuine courtin' couple. I'm askin' now what's the dear one's name, if that isn't thresspassin' on others who are in a firmer condition of friendship? Though, be rights, it's a fair an' showy nosegay I should be throwin' through a shyly opened window into the adorable lady's lap.

Sheila [*shyly*]. Me name is Sheila.

Brennan. Sheila is it? Ay, an' a Sheila are you. Ay, an' a suitable one too, for there's a gentle nature in the two soft sounds, an' a silver note in the echo, describin' grandly the pretty slendher lass me two ould eyes are now beholdin'.

Ayamonn [*going over and catching him by an arm to guide him out*]. I can't see you now, old friend, for the pair of us are heavily harnessed to a question that must be answered before either of us is a day older.

Brennan. Sure I know. An' isn't it only natural, too, that young people should have questions to ask and answers to give to the dewy problems that get in th' way of their dancin' feet?

Ayamonn [*impatiently*]. Come again, old friend, when time has halted us for an hour of rest.

Brennan. It isn't me, I'm sayin', that would be dense enough to circumvent your longin' to be deep down in the silent consequence of regardin' each other without let or hindrance. [*He goes towards Sheila, eagerly, pulling Ayamonn after him.*] It's easy seen, sweet lady, that you're well within the compass of your young man's knowledge, an' unaware of nothin', so I may speak as man to lady, so with cunnin' confidence, tell me what you think of the Bank of Ireland?

Ayamonn. Oh, for goodness' sake, old man. Sheila's no intherest in the Bank of Ireland. She cares nothing for money, or for anything money can buy.

Brennan [*staring at Ayamonn for a moment as if he had received a shock*]. Eh? Arra, don't be talkin' nonsense, man! Who is it daren't think of what money can buy? [*He crosses to the door in a trot on his toes, opens it, looks out, and closes it softly again. Then he tiptoes back to Sheila, bends down towards her, hands on knees, and whispers hoarsely*] I've just a little consideration of stocks and bonds nestin' in the Bank of Ireland, at four per cent — just enough to guard a poor man from ill, eh? Safe an' sound there, isn't it, eh? [*To Ayamonn*] Now, let the fair one speak out on her own. [*Twisting his head back to Sheila.*] Safe there as if St. Pether himself had the key of where the bonds are stationed, eh?

Sheila. I'm sure they must be, sir.

Brennan [*with chuckling emphasis*]. Yehess! Aren't you the sensible young lady; sure I knew you'd say that, without fear or favour. [*Turning towards Ayamonn.*] What do you say? You're a man, now, of tellin' judgement.

Ayamonn. Oh, the State would have to totther before you'd lose a coin.

Brennan [*gleefully*]. Go bang, absolutely bang! Eh?

Ayamonn. Go bang!

Brennan. Bang! [*To Sheila*] Hear that, now, from a man climbin' up to scholarship? Yehess! Stony walls, steely doors, locks an' keys, bolts an' bars, an' all th' bonds warm an' dhry, an' shinin' safe behind them.

Sheila. Safe behind them.

Brennan [*gleefully*]. Ay, so. An' none of it sthrollin' into Peter's Pence. [*Chuckling.*] Wouldn't the Pope be mad if he knew what he was missin'! Safe an' sound. [*To Ayamonn*] You think so, too, eh?

Ayamonn. Yes, yes.

Brennan [*soberly*]. Ay, of course you do. [*To Sheila — indicating Ayamonn*] A good breed, me sweet an' fair one, brought up proper to see things in their right light.

Ayamonn [*catching him impatiently by the arm*]. And now, old
    friend, we have to get you to go.

Brennan. Eh?

Ayamonn. To go; Sheila and I have things to talk about.

Brennan [*suddenly*]. An' what about the song, then?

Ayamonn. Song?

Brennan. Th' one for the Show. Isn't that what brought me up?
    At long last, afther hard sthrainin', me an' Sammy have got
    the tune down in tested clefs, crotchets, an' quavers, fair set
    down to be sung be anyone in thrue time. An' Sammy's
    below, in his gay suit for the Show, waitin' to be called up to
    let yous hear th' song sung as only Sammy can sing it.

Ayamonn. Bring him up, bring him up — why in hell didn't
    you tell me all this before?

Brennan [*stormily*]. Wasn't I thryin' all the time an' you wouldn't
    let a man get a word in edgeways. [*Gesturing towards Sheila.*]
    He'll jib at singin' in front of her. [*He whispers hoarsely towards
    Sheila.*] He's as shy as a kid in his first pair o' pants, dear
    lady.

Ayamonn [*impatiently pushing him out of the room*]. Oh, go on,
    go on, man, and bring him up.   [*Brennan goes out.*

Sheila [*earnestly*]. Wait till I'm gone, Ayamonn; I can't stop long,
    and I want to talk to you so much.

Ayamonn [*a little excited*]. Oh, you must hear the song, Sheila;
    they've been working to get the air down for a week, and it
    won't take a minute.

Sheila [*angrily*]. I've waited too long already! Aren't you more
    interested in what I want to say than to be listening to some
    vain fool singing a song?

Ayamonn [*a little taken aback*]. Oh, Sheila, what's wrong with
    you tonight? The young carpenter who'll sing it, so far from
    being vain, is as shy as a field-mouse, and you'll see, when he

starts to sing, he'll edge his face away from us. You do want
to hear it, Sheila, don't you?

Sheila [*appealingly*]. Let it wait over, Ayamonn; I can come to
hear it some other time. I do want to say something, very
serious, to you about our future meetings.

Ayamonn [*hastily*]. All right then; I'll hurry them off the minute
the song's sung. Here they are, so sit down, do, just for one
minute more.

    [*But she goes towards the door, and reaches it just as Old Brennan
    returns shoving in before him a young man of twenty-three, shy,
    and loth to come in. He is tall, but his face is pale and mask-like
    in its expression of resignation to the world and all around him.
    Even when he shows he's shy, the mask-like features do not alter.
    He is dressed in a white cut-away coat, shaped like a tailed
    evening dress, black waistcoat over a rather soiled shirt-front,
    frilled, and green trousers. He carries a sheet of manuscript music
    in his hand. Brennan unslings his melodeon from his back, fusses
    the young Singer forward; bumping against Sheila, who has
    moved towards the door, he pushes her back with a shove of his
    backside; and puts Ayamonn to the other end of the room with a
    push on the shoulder.*

Brennan [*as he pushes Sheila.*] Outa th' way, there! Stem your
eagerness for a second, will yous? All in good time. Give the
man a chance to get himself easy. [*As he pushes Ayamonn*]
Farther back, there, farther back! Give the performer a chance
to dispose himself. Isn't he a swell, wha'? The centre group's
to be dhressed the same way, while th' corner men'll be in
reverse colours — green coats, black trousers, an' white vest,
see? Th' whole assembly'll look famous. Benjamin's lendin'
all the set o' twelve suits for five bob, 'cause o' th' reason we're
runnin' th' Show for. [*To Sheila — in a hoarse whisper*] You stare
at the fire as if he wasn't here. He's extravagant in shyness, an'

sinks away into confusion at the stare of an eye — understand?
[*She slowly, and a little sullenly, sits down to stare into the fire.
The door is opened, and in comes Roory O'Balacaun with a
small roll of Irish magazines under an arm. He is a stout middle-
aged man, dressed in rough homespun coat, cap, and knee-
breeches, wearing over all a trench coat.*

Roory. Here y'are, Ayamonn, me son, avic's th' Irish magazines
I got me friend to pinch for you. [*He looks at the Singer.*]
Hello, what kind of a circus is it's goin' on here?

Ayamonn. Mr. Brennan Moore here's organising the singers for
the Minsthrel Show to help get funds in case we have to go
on sthrike, Roory.

Roory. I'm one o' th' men meself, but I don't stand for a foreign
Minsthrel Show bein' held, an' the Sword of Light gettin'
lifted up in th' land. We want no coon or Kaffir industry in our
country.

Brennan [*indignantly*]. Doesn't matter what you stand for before
you came here, you'll sit down now. Thry to regard yourself
as a civilised member of the community, man, an' hold your
peace for th' present. [*To the Singer*] Now, Sam, me son o'
gold, excavate the shyness out of your system an' sing as if
you were performin' before a Royal Command!

Roory [*with a growl*]. There's no royal commands wanted here.

Brennan [*with a gesture of disgusted annoyance*]. Will you for goodness' sake not be puttin' th' singer out? I used the term only
as an allegory, man.

Roory. Allegory man, or allegory woman, there's goin' to be no
royal inthrusions where the Sword o' Light is shinin'.

Ayamonn. Aw, for Christ's sake, Roory, let's hear the song!

Brennan [*to the Singer, who has been coughing shyly and turning
sideways from his audience*]. Now, Sam, remember you're not
in your working clothes, an' are a different man, entirely.

Chin up and chest out. [*He gives a note or two on the melodeon.*]
Now!
Singer [*singing*]:

> A sober black shawl hides her body entirely,
> Touch'd by th' sun and th' salt spray of the sea;
> But down in th' darkness a slim hand, so lovely,
> Carries a rich bunch of red roses for me.

[*He turns away a little more from his audience, and coughs shyly.*
Brennan [*enthusiastically*]. Sam, you're excellin' yourself! On
again, me oul' son!
Singer [*singing*]:

> Her petticoat's simple, her feet are but bare,
> An' all that she has is but neat an' scantie;
> But stars in th' deep of her eyes are exclaiming
> I carry a rich bunch of red roses for thee!

Brennan [*after giving a few curling notes on the melodeon*]. A second
Count McCormack in th' makin'! An' whenever he sung
Mother Mo Chree, wasn't there a fewroory in Heaven with the
rush that was made to lean over an hear him singin' it!
[*While Brennan has been speaking, the door has opened, and
Mullcanny now stands there gaping into the room. He is young,
lusty, and restless. He is wearing fine tweeds that don't fit too
well; and his tweed cap is set rakishly on his head. He, too, wears
a mackintosh.*
Mullcanny. Is this a home-sweet-away-from-home hippodhrome,
or what?
Brennan [*clicking his tongue in annoyance*]. Dtchdtchdtch!
Mullcanny. An' did I hear someone pratin' about Heaven, an' I
coming in? [*To Brennan — tapping him on the shoulder*] Haven't
you heard, old man, that God is dead?

Brennan. Well, keep your grand discovery to yourself for a minute or two more, please. [*To the Singer*] Now, Sam, apologisin' for th' other's rudeness, the last verse, please.

Singer [*singing*]:

> No arrogant gem sits enthron'd on her forehead,
> Or swings from a white ear for all men to see;
> But jewel'd desire in a bosom, most pearly,
> Carries a rich bunch of red roses for me!

Brennan [*after another curl of notes on the melodeon*]. Well, fair damsel and gentlemen all, what do you think of the song and the singer?

Ayamonn. The song was good, and the singer was splendid.

Mullcanny. What I heard of it wasn't bad.

Singer [*shyly*]. I'm glad I pleased yous all.

Roory [*dubiously*]. D'ye not think th' song is a trifle indecent?

Mullcanny [*mockingly*]. Indecent! And what may your eminence's specification of indecency be? [*Angrily*] Are you catalogued, too, with the Catholic Young Men going about with noses long as a snipe's bill, shthripping the gayest rose of its petals in search of a beetle, and sniffing a taint in the freshest breeze blowing in from the sea?

Brennan [*warningly*]. Lady present, lady present, boys!

Roory. It ill becomes a thrue Gael to stand unruffled when either song or story thries to introduce colour to the sabler nature of yearnin's in untuthored minds.

Brennan [*more loudly*]. Lady present, boys!

Sheila [*rising out of the chair and going towards the door*]. The lady's going now, thank you all for the entertainment. [*To Ayamonn*] I won't stay any longer to disturb the important dispute of your friends.

Ayamonn [*going over to her*]. Don't be foolish, Sheila, dear; but if you must go, you must. We'll see each other again tomorrow evening.

Sheila [*firmly*]. No, not tomorrow, nor the next night either.

Ayamonn [*while Brennan plays softly on the melodeon to hide embarrassment*]. When then?

Sheila. I can't tell. I'll write. Never maybe. [*Bitterly*] I warned you this night might be the last chance of a talk for some time, and you didn't try to make use of it!

Ayamonn [*catching her arm*]. I made as much use of it as you'd let me. Tomorrow night, in the old place, near the bridge, the bridge of vision where we first saw Aengus and his coloured birds of passion passing.

Sheila [*wildly*]. I can't; I won't, so there — oh, let me go!
  [*She breaks away from him, runs out, and a silence falls on the room for a few moments.*

Roory [*breaking the silence*]. Women is strange things! Elegant animals, not knowin' their own minds a minute.

Brennan [*consolingly*]. She'll come back, she'll come back.

Ayamonn [*trying to appear unconcerned*]. Aw, to hell with her!

Singer [*faintly*]. Can I go now?

Brennan. Wait, an' I'll be with you in a second.

Mullcanny [*to Ayamonn*]. I just dropped in to say, Ayamonn, that I'll be getting Haeckel's *Riddle of the Universe* tomorrow, afther long searching, and I'll let you have it the minute it comes into my hand.
  [*The door is suddenly flung open, and Eeada, followed by Dympna and Finnoola, with others, mingled with men behind them, rushes into the room in a very excited state. She comes forward, with her two companions a little behind, while the rest group themselves by the door.*

Eeada [*distractedly*]. It's gone She is, an' left us lonesome; vanished

She is like a fairy mist of an early summer mornin'; stolen
She is be some pagan Protestan' hand, envious of the love we
had for our sweet Lady of Eblana's poor!

Chorus. Our Lady of Eblana's gone!

Ayamonn. Nonsense; no Protestant hand touched Her. Where
was She?

Dympna. Safe in Her niche in th' hall She was, afther Her washin',
lookin' down on the comin's an' goin's of Her strugglin'
children: an' then we missed Her, an' th' niche was empty!

Chorus. Our Lady of Eblana's gone!

Single Voice. An' dear knows what woe'll fall on our poor
house now.

Brennan An' a good job, too. [*Passionately*] Inflamin' yourselves
with idols that have eyes an' see not; ears, an' hear not; an'
have hands that handle not; like th' chosen people settin'
moon-images an' sun-images, cuttin' away the thrue and
homely connection between the Christian an' his God! Here,
let me and me singer out of this unholy place!

[*He pushes his way through the people, followed by the Singer, and
goes out.*

Eeada [*nodding her head, to Ayamonn*]. All bark, but no bite! We
know him of old: a decent oul' blatherer. Sure, doesn't he
often buy violets and snowdhrops, even, for little Ursula,
below, tellin' her she mustn't put them before a graven image,
knowin' full well that that was th' first thing she'd hurry home
to do. An' she's breakin' her young heart below, now, because
her dear Lady has left her. [*Suspiciously*] If oul' Brennan had a
hand in Her removal, woe betide him.

Mullcanny [*mocking*]. Couldn't you all do betther than wasting
your time making gods afther your own ignorant images?

Ayamonn [*silencing him with a gesture*]. That's enough, Paudhrig.
[*To Eeada*] Tell little Ursula not to worry. Her Lady'll come

back. If your Lady of Eblana hasn't returned by tonight, I'll surrender my sleep afther my night's work to search for Her, and bring Her back safe to Her niche in the hall. No one in this house touched Her.

Eeada. An' you'll see She'll pay you back for your kindness, Ayamonn — [*looking at Mullcanny*] — though it's little surprised I'd be if, of Her own accord, She came down indignant, an' slipped off from us, hearin' the horrid talk that's allowed to float around this house lately.

Mullcanny [*mocking*]. Afraid of me, She was. Well, Ayamonn, I've some lessons to get ready, so I'll be off. I'll bring you the book tomorrow. [*To the crowd — mocking*] I hope the poor Lady of Eblana's poor'll find Her way home again.

                 [*He goes out through a surly-faced crowd.*

Ayamonn [*to Eeada*]. Don't mind Mullcanny. Good night, now; and don't worry about your dear statue. If She doesn't come back, we'll find another as bright and good to take Her place.

Eeada [*growling*]. The fella that's gone'll have a rough end, jeerin' things sacred to our feelin'.

     [*They all go out, and Ayamonn is left alone with Roory. Ayamonn takes off his doublet, folds it up, and puts it back in the basket. He goes into the other room and comes back with oilskin coat and thigh-leggings. He puts the leggings on over his trousers.*

Ayamonn [*putting on the leggings*]. Th' shunting-yard'll be a nice place to be tonight. D'ye hear it?

                 [*He listens to the falling rain, now heavier than ever.*

Roory. Fallin' fast. That Mullcanny'll get into throuble yet.

Ayamonn. Not he. He's really a good fellow. Gave up his job rather than his beliefs — more'n many would do.

Roory. An' how does he manage now?

Ayamonn. Hammering knowledge into deluded minds wishing

to be civil servants, bank clerks, an' constables who hope to take the last sacraments as sergeants in the Royal Irish Constabulary or the Metropolitan Police.

Roory. By God, he's his work cut out for him with the last lot!

[*The door is again opened and Eeada sticks her head into the room.*

Eeada. Your mother's just sent word that the woman she's mindin's bad, an' she'll have to stay th' night. I'm just runnin' round meself to make your mother a cup o' tea.

Ayamonn [*irritably*]. Dtch dtch — she'll knock herself up before she's done! When I lock up, I'll leave the key with you for her, Eeada.

[*He lights a shunter's lantern and puts out the lamp.*

Eeada. Right y'are.   [*She goes.*

Roory. What kid was it sketched th' angel on th' wall?

Ayamonn. Oh, I did that. I'd give anything to be a painter.

Roory. What, like Oul' Brennan o' th' Moor?

Ayamonn. No, no; like Angelico or Constable.

Roory [*indifferently*]. Never heard of them.

Ayamonn [*musingly*]. To throw a whole world in colour on a canvas though it be but a man's fine face, a woman's shape asthride of a cushioned couch, or a three-bordered house on a hill, done with a glory; even delaying God, busy forgin' a new world, to stay awhile an' look upon their loveliness.

Roory. Aw, Ayamonn, Ayamonn, man, put out your hand an' see if you're awake! [*He fiddles with the books on the table.*] What oul' book are you readin' now?

Ayamonn [*dressed now in oilskin leggings and coat, with an oilskin sou'wester on his head, comes over to look at the book in Roory's hand, and shines the lantern on it*]. Oh, that's Ruskin's *Crown of Wild Olive* — a grand book — I'll lend it to you.

Roory. What for? What would I be doin' with it? I've no time to waste on books. Ruskin. Curious name; not Irish, is it?

Ayamonn. No, a Scotsman who wrote splendidly about a lot of things. Listen to this, spoken before a gathering of business men about to build an Exchange in their town.

Roory. Aw, Ayamonn — an Exchange! What have we got to do with an Exchange?

Ayamonn [*impatiently*]. Listen a second, man! Ruskin, speakin' to the business men, says: 'Your ideal of life is a pleasant and undulating world, with iron and coal everywhere beneath it. On each pleasant bank of this world is to be a beautiful mansion; stables, and coach-houses; a park and hot-houses; carriage-drives and shrubberies; and here are to live the votaries of the Goddess of Getting-on — the English gentleman ——'

Roory [*interrupting*]. There you are, you see, Ayamonn — th' *English* gentleman!

Ayamonn. Wait a second — Irish or English — a gentleman's th' same.

Roory. 'Tisn't. I'm tellin' you it's different. What's in this Ruskin of yours but another oul' cod with a gift of the gab? Right enough for th' English, pinin' afther little things, ever rakin' cindhers for th' glint of gold. We're different — we have th' light.

Ayamonn. You mean th' Catholic Faith?

Roory [*impatiently*]. No, no; that's there, too; I mean th' light of freedom; th' tall white candle tipped with its golden spear of flame. The light we thought we'd lost; but it burns again, sthrengthenin' into a sword of light. Like in th' song we sung together th' other night. [*He sings softly:*]

> Our courage so many have thought to be agein',
> Now flames like a brilliant new star in th' sky;
> And Danger is proud to be call'd a good brother,
> For Freedom has buckled her sword on her thigh.

Ayamonn [*joining in*]:

> Then out to th' place where th' battle is bravest,
> Where th' noblest an' meanest fight fierce in th' fray,
> Republican banners shall mock at th' foemen,
> An' Fenians shall turn a dark night into day!

[*A pause as the two of them stand silent, each clasping the other's hand. Ayamonn opens the door to pass out.*

Roory [*in a tense whisper*]. Th' Fenians are in force again, Ayamonn; th' Sword o' Light is shinin'!

[*They go out, and Ayamonn closes the door as the Curtain falls.*

ACT II

The same as in Act I.

It is about ten o'clock at night. The rain has stopped, and there is a fine moon sailing through the sky. Some of its rays come in through the window at the side.

Ayamonn, in his shirt-sleeves, is sitting at the table. He has an ordinary tin money-box in his hand, and a small pile of coppers, mixed with a few sixpences, are on the table beside him. He is just taking the last coin from the slit in the box with the aid of a knife-blade. His mother is by the dresser piling up the few pieces of crockery used for a recent meal. The old one-wick lamp is alight, and stands on the table near to Ayamonn. Several books lie open there, too.

Ayamonn. There's th' last one out, now. It's quite a job getting them out with a knife.

Mrs. Breydon. Why don't you put them in a box with a simple lid on?

Ayamonn. The harder it is to get at, the less chance of me spending it on something more necessary than what I seek. [*He counts the money on the table.*] One bob — two — three — an' six-pence — an' nine — three an' ninepence; one an' threepence to get yet — a long way to go.

Mrs. Breydon. Maybe, now, th' bookseller would give you it for what you have till you can give him th' rest.

Ayamonn [*in agony*]. Aw, woman, if you can't say sense, say nothing! Constable's reproductions are five shillings second-hand, an' he that's selling is the bastard that nearly got me

254

jailed for running off with his Shakespeare. It's touch an' go
if he'll let me have it for the five bob.

Mrs. Breydon [*philosophically*]. Well, seein' you done without
it so long, you can go without it longer.

Ayamonn [*with firm conviction*]. I'll have it the first week we get
the extra shilling the men are demandin'.

Mrs. Breydon. I shouldn't count your chickens before they're
hatched.

Ayamonn [*joking a little bitterly*]. Perhaps our blessed Lady of
Eblana's poor will work a miracle for me.

Mrs. Breydon [*a little anxiously*]. Hush, don't say that! Jokin' or
serious, Ayamonn, I wouldn't say that. We don't believe in
any of their Blessed Ladies, but as it's somethin' sacred, it's
best not mentioned. [*She shuffles into her shawl.*] Though it's a
queer thing, Her goin' off out of Her niche without a one in
th' house knowin' why. They're all out huntin' for Her still.
[*The door opens, and Brennan comes in slowly, with a cute grin on
his face. He has a large package, covered with paper, under his
arm.*

Brennan. Out huntin' still for Her they are, are they? Well, let
them hunt; She's here! A prisoner under me arm!

Mrs. Breydon [*indignantly*]. Well, Mr. Brennan Moore, it's ashamed
of yourself you should be yokin' th' poor people to throubled
anxiety over their treasure; and little Ursula breakin' her
heart into th' bargain.

Ayamonn. It's god-damned mean of you, Brennan! What good
d'ye think you'll do by this rowdy love of your own opinions
— forcing tumult into the minds of ignorant, anxious people?

Brennan [*calmly*]. Wait till yous see, wait till yous see, before
yous are sorry for sayin' more. [*He removes the paper and shows
the lost image transfigured into a figure looking as if it had come
straight from the shop: the white dress is spotless, the blue robe*

radiant, and the gold along its border and on the crown is gleaming. He holds it up for admiration. Triumphantly] There, what d'ye think of Her now? Fair as th' first grand tinge of th' dawn, She is, an' bright as th' star of the evenin'.

Mrs. Breydon. Glory be to God, isn't She lovely! But hurry Her off, Brennan, for She's not a thing for Protestant eyes to favour.

Ayamonn [*a little testily*]. Put it back, Brennan, put it back, and don't touch it again.

Brennan. Isn't that what I'm going to do? Oh, boy alive, won't they get th' shock o' their lives when they see Her shinin' in th' oul' spot. [*He becomes serious.*] Though, mind you, me thrue mind misgives me for decoratin' what's a charm to the people of Judah in th' worship of idols; but th' two of you is witness I did it for the sake of the little one, and not in any tilt towards honour to a graven image.

Mrs. Breydon [*resignedly*]. It's done now, God forgive us both, an' me for sayin' She's lovely. Touchin' a thing forbidden with a startled stir of praise!

Ayamonn. Put it back, put it back, man, and leave it quiet where you got it first.

[*Brennan goes out, looking intently out, and listening, before he does so.*

Mrs. Breydon. He meant well, poor man, but he's done a dangerous thing. I'll be back before you start for work. [*With a heavy sigh.*] It won't take us long to tend her for the last time. The white sheets have come, th' tall candles wait to be lit, an' th' coffin's ordhered, an' th' room'll look sacred with the bunch of violets near her head. [*She goes out slowly — as she goes*] Dear knows what'll happen to th' three children.

[*Ayamonn sits silent for a few moments, reading a book, his elbows resting on the table.*

Ayamonn [*with a deep sigh — murmuringly*]. Sheila, Sheila, my heart cries out for you! [*After a moment's pause, he reads:*]

> But I am pigeon-livered, an' lack gall
> To make oppression bitther; or, ere this,
> I should have fatted all th' region kites
> With this slave's offal: Bloody, bawdy villain!

Oh, Will, you were a boyo; a brave boyo, though, and a beautiful one!

[*The door opens and Old Brennan comes in, showing by his half suppressed chuckles that he is enjoying himself. He wanders over the room to stand by the fire.*

Brennan [*chuckling*]. In Her old place she is, now, in Her new coronation robe; and funny it is to think it's the last place they'll look for Her.

Ayamonn. I'm busy, now.

Brennan [*sitting down by the fire*]. Ay, so you are; so I see; busy readin'. Read away, for I won't disturb you; only have a few quiet puffs at th' oul' pipe. [*A pause.*] Ah, then, don't I wish I was young enough to bury meself in th' joy of readin' all th' great books of th' world. Ah! but when I was young, I had to work hard.

Ayamonn. I work hard, too.

Brennan. 'Course you do! Isn't that what I'm sayin'? An' all th' more credit, too, though it must be thryin' to have thoughtless people comin' in an' intherferin' with the golden movements of your thoughts.

Ayamonn. It's often a damned nuisance!

Brennan. 'Course it is. Isn't that what I'm sayin'? [*As the door opens*] An' here's another o' th' boobies entherin' now. [*Roory comes in, and shuts the door rather noisily.*] Eh, go easy, there — can't you see Ayamonn's busy studyin'?

Roory [*coming and bending over Ayamonn*]. Are you still lettin' oul' Ruskin tease you?

Ayamonn [*angrily*]. No, no; Shakespeare, Shakespeare, this time! [*Springing from his chair*] Damn it, can't you let a man alone a minute? What th' hell d'ye want now?

Brennan [*warningly*]. I told you he was busy.

Roory [*apologetically*]. Aw, I only came with the tickets you asked me to bring you for the comin' National Anniversary of Terence Bellew MacManus.

Ayamonn. All right, all right; let's have them.

Roory. How many d'ye want? How many can you sell?

Ayamonn. Give me twelve sixpennies; if the sthrike doesn't come off I'll easily sell that number.

Roory [*counting out the tickets which Ayamonn gathers up and puts into his pocket*]. I met that Mullcanny on the way with a book for you; but he stopped to tell a couple of railwaymen that the Story of Adam an' Eve was all a cod.

Brennan [*indignantly*]. He has a lot o' the people here in a state o' steamin' anger, goin' about with his bitther belief that the patthern of a man's hand is nearly at one with a monkey's paw, a horse's foot, th' flipper of a seal, or th' wing of a bat!

Ayamonn. Well, each of them is as wonderful as the hand of a man.

Roory. No, Ayamonn, not from the Christian point of view. D'ye know what they're callin' him round here? Th' New Broom, because he's always sayin' he'll sweep th' idea of God clean outa th' mind o' man.

Brennan [*excited*]. There'll be dire damage done to him yet! He was goin' to be flattened out be a docker th' other day for tellin' him that a man first formin' showed an undoubted sign of a tail.

Ayamonn. Ay, and when he's fully formed, if he doesn't show the tail, he shows most signs of all that goes along with it.

Roory. But isn't that a nice dignity to put on th' sacredness of a man's conception!

Brennan [*whisperingly*]. An' a lot o' them are sayin', Ayamonn, that your encouragement of him should come to an end.

Ayamonn. Indeed? Well, let them. I'll stand by any honest man seekin' th' truth, though his way isn't my way. [*To Brennan*] You, yourself, go about deriding many things beloved by your Catholic neighbours.

Brennan. I contest only dangerous deceits specified be the Council o' Thrent, that are nowhere scheduled in th' pages of the Holy Scriptures.

Roory. Yes, Ayamonn, it's altogether different; he just goes about blatherin' in his ignorant Protestant way.

Brennan [*highly indignant*]. Ignorant, am I? An' where would a body find an ignorance lustier than your own, eh? If your Council o' Thrent's ordher for prayers for the dead who are past help, your dismal veneration of Saints an' Angels, your images of wood an' stone, carved an' coloured, have given you the image an' superscription of a tail, th' pure milk of the gospel has made a man of me, God-fearin', but stately, with a mind garlanded to th' steady an' eternal thruth!

[*While they have been arguing, Mullcanny has peeped round the door, and now comes into the room, eyeing the two disputants with a lot of amusement and a little scorn. They take no notice of him.*

Roory. Sure, man, you have the neighbourhood hectored with your animosity against Catholic custom an' Catholic thought, never hesitatin' to give th' Pope even a deleterious name.

Brennan [*lapsing, in his excitement, into a semi-Ulster dialect*]. We dud ut tae yeh in Durry, on' sent your bravest floatin' down dud in th' wathers of th' Boyne, like th' hosts of Pharaoh tumblin' in the rush of th' Rud Sea! Thut was a slup in th' puss tae your Pope!

Mullcanny. You pair of damned fools, don't you know that the Pope wanted King Billy to win, and that the Vatican was ablaze with lights of joy afther King James's defeat over the wathers of the Boyne?

Roory. You're a liar, he didn't!

Brennan. You're a liar, it wasn't!

[*They turn from Mullcanny to continue the row with themselves.*

Brennan. Looksee, if I believed in the ministhration of Saints on' Angels, I'd say thut th' good Protestant St. Puthrick was at the hud of what fell out at Durry, Aughrim, on' th' Boyne.

Roory [*stunned with the thought of St. Patrick as a Protestant*]. Protestant St. Pathrick? Is me hearin' sound, or what? What name did you mention?

Brennan. I said St. Puthrick — th' evangelical founder of our thrue Church.

Roory. Is it dhreamin' I am? Is somethin' happenin' to me, or is it happenin' to you? Oh, man, it's mixin' mirth with madness you are at thinkin' St. Pathrick ever looped his neck in an orange sash, or tapped out a tune on a Protestant dhrum!

Brennan [*contemptuously*]. I refuse to argue with a one who's no' a broad-minded mon. Abuse is no equivalent for lugic — so I say God save th' King, an' tae hull with th' Pope!

Roory [*indignantly*]. You damned bigot — to hell with th' King, an' God save th' Pope!

Mullcanny [*to Ayamonn*]. You see how they live in bittherness, the one with the other. Envy, strife, and malice crawl from the coloured slime of the fairy-tales that go to make what is called religion. [*Taking a book from his pocket*] Here's something can bear a thousand tests, showing neatly how the world and all it bears upon it came into slow existence over millions of

years, doing away for ever with the funny wonders of the
seven days' creation set out in the fairy book of the Bible.

Ayamonn [*taking the book from Mullcanny*]. Thanks, Pether, oul'
son; I'm bound to ave a good time reading it.

Mullcanny. It'll give you the true and scientific history of man as
he was before Adam.

Brennan [*in a woeful voice*]. It's a darkened mind that thries tae
lower us to what we were before th' great an' good God
fashioned us. What does ony sensible person want to know
what we were like before the creation of th' first man?

Ayamonn [*murmuringly*]. To know the truth, to seek the truth,
is good, though it lead to th' danger of eternal death.

Rory [*horror-stricken — crossing himself*]. Th' Lord between us
an' all harm!

Brennan [*whispering prayerfully*]. Lord, I believe, help Thou mine
unbelief.

Mullcanny [*pointing out a picture in the book*]. See? The human form
unborn. The tail — look; the os coccyx sticking a mile out;
there's no getting away from it!

Brennan [*shaking his head woefully*]. An' this is holy Ireland!

Roory [*lifting his eyes to the ceiling — woefully*]. Poor St. Pathrick!

Mullcanny [*mockingly*]. He's going to be a lonely man soon eh?
[*To Ayamonn*] Keep it safe for me, Ayamonn. When you've
read it, you'll be a different man. [*He goes to the door*] Well,
health with the whole o' you, and goodbye for the present.
[*He goes out.*

Roory. Have nothin' to do with that book, Ayamonn, for that
fellow gone out would rip up the floor of Heaven to see what
was beneath it. It's clapped in jail he ought to be!

Brennan. An' th' book banned!

Ayamonn. Roory, Roory, is that th' sort o' freedom you'd bring
to Ireland with a crowd of green branches an' th' joy of

shouting? If we give no room to men of our time to question many things, all things, ay, life itself, then freedom's but a paper flower, a star of tinsel, a dead lass with gay ribbons at her breast an' a gold comb in her hair. Let us bring freedom here, not with sounding brass an' tinkling cymbal, but with silver trumpets blowing, with a song all men can sing, with a palm branch in our hand, rather than with a whip at our belt, and a headsman's axe on our shoulders.

[*There is a gentle knock at the door, and the voice of Sheila is heard speaking.*

Sheila [*outside*]. Ayamonn, are you there? Are you in?

Brennan [*whispering*]. The little lass; I knew she'd come back.

Ayamonn. I don't want her to see you here. Go into the other room — quick. [*He pushes them towards it.*] An' keep still.

Roory [*to Brennan*]. An' don't you go mockin' our Pope, see?

Brennan [*to Roory*]. Nor you go singlin' out King Billy for a jeer.

Ayamonn. In with yous, quick!

Brennan. I prophesied she'd come back, didn't I, Ayamonn? that she'd come back, didn't I?

Ayamonn. Yes, yes; in you go.

[*He puts them in the other room and shuts the door. Then he crosses the room and opens the door to admit Sheila. She comes in, and he and Sheila stand silently for some moments, she trying to look at him, and finding it hard.*

Sheila [*at last*]. Well, haven't you anything to say to me?

Ayamonn [*slowly and coldly*]. I waited for you at the bridge today; but you didn't come.

Sheila. I couldn't come; I told you why.

Ayamonn. I was very lonely.

Sheila [*softly*]. So was I, Ayamonn, lonely even in front of God's holy face.

Ayamonn. Sheila, we've gone a long way in a gold canoe over

many waters, bright and surly, sometimes sending bitter spray
asplash on our faces. But you were ever listening for the beat
from the wings of the angel of fear. So you got out to walk
safe on a crowded road.

Sheila. This is a cold and cheerless welcome, Ayamonn.

Ayamonn. Change, if you want to, the burning kiss falling on the
upturned, begging mouth for the chill caress of a bony, bearded
Saint. [*Loudly*] Go with th' yelling crowd, and keep them brave
and yell along with them!

Sheila. Won't you listen, then, to the few words I have to say?

Ayamonn [*sitting down near the fire, and looking into it, though he
leaves her standing*]. Go ahead; I won't fail to hear you.

Sheila. God knows I don't mean to hurt you, but you must know
that we couldn't begin to live on what you're earning now —
could we? [*He keeps silent.*] Oh, Ayamonn, why do you waste
your time on doing foolish things?

Ayamonn. What foolish things?

[*A hubbub is heard in the street outside; voices saying loudly
'Give him one in the bake' or 'Down him with a one in th'
belly'; then the sound of running footsteps, and silence.*

Sheila [*when she hears the voices — nervously*]. What's that?

Ayamonn [*without taking his gaze from the fire*]. Some drunken row
or other.   [*They listen silently for a few moments.*

Ayamonn. Well, what foolish things?

Sheila [*timid and hesitating*]. You know yourself, Ayamonn:
trying to paint, going mad about Shakespeare, and consorting
with a kind of people that can only do you harm.

Ayamonn [*mockingly prayerful — raising his eyes to the ceiling*]. O
Lord, let me forsake the foolish, and live; and go in the way of
Sheila's understanding!

Sheila [*going over nearer to him*]. Listen, Ayamonn, my love; you
know what I say is only for our own good, that we may come

together all the sooner. [*Trying to speak jokingly*] Now, really, isn't it comical I'd look if I were to go about in a scanty petticoat, covered in a sober black shawl, and my poor feet bare! [*Mocking*] Wouldn't I look well that way!

Ayamonn [*quietly*]. With red roses in your hand, you'd look beautiful.

Sheila [*desperately*]. Oh, for goodness' sake, Ayamonn, be sensible! I'm getting a little tired of all this. I can't bear the strain the way we're going on much longer. [*A short pause.*] You will either have to make good, or ——   [*She pauses.*

Ayamonn [*quietly*]. Or what?

Sheila [*with a little catch in her voice*]. Or lose me; and you wouldn't like that to happen.

Ayamonn. I shouldn't like that to happen; but I could bear the sthrain.

Sheila. I risked a big row tonight to come to tell you good news: I've been told that the strike is bound to take place; there is bound to be trouble; and, if you divide yourself from the foolish men, and stick to your job, you'll soon be a foreman of some kind or other.

Ayamonn [*rising from his seat and facing her for the first time*]. Who told you all this? The Inspector?

Sheila. Never mind who; if he did, wasn't it decent of him?

Ayamonn. D'ye know what you're asking me to do, woman? To be a blackleg; to blast with th' black frost of desertion the gay hopes of my comrades. Whatever you may think them to be, they are my comrades. Whatever they may say or do, they remain my brothers and sisters. Go to hell, girl, I have a soul to save as well as you. [*With a catch in his voice*] Oh, Sheila, you shouldn't have asked me to do this thing!

Sheila [*trying to come close, but he pushes her back*]. Oh, Ayamonn, it is a chance; take it, do, for my sake!

[*Rapid footsteps are heard outside. The door flies open and Mull-*
canny comes in, pale, frightened, his clothes dishevelled, and a
slight smear of blood on his forehead. His bowler hat is crushed
down on his head, his coat is torn, and his waistcoat unbuttoned,
showing his tie pulled out of its place. He sinks into a chair.

Ayamonn. What's happened? Who did that to you?

Mullcanny. Give's a drink, someone, will you?

                    [*Ayamonn gets him a drink from a jug on the dresser.*

Mullcanny. A gang of bowseys made for me, and I talking to a
man. Barely escaped with my life. Only for some brave oul' one,
they'd have laid me out completely. She saved me from worse.

Ayamonn. How th' hell did you bring all that on you?

Mullcanny [*plaintively*]. Just trying to show a fellow the foolishness of faith in a hereafter, when something struck me on the
head, and I was surrounded by feet making kicks at me!

[*A crash of breaking glass is heard from the other room, and Brennan*
and Roory come running out of it.

Roory. A stone has done for th' window! [*He sees Mullcanny.*]
Oh, that's how th' land lies, is it? Haven't I often said that if
you go round leerin' at God an' His holy assistants, one day
He's bound to have a rap at you!

Brennan. Keep away from that window, there, in case another
one comes sailin' in.

[*Immediately he has spoken, a stone smashes in through the window.*
Brennan lies down flat on the floor; Mullcanny slides from the
chair and crouches on the ground; Roory gets down on his hands
and knees, keeping his head as low as possible, so that he resembles a
Mohammedan at his devotions; Sheila stands stiff in a corner, near
the door; and Ayamonn, seizing up a hurley lying against the
dresser, makes for the door to go out.

Brennan. I guessed this was comin'.

Ayamonn [*angrily*]. I'll show them!

Sheila [*to Ayamonn*]. Stop where you are, you fool!

[*But Ayamonn pays no attention to the advice and hurries out of the door.*

Roory [*plaintively and with dignity — to Mullcanny*]. This is what you bring down on innocent people with your obstinate association of man with th' lower animals.

Mullcanny [*truculently*]. Only created impudence it is that strives to set yourselves above the ape's formation, genetically present in every person's body.

Brennan [*indignantly*]. String out life to where it started, an' you'll find no sign, let alone a proof, of the dignity, wisdom, an' civility of man ever having been associated with th' manners of a monkey.

Mullcanny. And why do children like to climb trees, eh? Answer me that?

Roory [*fiercely*]. They love it more where you come from than they do here.

Sheila [*from her corner*]. It's surely to be pitied you are, young man, lettin' yourself be bullied by ignorant books into believing that things are naught but what poor men are inclined to call them, blind to the glorious and eternal facts that shine behind them.

Mullcanny [*pityingly*]. Bullied be books — eternal facts — aw! Yous are all scared stiff at the manifestation of a truth or two. D'ye know that the contraction of catharrah, apoplexy, consumption, and cataract of the eye is common to the monkeys? Knowledge you have now that you hadn't before; and a lot of them even like beer.

Roory. Well, that's something sensible, at last.

Brennan [*fiercely*]. Did they get their likin' for beer from us, or did we get our likin' of beer from them? Answer me that, you, now; answer me that!

Roory. Answer him that. We're not Terra Del Fooaygeeans, but sensible, sane, an' civilised souls.

Mullcanny [*gleefully*]. Time's promoted reptiles — that's all; yous can't do away with the os coccyges!

Brennan. Ladies present, ladies present.

Roory [*creeping over rapidly till his face is close to that of Mullcanny's — fiercely*]. We stand on the earth, firm, upright, heads cocked, lookin' all men in th' face, afraid o' nothin'; men o' goodwill we are, abloom with th' blessin' o' charity, showin' in th' dust we're made of, th' diamond-core of an everlastin' divinity!

Sheila [*excitedly*]. Hung as high as Gilderoy he ought to be, an' he deep in the evil of his rich illusions, spouting insults at war with th' mysteries an' facts of our holy faith!

Brennan [*to Sheila*]. Hush, pretty lady, hush. [*To the others*] Boys, boys, take example from a poor oul' Protestant here, never lettin' himself be offended be a quiver of anger in any peaceable or terrified discussion. Now, let that last word finish it; finis — the end, see?

Roory [*angrily — to Brennan*]. Finis youssel, you blurry-eyed, wither-skinned oul' greybeard, singin' songs in th' public streets for odd coppers, with all th' boys in th' Bank of Ireland workin' overtime countin' all you've got in their front room! Finis you!

Brennan [*indignantly*]. An office-boy, in a hurry, wouldn't stop to pick up from th' path before him the few coins I have. An' as for being withered, soople as you I am, hands that can tinkle a thremblin' tune out of an oul' melodeon, legs that can carry me ten miles an' more, an' eyes that can still see without hardship a red berry shinin' from a distant bush!

[*The door opens and Ayamonn and his mother come in. She runs over to the blossoms at the window, tenderly examining the plants growing there — the musk, the geranium, and the fuchsia.*

Mrs. Breydon [*joyfully*]. Unharmed, th' whole of them. Th'
stone passed them by, touchin' none o' them — thank God
for that mercy!

Ayamonn. What th' hell are you doin' on your knees? Get up,
get up. [*They rise from the floor shamefacedly.*] Th' rioters all
dispersed. [*To Mullcanny*] Mother was th' oul' one who saved
you from a sudden an' unprovided death. An' th' Blessed Image
has come back again, all aglow in garments new. Listen!

[*A murmur of song has been heard while Ayamonn was speaking,
and now Eeada, Dympna, Finnoola, and the Men appear at
the door — now wide open — half backing into the room singing
part of a hymn softly, their pale faces still wearing the frozen look
of resignation; staring at the Image shining bright and gorgeous as
Brennan has made it for them, standing in a niche in the wall,
directly opposite the door. Eeada, Dympna, Finnoola, and the
Men singing softly —*]

> Oh! Queen of Eblana's poor children,
> Bear swiftly our woe away;
> An' give us a chance to live lightly
> An hour of our life's dark day!
> Lift up th' poor heads ever bending,
> An' light a lone star in th' sky,
> To show thro' th' darkness, descending,
> A cheerier way to die.

Eeada [*coming forward a little*]. She came back to Her poor again,
in raiment rich. She came back; of Her own accord. She
came to abide with Her people.

Dympna. From her window, little Ursula looked, and saw Her
come in; in th' moonlight, along the street She came, stately.
Blinded be the coloured light that shone around about Her, the
child fell back, in a swoon she fell full on the floor beneath her.

1st Man. My eyes caught a glimpse of Her, too, glidin' back to where She came from. Regal an' proud She was, an' wondrous, so that me eyes failed; me knees thrembled an' bent low, an' me heart whispered a silent prayer to itself as th' vision passed me by, an' I fancied I saw a smile on Her holy face.

Eeada. Many have lied to see a strange thing this favoured night, an' blessin' will flow from it to all tempered into a lively belief; and maybe, too, to some who happen to be out of step with the many marchin' in the mode o' thruth. [*She comes a little closer to Mrs. Breydon. The others, backs turned towards the room, stand, most of them outside the door, a few just across the threshold, in a semicircle, heads bent as if praying, facing towards the Image.*] Th' hand of a black stranger it was who sent the stones flyin' through your windows; but ere tomorrow's sun is seen, they will be back again as shelther from th' elements. A blessin' generous on yous all — [*pause*] — except th' evil thing that stands, all stiff-necked, underneath th' roof!

Mullcanny [*mockingly*]. Me!

Sheila [*fiercely*]. Ay, you, that shouldn't find a smile or an unclenched hand in a decent man's house!

Mullcanny. I'll go; there's too many here to deal with — I'll leave you with your miracle.

Ayamonn. You can stay if you wish, for whatever surety of shelther's here, it's open to th' spirit seeking to add another colour to whatever thruth we know already. Thought that has run from a blow will find a roof under its courage here, an' a fire to sit by, as long as I live an' th' oul' rooms last!

Sheila [*with quiet bitterness*]. Well, shelter him, then, that by right should be lost in the night, a black night, an' bitterly lonely, without a dim ray from a half-hidden star to give him a far-away companionship; ay, an' a desolate rest under a thorny and dripping thicket of lean and twisted whins, too tired to

thry to live longer against th' hate of the black wind and th'
grey rain. Let him lie there, let him live there, forsaken,
forgotten by all who live under a kindly roof and close to a
cosy fire!

Mullcanny [*with a pretended alarm*]. Good God, I'm done, now!
I'm off before worse befall me. Good night, Ayamonn.

Ayamonn. Good night, my friend.   [*Mullcanny goes out.*

Brennan. We're keepin' decent people out of their beds — so
long, all.

Roory. I'll be with you some o' th' way, an' we can finish that
argument we had. Good night all.

[*He and Brennan go out together, closing the door after them. Sheila
stands where she was, sullen and silent.*

Mrs. Breydon. Shame on you, Sheila, for such a smoky flame to
come from such a golden lamp! [*Sheila stays silent.*] Tired out
I am, an' frightened be th' scene o' death I saw today. Dodge
about how we may, we come to th' same end.

Ayamonn [*gently leading her towards the other room*]. Go an' lie
down lady; you're worn out. Time's a perjured jade, an'
ever he moans a man must die. Who through every inch of
life weaves a patthern of vigour an' elation can never taste
death, but goes to sleep among th' stars, his withered arms
outstretched to greet th' echo of his own shout. It will be for
them left behind to sigh for an hour, an' then to sing their
own odd songs, an' do their own odd dances, to give a lonely
God a little company, till they, too, pass by on their bare way
out. When a true man dies, he is buried in th' birth of a
thousand worlds.

[*Mrs. Breydon goes into the other room, and Ayamonn closes the
door softly behind her. He comes back and stands pensive near the
fire.*

Ayamonn [*after a pause*]. Don't you think you should go too?

Sheila [*a little brokenly*]. Let me have a few more words with you, Ayamonn, before we hurry to our separation.

Ayamonn [*quietly*]. There is nothing more to be said.

Sheila. There's a lot to be said, but hasty time won't stretch an hour a little out to let the words be spoken. Goodbye.

Ayamonn [*without turning his head*]. Goodbye.

> [*Sheila is going slowly to the door when it partly opens, and half the head of Eeada peeps around it, amid an indistinct murmur as of praying outside.*

Eeada [*in half a whisper*]. Th' Protestan' Rector to see Mr. Breydon.

> [*The half of her head disappears, but her voice is heard saying a little more loudly*] This way, sir; shure you know th' way well, anyhow.

> [*The door opening a little more, the Rector comes in. He is a handsome man of forty. His rather pale face wears a grave scholarly look, but there is kindness in his grey eyes, and humourous lines round his mouth, though these are almost hidden by a short, brown, pointed beard, here and there about to turn grey. His black clothes are covered by a warm black topcoat, the blackness brightened a little by a vivid green scarf he is wearing round his neck, the fringed ends falling over his shoulders. He carries a black, broad-brimmed, soft clerical hat and a walking-stick in his left hand. He hastens towards Ayamonn, smiling genially, hand outstretched in greeting.*

Rector. My dear Ayamonn.   [*They shake hands.*

Ayamonn [*indicating Sheila*]. A friend of mine, sir — Sheila Moorneen. [*Moving a chair.*] Sit down, sir.

> [*The Rector bows to Sheila; she returns it quietly, and the Rector sits down.*

Rector. I've hurried from home in a cab, Ayamonn, to see you before the night was spent. [*His face forming grave lines*] I've a message for you — and a warning.

[*The door again is partly opened, and again the half head of Eeada appears, mid the murmurs outside, unheard the moment the door closes.*

Eeada. Two railwaymen to see you, Ayamonn; full house tonight you're havin', eh?

[*The half head goes, the door opens wider, and the two railwaymen come into the room. They are dressed drably as the other men are, but their peaked railway uniform caps (which they keep on their heads) have vivid scarlet bands around them. Their faces, too, are like the others, and stonily stare in front of them. They stand stock still when they see the Rector.*

1st Railwayman [*after a pause*]. 'Scuse us. Didn' know th' Protstan' Minister was here. We'll wait outside till he goes, Ayamonn.

Ayamonn. Th' Rector's a dear friend of mine, Bill; say what you want, without fear — he's a friend.

1st Railwayman [*a little dubiously*]. Glad to hear it. You know th' sthrike starts tomorrow?

Ayamonn. I know it now.

2nd Railwayman. Wouldn' give's th' extra shillin'. Offered us thruppence   instead — th'   lowsers!   [*Hastily — to   Rector*] 'Scuse me, sir.

1st Railwayman [*taking a document from his breast pocket*]. An' th' meetin's proclaimed.

Rector [*to Ayamonn*]. That's part of what I came to tell you.

1st Railwayman [*handing document to Ayamonn*]. They handed that to our Committee this evening, a warrant of warning.

Rector [*earnestly — to Ayamonn*]. I was advised to warn you, Ayamonn, that the Authorities are prepared to use all the force they have to prevent the meeting.

Ayamonn. Who advised you, sir — th' Inspector?

Rector. My churchwarden, Ayamonn. Come, even he has good in him.

Ayamonn. I daresay he has, sir; I've no grudge against him.

Rector [*convinced*]. I know that, Ayamonn.

Ayamonn [*indicating document — to 1st Railwayman*]. What are th' Committee going to do with this?

1st Railwayman. What would you do with it, Ayamonn?

Ayamonn [*setting it alight at the fire and waiting till it falls to ashes*]. That!

2nd Railwayman [*gleefully*]. Exactly what we said you'd do!

Sheila [*haughtily*]. It's not what any sensible body would think he'd do.

1st Railwayman [*ignoring her*]. Further still, Ayamonn, me son, we want you to be one of the speakers on the platform at the meeting.

Sheila [*bursting forward and confronting the railwaymen*]. He'll do nothing of the kind — hear me? Nothing of the kind. Cinder-tongued moaners, who's to make any bones about what you suffer, or how you die? Ayamonn's his reading and his painting to do, and his mother to mind, more than lipping your complaints in front of gun muzzles, ready to sing a short and sudden death-song!

1st Railwayman [*a little awed*]. To see Ayamonn we came, an' not you, Miss.

2nd Railwayman [*roughly*]. Let th' man speak for himself.

Ayamonn [*catching Sheila's arm and drawing her back*]. It's my answer they're seeking. [*To railwaymen*] Tell the Committee, Bill, I'll be there; and that they honour me when they set me in front of my brothers. The Minstrel Show must be forgotten.

Sheila [*vehemently — to the Rector*]. You talk to him; you're his friend. You can influence him. Get him to stay away, man!

Rector. It's right for me to warn you, Ayamonn, and you, men, that the Authorities are determined to prevent the meeting; and that you run a grave risk in defying them.

2nd Railwayman [*growling*]. We'll chance it. We've barked long
     enough, sir; it's time to bite a bit now.

Sheila [*to Rector*]. Warning's no good; that's not enough —
     forbid him to go. Show him God's against it!

Rector [*standing up*]. Who am I to say that God's against it?
     You are too young by a thousand years to know the mind of
     God. If they be his brothers, he does well among them.

Sheila [*wildly*]. I'll get his mother to bar his way. She'll do more
     than murmur grand excuses.

     [*She runs to the door of the other room, opens it, and goes in. After
        a few moments, she comes out slowly, goes to the chair left idle
        by the Rector, sits down on it, leans her arms on the table, and
        lets her head rest on them.*

Ayamonn. Well?

Sheila [*brokenly*]. She's stretched out, worn and wan, fast asleep,
     and I hadn't the heart to awaken her.

Rector [*holding out a hand to Ayamonn*]. Come to see me before
     you go, Ayamonn. Be sure, wherever you may be, whatever
     you may do, a blessing deep from my breast is all around you.
     Goodbye. [*To the railwaymen*] Goodbye, my friends.

Railwaymen. Goodbye, sir.

     [*The Rector glances at Sheila, decides to say nothing, and goes
        towards the door; Ayamonn opens it for him, and he goes out
        through the semicircle of men and women, still softly singing before
        the Statue of the Queen of Eblana's poor. Sheila's quiet crying
        heard as a minor note through the singing.*

         Oh, Queen of Eblana's poor children,
         Bear swiftly our woe away,
         An' give us a chance to live lightly
         An hour of our life's dark day!

CURTAIN

ACT III

A part of Dublin City flowering into a street and a bridge across the river Liffey. The parapets are seen to the right and left so that the bridge fills most of the scene before the onlooker. The distant end of the bridge leads to a street flowing on to a point in the far distance; and to the right and left of this street are tall gaunt houses, mottled with dubious activities, with crowds of all sorts of men and women burrowing in them in a pathetic search for a home. These houses stand along another street running parallel with the river. In the distance, where the street, leading from the bridge, ends in a point of space, to the right, soars the tapering silver spire of a church; and to the left, Nelson's Pillar, a deep red, pierces the sky, with Nelson, a deep black, on its top, looking over everything that goes on around him. A gloomy grey sky is over all, so that the colours of the scene are made up of the dark houses, the brown parapets of the bridge, the grey sky, the silver spire, the red pillar, and Nelson's black figure.

On one of the bridge parapets a number of the men seen in the previous scenes are gathered together, their expressionless faces hidden by being bent down towards their breasts. Some sit on the parapets, some lounge against the gaunt houses at the corner of the street leading from the bridge, and, in one corner, a man stands wearily against the parapet, head bent, an unlit pipe dropping from his mouth, apparently forgotten. The sun shines on pillar and church spire, but there is no sign of sun where these people are.

On the pavement, opposite to where the men sit, nearer to this end of the bridge, sit Eeada, Dympna, and Finnoola, dressed so in black that they appear to be enveloped in the blackness of a dark night.

In front of Eeada is a drab-coloured basket in which cakes and apples are spending an idle and uneasy time. Dympna has a shallower basket holding decadent blossoms, and a drooping bunch of violets hangs from a listless hand.

Eeada [*drowsily*]. This spongy leaden sky's Dublin; those tomby houses is Dublin too — Dublin's scurvy body; an' we're Dublin's silver soul. [*She spits vigorously into the street.*] An' that's what Eeada thinks of th' city's soul an' body!

Dympna. You're more than right, Eeada, but I wouldn't be too harsh. [*Calling out in a sing-song way*] Violets, here, on'y tuppence a bunch; tuppence a bunch, th' fresh violets!

Eeada [*calling out in a sing-song voice*]. Apples an' cakes, on'y tuppence a head here for th' cakes; ripe apples a penny apiece!

Dympna. Th' sun is always at a distance, an' th' chill grey is always here.

Finnoola. Half-mournin' skies for ever over us, frownin' out any chance of merriment that came staggerin' to us for a little support.

Eeada. That's Dublin, Finnoola, an' th' sky over it. Sorrow's a slush under our feet, up to our ankles, an' th' deep drip of it constant overhead.

Dympna. A graveyard where th' dead are all above th' ground.

Eeada. Without a blessed blink of rest to give them hope. An' she cockin' herself up that she stands among other cities as a queen o' counsel, laden with knowledge, afire with th' song of great men, enough to overawe all livin' beyond th' salty sea, undher another sun be day, an' undher a different moon be night. [*They drowse, with heads bent lower.*

1st Man [*leaning wearily against the parapet*]. Golden Gander'll do it, if I'm e'er a thrue prophet. [*Raising his voice a little*] He'll flash past th' winnin' post like an arra from th' bow, in the

five hundhred guinea West's Awake Steeplechase Championship.

2nd Man [*drowsily contradicting*]. In me neck he will! He'd have a
chance if it was a ramble. Copper Goose'll leave him standin',
if I'm e'er a thrue prophet.

Eeada [*waking up slightly*]. Prophets? Do me ears deceive me, or
am I afther hearin' somebody say prophets?

Dympna. You heard a murmur of it, Eeada, an' it's a bad word to
hear, remindin' us of our low estate at th' present juncture.
Th' prophets we once had are well hidden behind God be
now, an' no wondher, for we put small pass on them, an' God
in His generous anger's showin' us what it is to be saddled
with Johnnies-come-marchin'-home, all song an' shirt an'
no surety.

Finnoola [*shaking her head sadly*]. A gold-speckled candle, white
as snow, was Dublin once; yellowish now, leanin' sideways,
an' gutherin' down to a last shaky glimmer in th' wind o' life.

Eeada. Well, we've got Guinness's Brewery still, givin' us a
needy glimpse of a bether life an hour or so on a Saturday
night, though I hold me hand at praisin' th' puttin' of Brian
Boru's golden harp on every black porther bottle, destined to
give outsiders a false impression of our pride in th' tendher
an' dauntless memories of th' past.

[*The Rector and the Inspector appear at the farther end of the bridge,
and come over it towards where the men and women are. The
Rector is dressed in immaculate black, wears a glossy tall hat, and
carries a walking-stick. He has shed his topcoat, but wears his
green scarf round his neck. The Inspector is clad in a blue uniform,
slashed with silver epaulettes on the shoulders, and silver braid
on collar and cuffs. He wears a big blue helmet, back and front
peaks silver-bordered, and from a long silver spike on the top
flows a graceful plume of crimson hair. On the front is a great*

silver crown throned on a circle of red velvet. A sword, in a silver scabbard, hangs by his side. He is wearing highly-polished top-boots. They both pause on the bridge, the Rector looking pensively down over the parapet at the flowing river.

Inspector. It was a great wedding, sir. A beautiful bride and an elegant bridegroom; a distinguished congregation, and the Primate in his fine sermon did justice to the grand occasion, sir. Fittingly ended, too, by the organ with *The Voice that Breathed o'er Eden.*

Rector [*apparently not very interested*]. Oh yes, yes; quite.

Inspector. Historic disthrict, this, round here: headquarters of a Volunteer Corp in Grattan's time — not, of course, that I agree with Grattan. A great-great-grandfather of mine was one of the officers.

Rector. Oh yes; was he?

Inspector. Yes. Strange uniform he wore: richly black, with sky-blue facings, a yellow breast-piece, ribbed with red braid, and, capping all, a huge silver helmet having a yellow plume soaring over it from the right-hand side.

Rector [*smiling*]. Your own's not too bad, Mr. Churchwarden.

Inspector. Smart; but a bit too sombre, I think, sir.

Eeada [*whining towards them*]. On'y a penny each, th' rosy apples, lovely for th' chiselurs — Jasus! what am I sayin'? Lovely for th' little masters an' little misthresses, stately, in their chandeliered an' carpeted dwellin'-houses; or a cake — on'y tuppence a piece — daintily spiced, an' tastin' splendid.

Dympna [*whining towards them*]. Tuppence, here, th' bunch o' violets, fit for to go with th' white an' spotless cashmere gown of our radiant Lady o' Fair Dealin.'

Eeada [*deprecatingly*]. What are you sayin', woman? That's a Protestan' ministher, indeed, gentleman, Dympna!

Dympna. Me mind slipped for a poor minute; but it's pity he'll have on us, an' regulate our lives with what'll bring a sudden cup o' tea within fair reach of our hands.

Eeada. Apples, here, penny each, rosy apples, picked hardly an hour ago from a laden three; cakes tuppence on'y, baked over scented turf as th' dawn stepped over th' blue-gowned backs o' th' Dublin Mountains.

Dympna. Tuppence a bunch, th' violets, shy an' dhrunk with th' dew o' th' mornin'; fain to lie in the white bosom of a high-born lady, or fit into th' lapel of a genuine gentleman's Sunday courtin' coat.

[*The Rector takes a few coins from his pocket and throws them to the women, who pick them up and sink into silence again.*

Inspector. Swift, too, must have walked about here with the thorny crown of madness pressing ever deeper into his brain.

Rector [*indicating the men and women*]. Who are these?

Inspector [*indifferent*]. Those? Oh, flotsam and jetsam. A few of them dangerous at night, maybe; but harmless during the day.

Rector. I've read that tens of thousand of such as those followed Swift to the grave.

Inspector. Indeed, sir? A queer man, the poor demented Dean; a right queer man.

[*A sleepy lounger suddenly gives a cough, gives his throat a hawk, and sends a big spit on to one of the Inspector's polished boots then sinks back into sleep again.*

Inspector [*springing back with an angry exclamation*]. What th' hell are you after doing, you rotten lizard! Looka what you've done, you mangy rat!

[*He takes hold of the lounger and shakes him sharply.*

2nd Man [*sleepily resentful*]. Eh, there! Wha' th' hell?

Inspector [*furiously*]. You spat on my boots, you tousled toad — my boots, boots, boots!

2nd Man [*frightened and bewildered*]. Boots, sir? Is it me, sir? Not me sir. Musta been someone else, sir.

Inspector [*shaking him furiously*]. You, you, you!

2nd Man. Me, sir? Never spit in public in me life, sir. Makin' a mistake, sir. Musta been someone else.

Rector. Inspector Finglas! Remember you wear the King's uniform! Quiet, quiet, man!

Inspector [*subsiding*]. Pardon me. I lost my temper. I'm more used to a blow from a stone than a dirty spit on my boot.

Rector [*shuddering a little*]. Let us go from here. Things here frighten me, for they seem to look with wonder on our ease and comfort.

Inspector. Frighten you? Nonsense — and with me!

Rector. Things here are of a substance I dare not think about, much less see and handle. Here, I can hardly bear to look upon the same thing twice.

Inspector. There you are, and as I've said so often, Breydon's but a neat slab of a similar slime.

Rector. You wrong yourself to say so: Ayamonn Breydon has within him the Kingdom of Heaven. [*He pauses.*] And so, indeed, may these sad things we turn away from.

[*They pass out.*

Eeada [*thinking of the coins given*]. Two tiny sixpences — fourpence a head. Oh, well, beggars can't be choosers. But isn't it a hard life to be grindin' our poor bums to powder, for ever squattin' on the heartless pavements of th' Dublin streets!

Dympna. Ah, what is it all to us but a deep-written testament o' gloom: grey sky over our heads, brown an' dusty streets undher our feet, with th' black an' bitther Liffey flowin' through it all.

Eeada [*mournfully*]. We've dhrifted down to where there's nothin'. Younger I was when every quiet-clad evenin' carried a jaunty jewel in her bosom. Tormented with joy I was then as to whether I'd parade th' thronged sthreets on th' arm of a 16th Lancer, his black-breasted crimson coat a sight to see, an' a black plume droopin' from his haughty helmet; or lay claim to a red-breasted Prince o' Wales's Own, th' red plume in his hat a flame over his head.

Dympna. It was a 15th King's Own Hussar for me, Eeada, with his rich blue coat an' its fairyland o' yellow braid, two yellow sthripes down his trousers, an' a red bag an' plume dancin' on his busby.

Eeada. Lancers for me, Dympna.

Dympna. Hussars for me, Eeada.

Eeada. An' what for you, Finnoola?

Finnoola. What would a girl, born in a wild Cork valley, among the mountains, brought up to sing the songs of her fathers, what would she choose but the patched coat, shaky shoes, an' white hungry face of th' Irish rebel? But their shabbiness was threaded with th' colours from the garments of Finn Mac Cool of th' golden hair, Goll Mac Morna of th' big blows, Caoilte of th' flyin' feet, an' Oscar of th' invincible spear.

Eeada [*nudging Dympna*]. That was some time ago, if y'ask me. [*A cheer is heard in the distance, it has a defiant and confident sound, though its echo only reaches the bridge.*

Dympna [*drowsily but lifting her head a little to listen*]. Wha' was that? A cheer? [*Her head droops again*] I hate the sound o' cheerin'.

[*A group of workingmen come in. They are excited, and they speak loudly to each other.*

1st Workman [*exultingly*]. The dockers are with us to a man; and the lorry-drivers, too. They'll all be at our meetin'!

2nd Workman. With their bands an' banners.

3rd Workman [*timidly*]. I wonder will they call the soldiers out?

1st Workman [*loud and defiant*]. Let them; we'll stand up to
them!

3rd Workman [*doubtfully*]. What? Stand up against infanthry an'
the bang of their bullets?

2nd Workman. Ay; or against horse, fut, an' artillery — what
does it matter?

3rd Workman. If the soldiers are out, the police'll get tougher,
knowing the power that's behind them.

2nd Workman. If they do aself, what does it mather?

3rd Workman [*irritably — in a half-shout*]. Nothin' seems to
mather with yous two!   [*The echo of a rousing cheer is heard.*

1st Workman [*exultantly*]. Hear that! Ayamonn rousin' the disthrict west from where we're standin'! [*The echo of another
cheer comes from beyond the bridge.*]

2nd Workman [*exultantly*]. Hear that! Mick rousin' them up in the
streets around the upper bridge!

1st Workman. Come on, lads! We've work to do before the real
meetin' begins! [*He goes out over the bridge.*

2nd Workman. Crooning a song of death to some, ourselves,
we'll be, if they thry to stop us now.

[*They hurry out. Brennan, playing his melodeon has come slowly
over the bridge from the far side.*

Brennan [*giving himself confidence*]. Evenin', ladies an' gentlemen.
Good thing to be alive when th' sun's kind. [*They take no heed
of what he says. He begins to sing in a voice that was once a mellow
baritone, but now is a little husky with age, now and again quavering
a little on the higher notes in the song. Singing:*]

> I stroll'd with a fine maid far out in th' counthry,
> Th' blossoms around us all cryin' for dew;
> On a violet-clad bench, sure, I sat down beside her,
> An' tuck'd up my sleeves for to tie up her shoe.

An' what's that to anyone whether or no
If I came to th' fore when she gave me th' cue?
She clos'd her eyes tight as she murmur'd full low,
Be good enough, dear, for to tie up my shoe.

Eeada [*with muttered indignation*]. Isn't that outrageous, now;
  on a day like this, too, an' in a sober mood!
Dympna. In front o' decent women as well!
1st Man [*waking up suddenly*]. Disturbin' me dhreams of Golden
  Gandher gallopin' home to win in a canther!
Brennan [*singing*]:

Th' hawthorn shook all her perfume upon us,
Red poppies saluted, wherever they grew,
Th' joyous exertion that flaunted before me,
When I tuck'd up my sleeves for to fasten her shoe.
An' what's it to anyone, whether or no
I learn'd in that moment far more than I knew,
As she lifted her petticoat, shyly an' slow,
An' I tuck' up my sleeves for to fasten her shoe?

The heathery hills were all dancin' around us,
False things in th' world turn'd out to be thrue,
When she put her arms round me, an' kiss'd me an'
    murmur'd,
You've neatly an' tenderly tied up my shoe.
An' what's that to anyone whether or no,
I ventur'd quite gamely to see th' thing through,
When she lifted her petticoat, silent an' slow,
An' I tuck'd up my sleeves for to tie up her shoe?

[*Some pennies have been thrown from the windows of the houses.
Brennan picks them up, and taking off a shabby, wide-brimmed
hat, bestows a sweeping bow on the houses. During the singing*

of the last verse of the song, Ayamonn and Roory have strolled in, and have listened to the old man singing while they leant against the balustrade of the bridge. The scene has grown darker as the old man is singing his song, for the sun is setting.

2nd Man [*waking up suddenly*]. Off with you, old man, thinkin' to turn our thoughts aside from th' way we are, an' th' worn-out hope in front of us.

1st Man [*waking up — wrathfully*]. Get to hell outa that, with your sootherin' songs o' gaudy idleness!

Eeada. Makin' his soul, at his age, he ought to be, instead o' chantin' ditties th' way you'd fear what would come upon you in th' darkness o' th' night, an' ne'er a sword be your side either.

3rd Man. Away with you an' your heathen songs to parts renowned for ignorance an' shame!

Finnoola. Away to where light women are plenty, an' free to open purple purses to throw you glitterin' coins!

[*Brennan slings his melodeon on to his back, puts his hat back on his head, and wends his way across the bridge.*

Roory [*as he passes*]. Isn't it a wondher, now, you wouldn't sing an Irish song, free o' blemish, instead o' one thickly speckled with th' lure of foreign enthertainment?

[*Brennan heeds him not, but crosses the bridge and goes out. The men and women begin to sink into drowsiness again.*

Ayamonn. Let him be, man; he sang a merry song well, and should have got a fairer greeting.

Roory [*taking no notice of Ayamonn's remark — to the men and women*]. Why didn't yous stop him before he began? *Pearl of th' White Breasts*, now, or *Battle Song o' Munster* that would pour into yous Conn's battle-fire of th' hundhred fights. Watchman o' Tara he was, his arm reachin' over deep rivers an' high hills, to dhrag out a host o' sthrong enemies shiverin' in shelthers. Leadher of Magh Femon's Host he was, Guardian of Moinmoy, an' Vetheran of our river Liffey, flowin' through a city whose dhrinkin' goblets once were made of gold, ere wise men carried it with frankincense an' myrrh to star-lit Bethlehem.

Eeada [*full of sleep — murmuring low*]. Away you, too, with your spangled memories of battle-mad warriors buried too deep for words to find them. Penny, here, each, th' ripe apples.

Dympna [*sleepily — in a low murmur*]. Away, an' leave us to saunter in sleep, an' crave out a crust in the grey kingdom of quietness. Tuppence a bunch the fresh violets.

Finnoola [*sleepily*]. Run away son, to where bright eyes can see no fear, an' white hands, idle, are willin' to buckle a sword on a young man's thigh.

1st Man [*with a sleepy growl*]. Get to hell where gay life has room to move, an' hours to waste an' white praise is sung to coloured shadows. Time is precious here.

2nd and 3rd Men [*together — murmuringly*]. Time is precious here.

Ayamonn. Rouse yourselves; we hold a city in our hands!

Eeada [*in a very low, but bitter voice*]. It's a bitther city.

Dympna [*murmuring the same way*]. It's a black an' bitther city.

Finnoola [*speaking the same way*]. It's a bleak, black, an' bitther city.

1st Man. Like a batthered, tatthered whore, bullied by too long a life.

2nd Man. An' her three gates are castles of poverty, penance, an' pain.

Ayamonn. She's what our hands have made her. We pray too much and work too little. Meanness, spite, and common patth-erns are woven thick through all her glory; but her glory's there for open eyes to see.

Eeada [*bitterly — in a low voice*]. Take your fill of her glory, then;

for it won't last long with your headin' against them who hold
the kingdom an' who wield th' power.

Dympna [*reprovingly*]. He means well, Eeada, an' he knows things
hid from us; an' we know his poor oul' mother's poor feet
has worn out a pathway to most of our tumbling doorways, seekin' out ways o' comfort for us she sadly needs
herself.

Eeada [*in a slightly livelier manner*]. Don't I know that well!
A shabby sisther of ceaseless help she is, blind to herself for
seein' so far into th' needs of others. May th' Lord be restless
when He loses sight of her!

Finnoola. For all her tired look an' wrinkled face, a pure white
candle she is, blessed this minute by St. Colmkille of th'
gentle manner, or be Aidan, steeped in th' lore o' Heaven, or
be Lausereena of th' silver voice an' snowy vestments — th'
blue cloak o' Brigid be a banner over her head for ever!

The Other Two Women [*together*]. Amen.

Roory [*impatiently*]. We waste our time here — come on!

Ayamonn. Be still, man; it was dark when th' spirit of God first
moved on th' face of th' waters.

Roory. There's nothin' movin' here but misery. Gun peal an'
slogan cry are th' only things to startle them. We're useless
here. I'm off, if you're not.

Ayamonn. Wait a moment, Roory. No-one knows what a
word may bring forth. Th' leaves an' blossoms have fallen,
but th' three isn't dead.

Roory [*hotly*]. An' d'ye think talkin' to these tatthered second-
hand ghosts'll bring back Heaven's grace an' Heaven's beauty
to Kaithleen ni Houlihan?

Ayamonn. Roory, Roory, your Kaithleen ni Houlihan has th'
bent back of an oul' woman as well as th' walk of a queen.
We love th' ideal Kaithleen ni Houlihan, not because she is

false, but because she is beautiful; we hate th' real Kaithleen ni Houlihan, not because she is true, but because she is ugly.

Roory [*disgusted*]. Aw, for God's sake, man!

[*He hurries off angrily.*

Eeada [*calling scornfully after him*]. God speed you, scut!

Ayamonn [*placing a hand softly on Eeada's head*]. Forget him, an' remember ourselves, and think of what we can do to pull down th' banner from dusty bygones, an' fix it up in th' needs an' desires of today.

[*The scene has now become so dark that things are but dimly seen, save the silver spire and crimson pillar in the distance; and Ayamonn's head set in a streak of sunlight, looking like the severed head of Dunn-Bo speaking out of the darkness.*

Finnoola. Songs of Osheen and Sword of Oscar could do nothing to tire this city of its shame.

Ayamonn. Friend, we would that you should live a greater life; we will that all of us shall live a greater life. Our sthrike is yours. A step ahead for us today; another one for you tomorrow. We who have known, and know, the emptiness of life shall know its fullness. All men and women quick with life are fain to venture forward. [*To Eeada*] The apple grows for you to eat. [*To Dympna*] The violet grows for you to wear. [*To Finnoola*] Young maiden, another world is in your womb.

Eeada [*still a little gloomily*]. Th' soldiers will be chasin' us with gunfire; th' polis hoppin' batons off our heads; our sons an' husbands hurried off to prison, to sigh away th' time in gloomier places than those they live in now.

Ayamonn. Don't flinch in th' first flare of a fight. [*He looks away from them and gazes meditatively down the river.*] Take heart of grace from your city's hidden splendour. [*He points with an outstretched hand.*] Oh, look! Look there! Th' sky has thrown a gleaming green mantle over her bare shoulders, bordhered with crimson, an' with a hood of gentle magenta over her handsome head — look!

[*The scene has brightened, and bright and lovely colours are being brought to them by the caress of the setting sun. The houses on the far side of the river now bow to the visible world, decked in mauve and burnished bronze; and the men that have been lounging against them now stand stalwart, looking like fine bronze statues, slashed with scarlet.*

Ayamonn. Look! Th' vans an' lorries rattling down th' quays, turned to bronze an' purple by th' sun, look like chariots forging forward to th' battle-front.

[*Eeada, rising into the light, now shows a fresh and virile face, and she is garbed in a dark-green robe, with a silvery mantle over her shoulders.*

Eeada [*gazing intently before her*]. Shy an' lovely, as well as battle-minded!

[*Dympna rises now to look where Ayamonn is pointing. She is dressed like Eeada, and her face is aglow. The men have slid from the parapets of the bridge, turning, too, to look where Ayamonn is pointing. Their faces are aglow, like the women's, and they look like bronze statues, slashed with a vivid green. Finnoola rises, last, and stands a little behind the others, to look at the city showing her melody of colours. Finnoola is dressed in a skirt of a brighter green than the other two women, a white bodice slashed with black, and a flowing silvery scarf is round her waist.*

Finnoola. She's glowin' like a song sung be Osheen himself, with th' golden melody of his own harp helpin'!

1st Man [*puzzled*]. Something funny musta happened, for, 'clare to God, I never noticed her shinin' that way before.

2nd Man. Looka the loungers opposite have changed to sturdy

men of bronze, and th' houses themselves are gay in purple
an' silver!

3rd Man. Our tired heads have always haunted far too low a
level.

Ayamonn. There's th' great dome o' th' Four Courts lookin'
like a golden rose in a great bronze bowl! An' th' river
flowin' below it, a purple flood, marbled with ripples o'
scarlet; watch th' seagulls glidin' over it — like restless white
pearls astir on a royal breast. Our city's in th' grip o' God!

1st Man [*emotionally*]. Oh, hell, it's grand!

Eeada. Blessed be our city for ever an' ever.

Ayamonn [*lifting his right hand high*]. Home of th' Ostmen, of th'
Norman, an' th' Gael, we greet you! Greet you as you catch a
passing hour of loveliness, an' hold it tightly to your panting
breast! [*He sings:*]

> Fair city, I tell thee our souls shall not slumber
> Within th' warm beds of ambition or gain;
> Our hands shall stretch out to th' fullness of labour,
> Till wondher an' beauty within thee shall reign.

The Rest [*singing together*]:

> We vow to release thee from anger an' envy,
> To dhrive th' fierce wolf an' sly fox from thy gate,
> Till wise man an' matrons an' virgins shall murmur
> O city of splendour, right fair is thy fate!

Ayamonn [*singing*]:

> Fair city, I tell thee that children's white laughter,
> An' all th' red joy of grave youth goin' gay,
> Shall make of thy streets a wild harp ever sounding,
> Touch'd by th' swift fingers of young ones at play!

The Rest [*singing*]:

> We swear to release thee from hunger an' hardship,
> From things that are ugly an' common an' mean;
> Thy people together shall build a brave city,
> Th' fairest an' finest that ever was seen!

[*Finnoola has been swaying her body to the rhythm of the song, and now, just as the last part is ending she swings out on to the centre of the bridge in a dance. The tune, played on a flute by someone, somewhere, is that of a Gavotte, or an air of some dignified and joyous dance, and, for a while, it is played in fairly slow time. After some time it gets quicker, and Ayamonn dances out to meet her. They dance opposite each other, the people around clapping their hands to the tap of the dancers' feet. The two move around in this spontaneous dance, she in a golden pool of light, he in a violet-coloured shadow, now and again changing their movements so that she is in the violet-coloured shadow, and he in the golden pool.*

Eeada [*loudly*]. The finest colours God has to give are all around us now.

Finnoola [*as she dances*]. The Sword of Light is shining!

1st Man [*exultantly*]. Sons an' daughters of princes are we all, an' one with th' race of Milesius!

[*The dance comes to an end with Ayamonn and Finnoola having their arms round each other.*

Eeada. Praise God for th' urge of jubilation in th' heart of th' young.

1st Man. An' for th' swiftness of leg an' foot in th' heart of a dance.

2nd Man. An' for th' dhream that God's right hand still holds all things firmly.

[*The scene darkens slightly. Ayamonn loosens his hold on Finnoola*

and raises his head to listen to something. In the distance can be
heard the sound of many feet marching in unison.

Finnoola [*a little anxiously*]. What is it you're listenin' to?

Ayamonn. I must go; goodbye, fair maid, goodbye.

Finnoola. Is it goin' to go you are, away from the fine things
shinin' around us? Amn't I good enough for you?

Ayamonn [*earnestly*]. You're lovely stayin' still, an' brimmin'
over with a wilder beauty when you're dancin'; but I must
go. May you marry well, an' rear up children fair as Emer
was, an' fine as Oscar's son; an' may they be young when
Spanish ale foams high on every hand, an' wine from th' royal
Pope's a common dhrink! Goodbye.

[*He kisses her, and goes across the bridge, passing out of sight on*
the farther bank of the river. The figures left behind have shrunk
a little; the colours have faded a good deal, and all look a little
puzzled and bewildered. The loungers have fallen back to the walls
of the houses, and, though they do not lie against them, they stand
close to them, as if seeking their shelter. There is a fairly long
pause before anyone speaks. They stand apart, as if shy of each
other's company.

Eeada [*murmuringly*]. Penny each, th' ripe apples. Who was it that
spoke that time? Jasus! I musta been dhreamin'.

Dympna [*in a bewildered voice*]. So must I, th' way I thought I
was lost in a storm of joy, an' many colours, with gay clothes
adornin' me.

Finnoola [*puzzled and dreamy*]. Dhreamin' I musta been when I
heard strange words in a city nearly smothered be stars, with
God guidin' us along th' banks of a purple river, all of us clad
in fresh garments, fit to make Osheen mad to sing a song of
the revelry dancin' in an' out of God's own vision.

Eeada [*murmuringly, but a little peevishly*]. For God's sake give
over dwellin' on oul' songs sung by Osheen, th' way you'd be

kindlin' a fire o' glory round some poor bog-warbler chantin' hoarse ditties in a sheltered corner of a windy street. [*Very sleepily*] Th' dewy violets, here, on'y tuppence a bunch — Jasus, apples I mean!

[*Now the tramp-tramp of marching men is heard more plainly.*

Dympna [*a little more awake*]. Tuppence each, the bunch of vio —— What can that be, now?

1st Man [*gloomily, but with a note of defiance in his voice*]. Th' thramp of marchin' soldiers out to prevent our meetin' an' to stop our sthrike.

2nd Man [*in a burst of resolution*]. We'll have both, in spite of them!

[*The scene darkens deeply now. In the pause following the 2nd Man's remark, nothing is heard but the sound of the tramping feet; then through this threatening sound comes the sound of voices singing quietly, voices that may be of those on and around the bridge, or of those singing some little distance away.*

Voices [*singing quietly*]:

We swear to release thee from hunger and hardship,
From things that are ugly and common and mean;
Thy people together shall build a great city,
The finest the fairest that ever was seen.

CURTAIN

ACT IV

Part of the grounds surrounding the Protestant church of St. Burnupus. The grounds aren't very beautiful, for they are in the midst of a poor and smoky district; but they are trim, and, considering the surroundings, they make a fair show. An iron railing running along the back is almost hidden by a green and golden hedge, except where, towards the centre, a fairly wide wooden gate gives admittance to the grounds. Beyond this gateway, on the pathway outside, is a street lamp. Shrubs grow here and there, and in the left corner, close to the hedge, are lilac and laburnum trees in bloom. To the right is the porch of the church, and part of the south wall, holding a long, rather narrow window, showing, in coloured glass, the figures of SS. Peter and Paul. Some distance away from the porch is a rowan tree, also in blossom, its white flowers contrasting richly with the gay yellow of the laburnum and the royal purple of the lilac. The rest of the grounds are laid out in grass, except for the path leading from the gateway to the entrance of the church. It is a warm, sunny evening, the Vigil of Easter, and the Rector is sitting on a deck-chair, before a table, on which are some books and papers. He is evidently considering the services that are to be held in the church on the following day.

The Rector is wearing a thick black cassock lined with red cloth, and at the moment is humming a verse of a hymn softly to himself, as he marks down notes on a slip of paper before him. A square black skull-cap covers his head.

Rector [singing to himself, softly]:

As Thou didst rise from Thy grim grave,
So may we rise and stand to brave

Th' power bestow'd on fool or knave;
We beseech Thee!

[*The verger comes out from the porch and walks towards the Rector.
He is bald as an egg, and his yellowish face is parched and
woebegone-looking. He is a man of sixty, and shows it. His
ordinary clothes are covered with a long black mantle of thin stuff,
with a small cape-like addition or insertion of crimson velvet on
the shoulders.*

Rector [*noticing the verger beside him*]. Hymn 625: we must have
that as our opening hymn, Samuel.

Samuel. It's got to go in, sir.

Rector. As you say — it's got to go in. Did you want to speak
to me, Samuel?

Samuel. Excuse me, sir, for what I'm agoin' to say.

Rector [*encouragingly*]. Yes, yes, Samuel, go on.

Samuel [*mysteriously*]. Somethin's afther happenin', sir, that I
don't like.

Rector [*turning a little in his chair*]. Oh! What's that, Sam?

Samuel. Mr. Fosther was here this mornin' runnin' a hand
through th' daffodils sent for Easther, an' found somethin' he
didn't like.

Rector. Yes?

Samuel. It's not for me to remark on anything that manœuvres
out in front o' me, or to slip in a sly word on things done, said,
or thought on, be th' pastors, masthers, or higher individuals
of th' congregation; but, sometimes, sir, there comes a time
when a true man should, must speak out.

Rector [*with a sigh*]. And the time has come to say something now
— what is it, Sam?

Samuel [*in a part whisper*]. This mornin', sir, and th' dear spring
sun shinin' through th' yellow robes of Pether an' th' purple

robes o' Paul, an' me arrangin' th' books in th' pews, who comes stealin' in, but lo and behold you, Fosther an' Dowzard to have a squint round. Seen' they're Select Vesthrymen, I couldn't ask them why they were nosin' about in th' silence of th' church on an ordinary week-day mornin'.

Rector [*patiently*]. Yes, but a long time ago, you said something about daffodils.

Samuel. I'm comin' at a gallop to them, sir.

Rector. Good; well, let's hear about the daffodils.

Samuel. Aha, says I, when I seen th' two prowlers with their heads close together, whisperin', aha, says I, there's somethin' on th' carpet.

Rector. Is what you have to tell me something to do with Dowzard and Foster, or the daffodils?

Samuel. Wait till you hear; sometimes Fosther an' Dowzard'll be to th' fore, an' sometimes th' daffodils. What can these two oul' codgers be up to? says I, sidlin' up to where they were, hummin' a hymn.

Rector. Humming a hymn? I'm glad to hear it; for I'd be surprised to hear either of them humming a hymn.

Samuel. Me it was, sir, who was hummin' th' hymn; for in a church, I like me thoughts to go with th' work I'm doin', if you know what I mean.

Rector [*impatiently*]. It'll be nightfall before you get to the daffodils, man.

Samuel. Wait till you hear, sir. There I was gettin' close to them be degrees, when, all of a sudden, didn't Fosther turn on me, shoutin' 'Are you goin' to be a party to th' plastherin' of Popish emblems over a Protestan' church?'

Rector. Popish emblems?

Samuel. Th' daffodils, sir.

Rector. The daffodils? But they simply signify the new life that

Spring gives; and we connect them in a symbolic way, quite innocently, with our Blessed Lord's Rising. And a beautiful symbol they are: daffodils that come before the swallow dares, and take the winds of March with beauty. Shakespeare, Sam.

Samuel [*lifting his eyes skywards and pointing upwards*]. Altogether too high up for poor me, sir. [*He bends down close to the Rector's ear.*] When he seen the cross o' daffodils made be Breydon, he near went daft. [*A pause, as if Samuel expected the Rector to speak, but he stays silent.*] God knows what'll be th' upshot if it's fixed to the Communion Table, sir. [*Another slight pause.*] Is it really to go there, sir? Wouldn't it look a little more innocent on th' pulpit, sir?

Rector [*in a final voice*]. I will place it myself in front of the Communion Table, and, if Mr. Foster or Mr. Dowzard ask anything more about it, say that it has been placed there by me. And, remember, when you say Mr. Foster and Mr. Dowzard, it's to be Mr. Breydon too. [*He hands some leaflets to Samuel.*] Distribute these through the pews, Sam, please. The arranging of the flowers is finished, is it?

Samuel. Yessir; all but the cross.

Rector. I will see to that myself. Thanks, Sam.

[*Samuel goes off into the church, and the Rector, leaning back in his chair with a book in his hand, chants softly.*]

Rector [*chanting*]:

> May wonders cease when we grow tame,
> Or worship greatness in a name;
> May love for man be all our fame,
> We beseech Thee!

[*As he pauses to meditate for a moment, Mrs. Breydon is seen coming along, outside the hedge. She enters by the gate, and comes over to the Rector. Sheila has come with her, but lags a little behind when they enter the grounds. The Rector rises quickly from his chair to greet Mrs. Breydon.*

Rector [*warmly*]. My dear Mrs. Breydon! Hasn't it been a lovely day? The weather promises well for Easter.

Mrs. Breydon. It would be good if other things promised as well as the weather, sir.

Rector. We must be patient, and more hopeful, my friend. From the clash of life new life is born.

Mrs. Breydon. An' often new life dies in th' clash too. Ah, when he comes, sir, speak th' word that will keep my boy safe at home, or here.

Rector [*laying a gentle hand on her arm*]. I wish I could, dear friend; I wish I could.

Mrs. Breydon. His mind, like his poor father's, hates what he sees as a sham; an' shams are powerful things, mustherin' at their broad backs guns that shoot, big jails that hide their foes, and high gallows to choke th' young cryin' out against them when th' stones are silent.

Rector. Let those safely sheltered under the lawn of the bishop, the miniver of the noble, the scarlet and ermine of the judge, say unto him, this thing you must not do; I won't, for sometimes out of the mouths of even babes and sucklings cometh wisdom.

Sheila. If what's against him be so powerful, he is helpless; so let this power go on its way of darkened grandeur, and let Ayamonn sit safe by his own fireside.

[*To the left, on the path outside the hedge, the Inspector, in full uniform, appears, evidently coming to see the Rector; on the right, followed by the men and women of the previous scenes, appears Ayamonn. He and the Inspector meet at the gate. The Inspector and he halt. The Inspector indicates he will wait for Ayamonn to pass, and Ayamonn comes into the grounds towards the Rector.*

The Inspector follows, but, in the grounds, stands a little apart, nearer the hedge. The men and women spread along the path outside, and stay still watching those in the grounds from over the hedge. They hold themselves erect, now; their faces are still pale, but are set with seams of resolution. Each is wearing in the bosom a golden-rayed sun. Brennan comes in and, crossing the grass, sidles over to sit down on the step of the porch.

Rector [*shaking Ayamonn's hand*]. Ah, I'm so glad you've come; I hope you'll stay.

Ayamonn [*hastily*]. I come but to go. You got the cross of daffodils?

Rector. Your mother brought it to us; it will hang in front of our church's greatest promise. Come and place it there with your own loyal hands, Ayamonn.

Inspector. Loyal hands engaged in rough rending of the law and the rumpling-up of decency and order; and all for what? For what would but buy blacking for a pair of boots, or a sheet of glass to mend a broken window!

Brennan [*from his seat on the porch's step*]. He's right, Ayamonn, me son, he's right: money's the root of all evil.

Ayamonn [*to the Inspector*]. A shilling's little to you, and less to many; to us it is our Shechinah, showing us God's light is near; showing us the way in which our feet must go; a sun-ray on our face; the first step taken in the march of a thousand miles.

Inspector [*threateningly*]. I register a lonely warning here that the people of power today will teach a lesson many will remember for ever; though some fools may not live long enough to learn it.

Mrs. Breydon. Stay here, my son, where safety is a green tree with a kindly growth.

Men and Women [*in chorus — above*]. He comes with us!

Sheila. Stay here where time goes by in sandals soft, where days fall gently as petals from a flower, where dark hair, growing grey, is never noticed.

Men and Women [*above*]. He comes with us!

Ayamonn [*turning towards them*]. I go with you!

Inspector [*vehemently*]. Before you go to carry out all your heated mind is set to do, I warn you for the last time that today swift horses will be galloping, and swords will be out of their scabbards!

Rector [*reprovingly — to Inspector*]. I hope you, at least, will find no reason to set your horses moving.

Inspector [*stiffly*]. I'll do my duty, sir; and it would be a good thing if someone we all know did his in that state of life unto which it has pleased God to call him.

Rector [*losing his temper*]. Oh, damn it, man, when you repeat the Church's counsel, repeat it right! Not *unto which it has pleased God to call him*, but *unto which it shall please God to call him*.

Inspector [*losing his temper too*]. Damn it, man, do you believe that what the fellow's doing now is the state of life unto which it has pleased God to call him?

Rector [*hotly*]. I have neither the authority nor the knowledge to deny it, though I have more of both than you, sir!

[*The Inspector is about to answer angrily, but Sheila catches his arm.*

Sheila. Oh, cancel from your mind the harder things you want to say, an' do your best to save us from another sorrow!

Inspector [*shaking off Sheila's hand roughly, and going to the gateway, where he turns to speak again*]. Remember, all! When swords are drawn and horses charge, the kindly Law, so fat with hesitation, swoons away, and sees not, hears not, cares not what may happen.

Mrs. Breydon [*angrily — up to the Inspector*]. Look at th' round

world, man, an' all its wondhers, God made, flaming in it,
an' what are you among them, standing here, or on a charging
horse, but just a braided an' a tasselled dot!

[*The Inspector hurries off, to pause, and stands outside the hedge, to
the right, the men and women shrinking back a little in awe to
give him a passage.*

Mrs. Breydon [*to Ayamonn*]. Go on your way, my son, an' win.
We'll welcome another inch of the world's welfare.

Rector [*shaking his hand*]. Go, and may the Lord direct you!
[*He smiles.*] The Inspector's bark is louder than his bite is deep.

Ayamonn. For the present — goodbye!

[*Ayamonn hurries away through the gate, pausing, outside the
hedge to the left, turning to give a last look at the Inspector.*

Inspector. Bear back, my boy, when you see the horsemen
charging!

[*He goes out by the right, and Ayamonn goes out left, followed by
the men and the women. There is a slight pause.*

Rector [*briskly — to banish a gloomy feeling*]. Now, Mrs. Breydon,
you run along to the vestry, and make us a good cup of tea —
I'm dying for one. [*To Sheila*] You'll join us, Miss Moorneen,
won't you?

Sheila [*immediately anxious*]. Oh no, thanks. I . . . I shouldn't
even be here. I'm a Catholic, you know.

Rector. I know, and I'd be the last to ask you to do anything you
shouldn't; but rest assured there's no canonical law against
taking tea made by a Protestant. Off you go, and help Mrs.
Breydon. I'll join you in a moment.

[*Sheila and Mrs. Breydon go off by the south wall of the church.*

Brennan [*as the Rector is gathering his books and papers from the
table*]. Hey, sir; hey there, sir! It won't shatther th' community
at large this disturbance, will it, eh?

Rector. I hope not.

Brennan [*with a forced laugh*]. No, no, of course not. Bank of Ireland'll still stand, eh? Ay. Ravenous to break in, some of them are, eh? Ay, ay. Iron doors, iron doors are hard to open, eh?

Rector [*going off to get his tea*]. I suppose so.

Brennan. Ay, are they. He supposes so; only supposes — there's a responsible man for you!

[*The verger comes into the porch and bends over Brennan.*

Samuel [*in a hoarse whisper*]. Come in an' have a decko at our grand cross.

Brennan. Cross? What cross?

Samuel. One o' daffodils for Easther, to be put in front of th' Communion Table.

Brennan. Popery, be God!

[*Booing is heard a little distance away, followed by the rattling fall of a shower of stones.*

Brennan. What's that; what's happenin'?

Samuel [*going to back, and looking down the street*]. A crowd flingin' stones; flingin' them at two men runnin' for their life.

Brennan [*nervously*]. Let's get into the church, quick. Throuble's beginnin' already.

[*They both go into the church, and Samuel closes the door. A crowd can be heard booing. Men and women, among them Eeada, Finnoola, Dympna, the Railwaymen, and the Lurchers who were on the bridge, pass across outside the hedge. The Leader carries a red flag, and all march with determination. They are all singing the following song:*

Leaders [*singing*]:

If we can't fire a gun, we can fire a hard stone,
Till th' life of a scab shrivels into a moan;

Crowd [*chorusing*]:

> Let it sink in what I say,
> Let me say it again —
> Though the Lord made an odd scab, sure, He also made
>   men!

Leaders [*singing*]:

> Th' one honour he'll get is a dusty black plume,
> On th' head of th' nag taking him to the tomb;

Crowd [*chorusing*]:

> Let it sink in what I say,
> Let me say it again:
> Th' scab's curs'd be th' workers, book, candle an' bell!

[*They cross over and disappear. After a pause, Dowzard and
   Foster come running in; they hurry through the gateway, and
   dash over to the church's porch.*

[*Dowzard is a big, beefy, red-faced man, rolls of flesh pouring out
   over the collar of his coat. His head is massive and bald, with
   jet-black tufts behind his ear, and a tiny fringe of it combed across
   high over his forehead. Foster is small and scraggy, with aggres-
   sion for ever lurking in his cranky face, ready to leap into full view
   at the slightest opportunity. His cheeks and lips are shaven, but
   spikes of yellowish whiskers point defiantly out from under his
   chin. His voice is squeaky and, when it is strengthened in anger,
   it rises into a thin piping scream. Both are dressed in the uniforms
   of railway foremen, blue cloth, with silver buttons, and silver
   braid on Dowzard's peaked hat and coat-sleeves, and gold braid
   on those of Foster. Both have their coats tightly buttoned up on them.
   They take off their peaked caps and wipe sweat from their
   foreheads. Dowzard pushes the door.*

Dowzard. We're safe here in th' grounds; Church grounds sacred. Unguarded, verminous villains — Papists, th' lot o' them!

Foster [*venomously*]. On' one o' their leaders a Select Vestryman. On' thot domned Rector stondin' by him. Steeped in Popery: sign o' th' cross; turnin' eastward sayin' th' Creed; sung Communion — be Gud, it's a public scondal!

Dowzard. Some o' them stones scorched me ear passin' by. We shouldn't have worn our uniforms. Gave us away. I knew we were in for it when they called us scabs.

Foster. Scobs themselves! Smoky, vonomous bastards! I tull you I'd wear me uniform in th' Vutican. [*He unbuttons his coat and shows that he is wearing a vivid orange sash, bordered with blue.*] Thor's me sash for all tae see. You should ha' stud with me, mon; stud like th' heroes o' Dully's Brae!

Dowzard [*shouting and knocking at door*]. Ey, there, in there, come out, open th' blasted door an' help a half-dead man!

[*The church door is opened, and the Rector, followed by the verger and Brennan, comes out into the grounds.*

Rector. What's wrong; what has happened?

Dowzard. Th' Pope's bullies with hard stones have smitten us sore. Honest men, virtuous an' upright, loyal to th' law an' constitution, have this day been smitten sore with Popish stones — oh, me poor head!

Foster. St. Bartholomew's Day's dawnin' again, I'm tullin' yous, an' dismumbered Protestants'll lie on all th' sthreets!

Rector. You can't be badly hurt when you complain so grandly.

Foster. Stand up for th' ruffians be makin' luttle of our hurts, so do, ay, do. [*Noticing Brennan who has edged towards the gate and is about to go away.*] Eh, you, aren't you goin' to stay an' put tustimony to the fullness o' th' Protestan' feth?

Brennan [*with slight mockery*]. Ay, I would, an' welcome, if I

hodn't to go, forbye, at this hour of on uvery day, I mak' ut a
rule tae be sturdy in th' readin' of a chaphter o' God's word so's
I won't hold on tae wordly things too strongly. [*He goes out.*

Foster [*fiercely*]. A jully-fush Protestant! [*To the Rector*] Look see,
I tull you th' fires o' Smithfield 'ull be blazin' round Protestant
bodies again, an' coloured lights 'ull be shown in th' Vatican
windows soon!

Dowzard. An' we'll be th' first to go up in th' flames.

Rector [*laughing contemptuously*]. Nonsense, oh, nonsense.

Foster [*almost screaming*]. It's not nonsense, mon! Every sable-robed
Jesuit's goin' about chucklin', his honds twitchin' to pounce
out on men like me here, an' Eddie Dowzard there, tae
manacle us, head, hond, and fut, for th' wheel, th' thumb-
screw, an' th' rack, an' then finish us up at th' stake in a hoppy
Romish auto-dey-fey! The Loyola boyos are out to fight
another buttle with th' men o' King Bully!

Rector [*amused*]. Well, let the Loyola boyos and King Bully fight it
out between them. I'm too busy to join either side. Goodbye.

Foster [*catching his arm as he is going — viciously*]. You're no'
goin' tae be lut slide off like thot, now, with your guilty
conscience, mon. There's things to be done, and things tae
be ondone in yon church, there; ay, ay.

Rector [*quietly*]. Indeed?

Foster [*angrily — to Dowzard*]. Uh, speak, speak a word, mon, on'
don't leave ut all tae me.

Dowzard. First, sir, we want you to get rid o' Breydon from the
Vesthry an' from th' church.

Rector. Oh, indeed?

Foster [*almost screaming*]. It's no' oh, indeed; answer th' question —
plain yes or no!

Rector [*coldly*]. Gentlemen, Mr. Breydon stays in the Vestry till
the parishioners elect someone else; as for the church, God

has seen fit to make him a member of Christ, and it is not
for me, or even for you, gentlemen, to say that God did
wrong.

Dowzard [*sneeringly*]. An' when did that wondherful thing
hoppen?

Rector. At his baptism, as you yourself should know.

Foster [*with an agonised squeal*]. Popery, Popery, nothin' but
Popery! Th' whole place's infusted with it!

[*The verger appears at the porch door with the cross of daffodils in
his hand. It has a Keltic shape, the shafts made of the flowers, and
the circle of vivid green moss. The verger shows it to Dowzard,
behind the Rector's back, and Dowzard sidling over, takes it
from him, the verger returning into the church again.*

Rector. And now be good enough, Mr. Foster, to let my arm go.

[*In the distance, a bugle-call sounding the charge is heard. Foster
lets go of the Rector's arm; and they all listen.*

Foster [*gleefully*]. Aha, there's the bugle soundin' th' charge, an'
soon the King's horses an' th' King's men'll be poundin' th'
riothers undher their feet! Law an ordher in th' State an' law an'
ordher in th' Church we must have. An' we're fightin' here as
they're fightin' there — for th' Crown an' ceevil an' releegious
liberty!

[*The sound of galloping horses is heard, followed by several volleys
of rifle-fire. They all listen intently for a few moments.*

Foster [*gleefully*]. Hear that now? Your Breydon fullow'll soon
be doshin' in here for th' church to hide him.

Rector. The cross of Christ be between him and all harm!

Dowzard [*dancing out in front of the Rector, holding out the cross —
with exultant glee*]. The cross — a Popish symbol! There y'urre,
see? A Popish symbol flourished in th' faces o' Protestant
people! [*With a yell*] Ichabod!

Foster [*venomously*]. I'll no' stick it, no; I'll no' stick it. Look-see, th' rage kindlin' godly Luther is kindlin' me! Here, go, gimme a holt of thot. [*He snatches the cross of flowers from Dowzard, flings it on the ground, and dances on it.*] Th' bible on' th' crown! The twa on' a half, th' orange on' blue; on' th' Dagon of Popery undher our Protestant feet!

Dowzard [*wildly*]. Th' dhrum, th' dhrum, th' Protestant dhrum!

[*While Foster and Dowzard have been dancing about and shouting their last few words, the men and women have run frightened along the path, behind the hedge. Those running from the right, turn, and run back to the left; those running from the left, turn, and run back to the left again, passing each other as they run. They suddenly see the men and women running about behind the hedge, and at once plunge into the porch, almost knocking the Rector down.*

Foster [*as they fly — to the Rector*]. Out uh th' way, mon, out uh th' way!

[*After a pause Eeada comes running through the gate, into the garden, over to the Rector.*

Eeada [*beseechingly*]. Oh, sir, please let me into the church, till all th' sthrife is over — no place's safe with the soldiers firin' an' th' police runnin' mad in a flourish o' batons!

Rector [*reassuringly*]. Be calm, be quiet, they won't touch a woman. They remain men, however furious they may be for the moment.

Eeada. Arra, God help your innocence! You should ha' seen them sthrikin' at men, women, an' childher. An' me own friend, Dympna, in hospital gettin' her face laced with stitches, th' way you'd lace a shoe! An' all along of followin' that mad fool, Breydon!

Rector. Go in, then. [*To the verger, who has come to the entrance*] See her safe.

[*Eeada and the verger go into the church. Finnoola comes slowly along the path outside the hedge, holding on to the railings as she moves, step by step. When she comes to the gateway, she sinks down on the ground and turns a white and distorted face towards those in the grounds.*

Finnoola [*painfully*]. For th' love o' God, one of you tell me if th' Reverend something Clinton's here, or have I to crawl a long way further?

Rector [*hurrying over to her*]. He's here; I'm he, my good woman. What is it you want of me?

Finnoola. I've a message for you from Ayamonn Breydon.

Rector [*eagerly*]. Yes, yes; where is he?

Finnoola. He's gone.

Rector. Gone? Gone where?

Finnoola. Gone to God, I hope.   [*A rather long pause.*

Rector [*in a low voice*]. May he rest in peace! And the message?

Finnoola. Yes. He whispered it in me ear as his life fled through a bullet-hole in his chest — th' soldiers, th' soldiers. He said this day's but a day's work done, an' it'll be begun again tomorrow. You're to keep an eye on th' oul' woman. He wants to lie in th' church tonight, sir. Me hip's hurt; th' fut of a plungin' horse caught me, an' I flat on th' ground. He sent a quick an' long farewell to you. Oh, for Christ's sake get's a dhrink o' wather! [*The verger runs for a drink.*] We stood our groun' well, though. [*The verger comes back with the water, and she drinks.*] Now I can have a thrickle of rest at last.

         [*She stretches herself out on the ground.*

Rector. Where did you leave him? Where is he lying now? [*She lies there, and makes no answer. He picks up the broken cross of flowers and is silent for a few moments. With head bent low — sorrowfully*] Oh, Ayamonn, Ayamonn, my dear, dear friend. Oh, Lord, open Thou mine eyes that I may see Thee, even as in a glass, darkly, in all this mischief and all this woe!

[*The curtain comes down to indicate the passing of some hours.
When it rises again, it is evening. The lamp over the porch door
is lighted, and so is the church, the light shining through the
yellow robe of St. Peter and the purple robe of St. Paul from the
window in the church's wall. The church organ is playing, very
softly, a dead march. The lamp on the path, outside the hedge,
isn't yet lighted. The dark figures of men and women can be
faintly seen lining themselves along the hedge. Mrs. Breydon is
standing in the grounds, near to the gateway. Foster and Dowzard
stand on the steps of the porch. A little in front, with his back
turned towards them, stands the Rector, now with white surplice
over his cassock, his stole around his neck, and the crimson-
lined hood of a Doctor of Divinity on his shoulders. Sheila, holding
a bunch of crimson roses in her hand, stands under the rowan
tree. Partly behind the tree, the Inspector is standing alone. A
lamplighter comes along the path, carrying his pole with the little
flower of light in the brass top. He lights the lamp on the path,
then comes over to peer across the hedge*]

Lamplighter. What's up? What's on? What's happenin' here?
What's they all doin' now?

1st Man. Bringin' th' body o' Breydon to th' church.

Lamplighter. Aw, is that it? Guessed somethin' was goin' on.

1st Man. He died for us.

Lamplighter. Looka that, now! An' they're all accouthered in
their best to welcome him home, wha'? Aw, well, th' world's
got to keep movin', so I must be off; so long!   [*He goes.*

Dowzard [*speaking to the Rector's back*]. For th' last time, sir, I
tell you half of the Vestry's against him comin' here; they don't
want our church mixed up with this venomous disturbance.

Rector [*without moving, and keeping his eyes looking towards the
gateway*]. All things in life, the evil and the good, the orderly
and disorderly, are mixed with the life of the Church Militant

here on earth. We honour our brother, not for what may have
been an error in him, but for the truth for ever before his face.
We dare not grudge him God's forgiveness and rest eternal
because he held no banner above a man-made custom.

Foster [*savagely*]. Aw, looksee, I'm no' a mon to sut down on'
listen to a tumblin' blether o' words — wull ye, or wull ye
not, give intil us?

[*In the distance a bagpipe is heard playing* Flowers of the Forest.
*Mrs. Breydon's body stiffens, and Sheila's head bends lower on
her breast.*

Rector. It is a small thing that you weary me, but you weary my
God also. Stand aside, and go your way of smoky ignorance,
leaving me to welcome him whose turbulence has sunken into
a deep sleep, and who cometh now as the waters of Shiloah
that go softly, and sing sadly of peace.

[*As he is speaking, the lament ceases, and a moment after, a stretcher
bier, bearing the covered-up body of Ayamonn, appears at the
gateway. It is carried down towards the church, and the Rector
goes to meet it.*

Rector [*intoning*]. Lord, Thou has been our refuge from one
generation to another. For a thousand years in Thy sight are
but as yesterday. [*He chants:*]

> All our brother's mordant strife
> Fought for more abundant life;
> For this, and more — oh, hold him dear.
> Jesu, Son of Mary, hear!
>
> Gather to Thy loving breast
> Ev'ry laughing thoughtful jest,
> Gemm'd with many a thoughtful tear.
> Jesu, Son of Mary, hear!

When Charon rows him nigh to shore,
To see a land ne'er seen before,
Him to rest eternal steer.
Jesu, Son of Mary, hear!

[*The bier is carried into the church, and, as it passes, Sheila lays the bunch of crimson roses on the body's breast.*

Sheila. Ayamonn, Ayamonn, my own poor Ayamonn!

[*The Rector precedes the bier, and Mrs. Breydon walks beside it, into the church, the rest staying where they are. There is a slight pause.*

Dowzard. We'd betther be goin'. Th' man's a malignant Romaniser. Keep your eye on th' rabble goin' out.

Foster [*contemptuously*]. There's little fight left in thom, th' now. I'll no' forgive thot Inspector fur refusin' to back our demond.

[*They swagger out through the gateway and disappear along the path outside the hedge, as those who carried the bier come out of the church.*

2nd Man. That's the last, th' very last of him — a core o' darkness stretched out in a dim church.

3rd Man. It was a noble an' a mighty death.

Inspector [*from where he is near the tree*]. It wasn't a very noble thing to die for a single shilling.

Sheila. Maybe he saw the shilling in th' shape of a new world.

[*The 2nd and 3rd Men go out by the gateway and mingle with the rest gathered there. The Inspector comes closer to Sheila.*

Inspector. Oughtn't you to go from this gloom, Sheila? Believe me, I did my best. I thought the charge would send them flying, but they wouldn't budge; wouldn't budge, till the soldiers fired, and he was hit. Believe me, I did my best. I tried to force my horse between them and him.

Sheila [*calmly*]. I believe you, Inspector Finglas.

Inspector [*gently catching her by the arm*]. Tom to you, dear. Come, Sheila, come, and let us put these things away from us as we saunter slowly home.

Sheila [*with a quiver in her voice*]. Oh, not now; oh, not tonight! Go your own way, and let me go mine, alone tonight.

Inspector [*taking her hand in his*]. Sheila, Sheila, be sparing in your thought for death, and let life smile before you. Be sparing in thought of death on one who spent his life too rashly and lost it all too soon. Ill-gotten wealth of life, ill-gone for ever!

Sheila [*withdrawing her hand from his gently*]. Oh, Tom, I hope you're right; you are right, you must be right.

[*They have walked to the gateway, and now stand there together, the men and women along the hedge eyeing them, though pretending to take no notice.*

Inspector. You'll see it clearer, dear, when busy Time in space has set another scene of summer's glory, and new-born spring's loud voice of hope hushes to silence th' intolerant dead.

Sheila [*musingly*]. He said that roses red were never meant for me; before I left him last, that's what he said. Dear loneliness tonight must help me think it out, for that's just what he said. [*Suddenly — with violence*] Oh, you dusky-minded killer of more worthy men!

[*She runs violently away from him, and goes out, leaving him with the men and women, who stand idly by as if noticing nothing.*

Inspector [*after a pause*]. What are ye doing here? Get home! Home with you, you lean rats, to your holes and haunts! D'ye think th' like o' you alone are decked with th' dark honour of trouble? [*Men and women scatter, slowly and sullenly, till only Brennan, with his melodeon on his back, is left, leaning by the gate. To Brennan*] Heard what I said? Are you deaf, or what?

Brennan [*calmly*]. I'm a Protestant, an' a worshipper in this church.

Inspector. One of the elect! So was Breydon. Well, keep clear of unruly crowds — men don't wait to ask the way you worship when they raise their arms to strike.

[*He goes slowly away down the path. A few moments pass, then the Rector and Mrs. Breydon come out of the church. He arranges a shawl round her shoulders.*

Rector. There; that's better! My wife insists you stay the night with us, so there's no getting out of it.

Mrs. Breydon. She's kind. [*She pauses to look at the rowan tree.*] There's th' three he loved, bare, or dhrenched with blossom. Like himself, for fine things grew thick in his nature: an' lather come the berries, th' red berries, like the blood that flowed today out of his white body. [*Suddenly — turning to face the church.*] Is it puttin' out th' lights he is?

Rector. Yes, before he goes home for the night.

Mrs. Breydon. Isn't it a sad thing for him to be lyin' lonesome in th' cheerless darkness of th' livelong night!

Rector [*going to the porch and calling out*]. Sam, leave the lights on tonight.   [*The church, which had dimmed, lights up again.*

Rector, He's not so lonesome as you think, dear friend, but alive and laughing in the midst of God's gay welcome. Come.

[*They slowly go through the gate and pass out. The verger comes from the church and swings the outer door to, to lock up for the night. Brennan comes down into the grounds.*

Samuel [*grumbling*]. Light on all night — more of his Romanisin' manœuvres.

Brennan. Eh, eh, there; houl' on a second!

Samuel. What th' hell do you want?

Brennan. Just to sing a little song he liked as a sign of respect an' affection; an' as a finisher-off to a last farewell.

Samuel [*locking the door*]. An what d'ye take me for? You an' your song an' your last farewell!

Brennan [*giving him a coin*]. For a bare few minutes, an' leave th'
  door open so's th' sound'll have a fair chance to go in to him.
  [*The verger opens the door.*] That's it. You're a kind man, really.
  [*Brennan stands facing into the porch, the verger leaning against
  the side of it. Brennan unslings his melodeon, plays a few preliminary
  notes on it, and then sings softly:*]

> A sober black shawl hides her body entirely,
> Touch'd be th' sun an' th' salt spray of th' sea;
> But down in th' darkness a slim hand, so lovely,
> Carries a rich bunch of red roses for me!

>   [*The rest of the song is cut off by the ending of the play.*

CURTAIN

RED ROSES FOR ME

A so-ber black shawl hides her bod-y en-ti-re-ly, Touch'd by th'

sun and th' salt spray of th' sea; But down in th' dark-ness a

slim hand, so love-ly, Car-ries a rich bunch of red ro-ses for me.—

TH' BOULD FENIAN MEN

Our cour-age so ma-ny have thought to be age-in', Now

flames like a bril-liant new star in th' sky; An' Dan-ger is proud to be

call'd a new bro-ther, Since Freedom has buckled her sword on her thigh. Then

out to th' place where th' bat-tle is brav-est, Where th'

noblest an' meanest fight fierce in th' fray, Re-pub-lic-an ban-ners shall

mock at th' foe-men, An' Fen-ians shall turn a dark night in-to day!

OH, QUEEN OF EBLANA'S POOR CHILDREN

Oh, Queen of Eb - la-na's poor child - ren, Bear swift-ly our woe a-

way; An' give us a chance to live light - ly An hour of our life's dark

day! Lift up th' poor heads ev-er bend - ing, An' light a lone star in th'

sky, To show thro' th' dark-ness, de-scend-ing, A cheer-i-er way to die.

I TUCK'D UP MY SLEEVES

I stroll'd with a fine maid far   out in th' coun-try, Th'

blos - soms a - round us   all   cry - in' for dew;___ On a

dai-sy deckt bench, sure, I sat down be-side her, An' tuck'd up my sleeves for to

tie up her shoe. An' what's that to a - ny one wheth-er or no, If I

came to th' fore when she gave me th' cue? She clos'd her eyes tight as she

mur-mured full low, Be good e-nough, dear, for to tie up my shoe.

FAIR CITY

Fair ci - ty, I tell thee our souls shall not slum-ber With- in th' warm

beds of am - bi - tion or gain; Our hands shall stretch out to th'

full-ness of la-bour, Till won-dher an' beau-ty with - in thee shall reign!

WE BESEECH THEE

As Thou didst rise from Thy— grim grave, So may we

rise to stand and brave Th' pow'r be - stow'd on

fool — or knave.— We be - seech Thee!

THE SCAB

If we can't fire a gun, we can fire a hard stone, Till th'

life of th' scab shriv-els in-to a moan. Let it sink in what I say, Let me

say it a - gain— Tho' th' Lord God made an odd scab He al - so made men!

BROTHERS

All our bro - ther's mord - ant strife

Fought for more a - bund - ant life; For

this, and more, oh, hold him dear.

Je - su, Son of Ma - ry, hear!